MORE
HEARTSMART™
COOKING
with Bonnie Stern

Dear Lise & Holt:

Some of Chuck's favorite recipes
are in this book, and I cannot
tell you how much it pleases me to include
them.
Good cooking

— Bonnie Stern.

— a Canadian eh.

RANDOM HOUSE
OF CANADA

HEART
AND STROKE
FOUNDATION
OF CANADA

®  becel IS A REGISTERED TRADE MARK OF THOMAS J. LIPTON,
TORONTO, CANADA, M4W 3R2.

Canadian Cataloguing in Publication Data

Stern, Bonnie
    More heartsmart cooking with Bonnie Stern

Includes index.
ISBN: 0-679–30841–5

1. Heart – Diseases – Diet therapy – Recipes.
2. Low-fat diet – Recipes. I. Title

RC684.D5S73 1997   641.5'6311   C96-931601–1

Photography: Robert Wigington
Food styling: Olga Truchan
Prop styling: Maggi Jones
Photographic assistant: Mark Paré
Back cover author photograph: Lorella Zanetti
Illustrations: Wayne Terry
Design: Andrew Smith
Page layout and composition: Joseph Gisini / Andrew Smith Graphics Inc.

Printed and bound in Canada

10 9 8 7 6 5 4 3 2

Front cover: Sea Bass with Couscous Crust and Tomato Olive Vinaigrette (page 148)

CONTENTS

Acknowledgements **5**

Author's Acknowledgements......................................**6**

Preface **8**

Introduction **9**

Healthful Cooking for Every Occasion **27**

About the Nutrient Analysis **32**

Recipes

    Appetizers...**33**

    Soups **55**

    Salads **77**

    Pastas **95**

    Meatless Main Courses **113**

    Fish and Seafood **139**

    Poultry..**159**

    Meat **181**

    Vegetables and Side Dishes **205**

    Breakfasts and Brunches **225**

    Breads...**245**

    Desserts...**263**

Appendices...**285**

    Canadian Diabetes Association Food Choice System.....**291**

Index..**297**

For Raymond —
my grade three sweetheart
who kept me waiting twenty years
before he was finally ready to get married,
but was worth waiting for.

ACKNOWLEDGEMENTS

The Heart and Stroke Foundation would like to thank the following people for their assistance in the development and review of the introductory chapter of *More HeartSmart Cooking with Bonnie Stern*. Their expertise and advice was invaluable in assisting in the translation of the scientific principles of healthy eating into practical information that every Canadian can act upon.

Members of the National Nutrition Advisory Committee and Nutrition Taskforce, Ontario:
Gail Leadley, RD; Suzanne Mahaffy, PDt.; Bretta Maloff, M.Ed.,RD;
Laura Sevenhuysen, M.Ed, RD; Kathy Furgala, RD; Jane Loppe, RD

Members of the Health Promotion Initiative Review Committee:
Joanne Carrier, APR; Gwen Dubois-Wing, RN, M.S.; Barb Riley, M.Sc.;
James C. Welsh, PhD

Barbara Selley, RD; Sharyn Joliat, M.Sc.,RD; Niki Guner, MBA; Richard Gallop;
Mary-Elizabeth Harriman, B.A.Sc.; Doug MacQuarrie, M.Ed.; Bonnie Stern, B.A.;
Bonnie Laing; Carol Dombrow, RD

A special thanks to:
• the Cookbook Taskforce who spent many hours bringing this book to fruition:
Richard Gallop, Niki Guner, Vicky Hum, Doug MacQuarrie, Linda Samis, Doug Pepper,
Bonnie Stern, Carol Dombrow, Lilianne Bertrand, Helga Breier, Elissa Freeman
• the writers of the introduction: Rena Mendelson, M.S., D.Sc., RD, Leslie Berndl, M.Sc., RD
and Bonnie Laing
• the nutritional analysis experts: Barbara Selley, RD and Sharyn Joliat, M.Sc., RD
of Info Access (1988) Inc.
• the editors of the recipes and the book: Shelley Tanaka and Sarah Davies
• Tara Giffin, M.H.Sc., P.Dt. for her expert assistance in the development of the book and
Lynn McAuliffe for her assistance with the final editing

becel® is dedicated to educating Canadians
about leading a heart healthy life. Supporting the educational initiatives of the
Heart and Stroke Foundation forms an integral part of this commitment.

The Heart and Stroke Foundation gratefully acknowledges the generous support of becel® in helping to make this cookbook possible. The financial support received from our sponsor does not constitute an endorsement by the Heart and Stroke Foundation or the author for the sponsor's products.

AUTHOR'S ACKNOWLEDGEMENTS

When *Morningside*'s Peter Gzowski saw the acknowledgements in *Simply HeartSmart Cooking*, he laughed and said, "Gee, didn't you do any of this book alone?"

Well, no, and it is the same story with this book. Although I believe my books are very personal and convey my taste, techniques and feelings about food, it takes many people to put together a project like this, and I've been lucky enough to work with the best in every field.

This is the second book I have written in conjunction with the Heart and Stroke Foundation of Canada. When I toured the country to promote our first book, I was amazed at the dedication and commitment of the volunteers who work so hard for this organization. I want to thank them for all their support in bringing these books to people's attention — sometimes a personal recommendation from someone you trust can make all the difference. Thanks to volunteers and staffers alike, especially Carol Dombrow, Rick Gallop, Doug MacQuarrie, Lilianne Bertrand, Helga Breier, Elissa Freeman, Tara Giffin, Niki Guner, Lynn McAuliffe, Vicky Hum, Linda Samis, Barbara Selley and Sharyn Joliat from Info Access, and Rena Mendelson, Leslie Berndl and Bonnie Laing, who wrote the Introduction.

Random House, once again, went all out to engage the finest talents to work on this project. Thanks to Vicki Black, Pat Cairns, Laurie Coulter, Sarah Davies, Joseph Gisini, Sheila Kay, David Kent, Kathryn Mulders, Doug Pepper, Duncan Shields, Andrew Smith, Beverley Sotolov, Lorraine Symmes, Alan Terakawa, Wayne Terry, Olga Truchan and Robert Wigington. And thanks to Susan Yates and Sidney Cohen, who produced the video that complements this book.

Ideas and recipes come from many sources: friends, colleagues and guest teachers at my school have all contributed ideas for recipes or have taught me new techniques or flavour combinations. Thanks to Darina Allen, John Ash, Hubert Aumeier, Rick Bayless, Fran Berkoff, Gwen Berkowitz, Giuliano Bugialli, Biba Caggiano, Hugh Carpenter, Shelley and Ruth Cohen, Mitchell Davis, Jim Dodge, Arlene Feltman-Sailhac, Fred Ferretti, Bernie Glazman, Barbara Glickman, Simone Goldberg, Andrea Iceruk, Madhur Jaffrey, Hubert Keller, Loni Kuhn, Susur Lee, Anne Lindsay, Patti and Earl Linzon, Nick Malgieri, Lydie Marshall, Carole Martin, Bob Masching, Christopher McDonald, Mark McEwan, Alice Medrich, Hart Melvin, Carlo Middione, Linda and Paul Molitor, Caprial Pence, Jacques Pepin, Mary Risley, Joel and Linda Rose, Nancy Lerner and Richard Rotman, Lynn and Norm Saunders, Nina Simonds, Irene Tam, Sam Twining, Edward Weil, Lynn and Barrie Wexler, Cynthia Wine, Margaret Visser, Eileen Yin-Fei Lo and Evelyn Zabloski.

Writing a book is only part of the challenge. The hard part is getting the message out. I have had tremendous support from the press for which I am very grateful. I'd especially like to thank Marion Kane at the *Toronto Star*, Elizabeth Baird at *Canadian Living Magazine*, Elizabeth Lancaster at *Eye on Toronto*, France Fontana-Hart at *The Dini Petty Show*, Peter Gzowski at *Morningside*, and Fiona Conway at *Canada AM*. Thanks also to Debbie Bassett, Wei Chen, Carla Collins, Bonnie Baker Cowan, Judy Creighton, Cynthia David, Alison Fryer, Randy Gulliver, Gerald Haddon, Deby Holbik, Mildred Istona, Mary Ito, Dan Matheson, Dini Petty, Valerie Pringle, Daphna Rabinovitch, Monda Rosenberg, Judy Schultz and Robin Ward.

My cooking school and cookware shop opened twenty-three years ago and for the first five years I was the only employee. No one can possibly appreciate their staff more than I do. Thanks to Anne Apps, Lorraine Butler, Sadie Darby, Letty Lastima, Maureen Lollar, Jacques Marie, Francine Menard, Melissa Mertl, Linda Stephen and especially Rhonda Caplan, who tested the recipes for this book. Thanks also to auxiliary staff Janet Anderson, Brian Campbell, Marie Formosa, Julie Lewis, Arnold Matthews, Emily Richards, Rose Snukal, Helen Walker, Alison Weinstein and Lorella Zanetti.

Indirectly, my father taught me a lot about food. He always says, "There's no such thing as a free lunch," and he's right! My cautious and worrisome nature definitely runs in the family, but it also keeps me focused. Thanks to Max and Ruth Stern; my children, Mark and Anna, who keep me humble ("We love you, Mom, but we won't eat this!"); my stepdaughter, Fara, who keeps me in touch with Generation X (and Generation V); my husband, to whom this book is dedicated; Charles, Meredith, Wayne and Jane Krangle, who get to try "cuisine experimentale" at our family cottage; and Bruce and Hedy Felstein, Jack Rupert, Shawn Duckman, Tina Lastima, Daphne Smith and Dely Balagtas.

I wouldn't trust just anyone to worry for me, so I want to thank my lawyer, Marian Hebb, who is a superb worrier, for taking some of the burden off my shoulders. And I want to thank my editor, Shelley Tanaka, who makes me sound so much better that I would like to submit my daily conversations to her before I even say good morning.

Finally, a very special thank-you to all my students for supporting me in what I love to do best — teach. Thanks for coming to my classes, thanks for using my recipes to share food with your family and friends, and thanks for bringing people back to the dinner table for love and comfort as well as nourishment.

BONNIE STERN
TORONTO, 1997

PREFACE

The Heart and Stroke Foundation of Canada is pleased to be able to provide you with our next exciting cookbook from Bonnie Stern. Our last Bonnie Stern book — *Simply HeartSmart Cooking* — was an overwhelming success and this book is produced in response to your request for more delicious, lower fat, higher fibre recipes. This book will meet all of your expectations and the recipes will help you put the theory into practice. Beyond adding more delicious recipes to your collection, this book will enhance your knowledge about food, learning about new ingredients, new tastes and flavours.

The Heart and Stroke Foundation is committed to helping Canadians improve their nutrition habits. The introduction of the book provides an opportunity for us to provide guidance and information to assist you in putting HeartSmart eating into action. Written by two very experienced dietitians, Rena Mendelson and Leslie Berndl, we hope the introduction will motivate you to make changes in your lifestyle. It provides you with the ideas, tools and motivation you need to understand and follow the "total diet" approach to eating. We have also included ideas on incorporating physical activity into your day-to-day activities.

In addition, the Heart and Stroke Foundation and Bonnie Stern are launching a video, *HeartSmart Cooking Class with Bonnie Stern,* to complement this book. The video allows you to attend a Bonnie Stern Cooking Course right in your own home. A number of the recipes that you will find in this book are demonstrated on the video, providing you with an opportunity to learn techniques that will be helpful in preparing many HeartSmart recipes.

I truly hope you enjoy your new book — our latest contribution to helping you enjoy yourself while you eat better.

GARY SUTHERLAND, PRESIDENT
HEART AND STROKE FOUNDATION OF CANADA

INTRODUCTION

A "TOTAL DIET" APPROACH TO FOOD AND ACTIVITY

Welcome to this new book of recipes, ideas, tips and guidelines, served up by the Heart and Stroke Foundation of Canada. If you're a fan of good food and healthy living, you may already be familiar with the other "heart" cookbooks and their great recipes and ideas.

This book is dedicated to the principle of "total diet" in meal planning and food preparation. What is it?

> The "total diet" approach to food selection, meal planning and eating stresses the three basic concepts of Canada's Food Guide to Healthy Eating:
>
> • Balance   • Variety   • Moderation
>
> "Total diet" means you should look at the big picture – what you eat over the course of the day or week, not just at one meal. It encourages you to choose from a wide selection of foods, knowing that no one food is especially "good" or "bad." It is the overall blend of food selections that determines the quality of your diet and health.

On the following pages, you will find all the ideas, tools and motivation you need to follow the "total diet" approach. The benefits of this approach are many — a reduction of total fat and an increase in fibre in your diet, as well as a wonderful range of flavours in the food you eat.

To round out the picture, there are useful sections on meal planning and shopping, as well as hints on how stepping up your physical activity can improve your vitality and sense of well-being.

Last but not least, are the sumptuous recipes Bonnie Stern has developed. These delicious dishes, covering everything from soups and appetizers to low-fat desserts, prove that you can cut back on fat without sacrificing taste.

THE CORNERSTONES OF HEALTHY LIVING

The three main principles of the "total diet" approach are:
• Balance
• Variety
• Moderation

The fourth principle is not connected to what you eat, but it is as important — physical activity. Together, these principles can help you make the best possible choices in the food you eat and the energy you use up.

Balance

Canada's Food Guide to Healthy Eating defines balance as the way in which you choose foods from all of the four food groups in order to get the essential nutrients the body needs to stay healthy. The Guide gives a recommended range of servings from each group.

Balance is needed because each food group plays a different role in providing the nutrition your body needs. Each group has key nutrients:

• Grain products – fibre, carbohydrates, B-vitamins
• Vegetables & Fruit – vitamins A & C, fibre
• Milk products – protein, calcium, riboflavin
• Meat & Alternatives – protein, iron, B-vitamins

Canada's Food Guide to Healthy Eating also mentions "other" foods, those which are high in fats and sugar, such as butter, candies, soft drinks and chips. For those who are calorie conscious, they can add extra calories without providing many nutrients. But in moderation, they can add to the pleasure of eating. The key word is moderation.

Variety

Not only is variety the spice of life, it can add to the quality of your eating experience. What you should aim for is a blend of flavours, textures and nutrients in the food you eat.

Variety is important because no single food contains all the nutrients you need. Even within a food group, different foods supply different nutrients.

For example, apples are a source of fibre while oranges are an excellent source of vitamin C; green vegetables are an important source of folic acid and minerals; orange vegetables are a good source of beta carotene.

As well as providing key nutrients, all foods contain trace elements that contribute to overall health.

Choosing a variety of foods will not only delight your taste buds, but will also help in moderating the amount of fat, salt, caffeine and alcohol you consume.

Remember that variety extends to the way you prepare foods, too. Here is a list of lower-fat methods of cooking:

• Grilling, on top of the stove or on a barbecue
• Baking
• Stir-frying
• Cooking in a non-stick skillet
• Steaming
• Roasting
• Broiling
• Boiling

And raw, of course, in the case of vegetables and fruit. All of the cooking methods above can be used to cut back on the amount of fat a cooked dish retains. The recipes in this book also show you other lower-fat ways to prepare your family's favourite dishes.

FATS

Many Canadians eat too much fat. A recommended fat intake for a day is:

Man: 90 grams of fat or less

Woman: 65 grams of fat or less

Not only the amount but the type of fat can affect your health. Some fats can help lower blood levels of bad cholesterol, while others raise it.

The message is: eat less fat and, of the fat you do eat, choose heart-friendly types.

TRACE ELEMENTS

Trace elements are minerals such as iodine or chromium, which the body needs in very small amounts.

- Polyunsaturates, found in safflower, corn, soybean, sesame seed and nut oils and soft tub margarines made from these oils. Some nuts, too, such as walnuts and pine nuts.

- Monounsaturates, found in olive and canola oil and soft tub margarines made with these oils. Some nuts, such as almonds, pecans and pistachios.

- Omega-3 fat, a type of polyunsaturated fat that helps prevent stickiness and clotting of blood. Found in fatty fish such as salmon, trout and mackerel, as well as in canola oil.

**HEART-HARMING
FATS THAT CAN
RAISE THE LEVEL OF
'BAD' CHOLESTEROL**

- Saturates, found in animal sources of fat such as meat, poultry, dairy products, as well as tropical oils such as palm, palm kernel and coconut oils, and food made with these oils, such as cookies, cakes and candies.

- Trans fatty acids have the same effect as saturated fat. They are created when vegetable oils are hydrogenated, turning a liquid oil into a hard shortening. Found in shortenings and foods made from shortening: cookies, crackers, baked goods.

Moderation

Moderation is about the amount you consume of any one food or food group. The message is: Too much of a good thing can create problems, even if the food that is overconsumed is nutritious.

When too much of any one food or food group is consumed, it can crowd out other foods and food groups. For example, a toddler drinking four cups (1 litre) of milk a day might not feel hungry enough to eat the foods from the other food groups, thereby missing out on nutrients which are important to overall health. Milk is part of a healthy diet but too much of any food is not good.

This is particularly true when it comes to "other foods." For example, eating a large bag of potato chips before dinner could cause you to eat less for dinner.

No one food, whether it is from the "other foods" or from a food group, should be considered "bad" or unhealthy. It is only the amount of these foods and the pattern of eating over time that has an effect on your health. There is room for any and all foods in the "total diet" approach, as long as the amounts are moderate.

To make sure your food habits are moderate, take a cue from Canada's Food Guide For Healthy Eating. The recommended servings and serving sizes from each group provide guidelines for how much of each food group you should be consuming to maintain a healthy balance.

Physical Activity

Balance, variety and moderation are essential to a healthy lifestyle. But apart from the food you take in, consider the energy you put out. Physical activity is the non-eating component of the "total diet" approach.

Increasing physical activity, whether in your daily tasks or in the form of a fitness program, will reward you in many ways:
- Reduced risk of heart disease, as well as many other diseases
- Increased energy and enjoyment of life
- Stress reduction and relaxation
- Increased strength and flexibility

That's a lot for a little effort every day.

EVERYDAY ACTIVITY

Luckily, it's easy to increase your level of physical activity. Start with the tasks and efforts you make every day. Whether at work or home, there are opportunities for you to step up your physical activity level.
- Walk whenever you can. For example, get off the bus one stop early and walk the rest of the way home.
- Find a safe parking space the furthest away from your destination and walk the rest of the way.

- Leave the car at home and walk for minor shopping trips.
- Liven up your household and your routine by getting a dog and walking it regularly.
- Look for opportunities to use the stairs at work, at home or anywhere. It's good exercise.
- Shovel the sidewalk in winter and do garden work in the summer. It will keep you active all year.
- When getting together with friends, plan an activity instead of a trip to the movies — cycling, swimming, a walk through a conservation area.

A COMMITMENT TO FITNESS

The more you increase your level of physical activity, the greater the rewards in terms of well-being.

Joining a club or a sports league, signing up for lessons, forming your own neighbourhood or workplace fitness group or buying a fitness video are all options you might consider. Here are some suggestions to keep in mind.

- Base your plans on your personal lifestyle and goals. If the activity fits in easily with your life, you'll do it more often.
- Choose a sport or activity you like. If it is fun, you'll continue it for the rest of your life. If you find it dreary, you will lose interest very quickly.
- If you work and have small children, a fitness centre near work is a good idea, so that you can work out at lunchtime, before or after work.
- If you have the space at home and the money, set up your own home fitness centre.
- Watching television or your children at play can be done from a stationary bike or stairmaster.
- Plan family activities that involve fitness — a family cycle, a game, family swimming at the local recreation centre, a weekend jog or walk.
- Interested in making new friends? Take up a new sport or revive your interest in an old one.

By making good food choices and becoming more physically active, you will be well on the way towards a greater feeling of well-being and better health, two goals worth achieving.

LIMIT SALT, ALCOHOL AND CAFFEINE

Moderation is especially important when it comes to salt, alcohol and caffeine.

- Salt can be reduced by consuming fewer convenience foods, avoiding high-salt snack foods such as chips and pretzels, and using less salt in cooking and at the table. Taste before you shake.
- Alcohol intake, if you drink, should be kept to one drink a day, defined as: 12 oz (350 mL) beer, 5 oz (150 mL) wine or 1½ oz (45 mL) spirits.
- Caffeine, in the form of coffee, tea or cola drinks, is not harmful if you limit your intake to the equivalent of 4 cups (1 litre) of coffee per day.

Health Canada   Santé Canada

CANADA'S
Food Guide
TO HEALTHY EATING

Enjoy a variety
of foods from each
group every day.

Choose lower-
fat foods
more often.

Grain Products
Choose whole grain
and enriched
products more
often.

Vegetables & Fruit
Choose dark green and
orange vegetables and
orange fruit more often.

Milk Products
Choose lower-fat
milk products more
often.

Meat & Alternatives
Choose leaner meats,
poultry and fish, as well
as dried peas, beans and
lentils more often.

Canada

CANADA'S
Food Guide
TO HEALTHY EATING
FOR PEOPLE FOUR YEARS AND OVER

Different People Need Different Amounts of Food

The amount of food you need every day from the 4 food groups and other foods depends on your age, body size, activity level, whether you are male or female and if you are pregnant or breast-feeding. That's why the Food Guide gives a lower and higher number of servings for each food group. For example, young children can choose the lower number of servings, while male teenagers can go to the higher number. Most other people can choose servings somewhere in between.

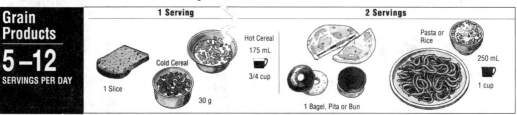

Grain Products
5–12
SERVINGS PER DAY

1 Serving
1 Slice
Cold Cereal
30 g
Hot Cereal
175 mL
3/4 cup

2 Servings
1 Bagel, Pita or Bun
Pasta or Rice
250 mL
1 cup

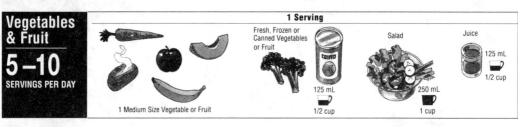

Vegetables & Fruit
5–10
SERVINGS PER DAY

1 Serving
1 Medium Size Vegetable or Fruit
Fresh, Frozen or Canned Vegetables or Fruit
125 mL
1/2 cup
Salad
250 mL
1 cup
Juice
125 mL
1/2 cup

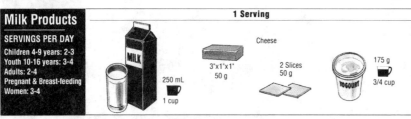

Milk Products
SERVINGS PER DAY
Children 4-9 years: 2-3
Youth 10-16 years: 3-4
Adults: 2-4
Pregnant & Breast-feeding
Women: 3-4

1 Serving
MILK
250 mL
1 cup
Cheese
3"x1"x1"
50 g
2 Slices
50 g
175 g
3/4 cup

Other Foods

Taste and enjoyment can also come from other foods and beverages that are not part of the 4 food groups. Some of these foods are higher in fat or Calories, so use these foods in moderation.

Meat & Alternatives
2–3
SERVINGS PER DAY

1 Serving
Meat, Poultry or Fish
50-100 g
Fish
1/3–2/3 Can
50–100 g
1-2 Eggs
Beans
125-250 mL
TOFU
100 g
1/3 cup
Peanut Butter
30 mL 2 tbsp

Enjoy eating well, being active and feeling good about yourself. That's VITALIT

© Minister of Supply and Services Canada 1992   Cat. No. H39-252/1992E   No changes permitted. Reprint permission not required.
ISBN 0-662-19648-1

MAKING THE "TOTAL DIET" APPROACH WORK FOR YOU

Understanding the elements of a healthy diet is one thing; putting it into action is another. This section deals with the practical ways you can make healthy food choices. It covers meal planning, grocery shopping, recipe selection and modification, plus strategies for eating out.

Meal planning

To make the most of the "total diet" approach, plan your meals and snacks. This will cut down on the number of on-the-spot food decisions that often result in poor choices.

Taking a little time to plan meals will actually save you time when it comes to meal preparation. It will also allow you to see that the nutritional needs of you and your family are met.

Here are some suggestions which will make meal planning simple and easy to do.

- Plan one week at a time to ensure that you include a wide variety of foods from each of the four food groups. The meal plan will then form the basis of your shopping list.
- In planning each of the daily meals, check out your choices with Canada's Food Guide To Healthy Eating on pages 13 and 14. Your food choices should match up with the recommended number of daily servings in each food group.
- Instead of planning meals around the meat component, try starting with the variety of grains available — couscous, rice, pasta, bulgur. Then add the seasonal vegetable that would complement the grain. Lastly, add the meat or alternative choice.
- If 5 to 12 servings of grains seems like a lot, remember a serving is only half a cup (125 mL) of cooked pasta. Serve 2 or 3 at a meal — a cup (250 mL) of pasta and a slice of bread on the side. Likewise, remember that a serving size for meat is only 2 to 3 ounces (50 – 100 g), about the size of a deck of cards.
- Snack planning is just as important as meal planning, and a good way to add to the food group servings — low-fat crackers or biscuits from the grain products group; veggies and dip (see recipe on page 40) or fresh fruit from the vegetables and fruit group.

FOUR STEPS TO SUCCESSFUL MEAL PLANNING

Putting together a meal plan that will work for you and your family requires four simple steps.

1) Learning what variety and amounts of food you need to be healthy
2) Examining how your eating habits measure up against the goals

3) Adjusting your menu by adding or subtracting foods
4) Making a new plan, with a shopping list to match, remembering to include the foods your family likes

Once you are used to going through these steps, you can do your weekly plan in minutes.

Step One: Foods needed to be healthy
The basis of any meal plan is Canada's Food Guide to Healthy Eating, found on pages 13 and 14. In addition to describing the foods in the four food groups, the Guide promotes the principles of balance, variety and moderation. It also recommends:

• Boosting the intake of fruits, vegetables and whole grains, to increase fibre
• Reducing fat intake by choosing lower-fat foods

In a nutshell, here is what you should be consuming daily:

Grain Products

You need at least five servings per day.

Choose whole grain and enriched products more often.

Examples of one serving:

One slice whole grain bread

¾ cup (175 mL) whole grain cereal such as oatmeal or bran flakes

½ cup (125 mL) cooked rice or pasta

Half a whole grain bun

Milk Products

You need at least two servings per day. Children and adolescents need at least three servings per day. For pre-schoolers (2 to 4 years old) two of the servings should be fluid milk for the vitamin D content.

Choose lower-fat milk products more often.

Examples of one serving:

1 cup (250 mL) milk

2 ounces (50 g) cheese

¾ cup (175 g) yogurt

Vegetables & Fruit

You need at least five servings per day.

Choose dark green and orange vegetables and orange fruit more often.

Examples of one serving:

1 cup (250 mL) salad greens

½ cup (125 mL) raw, canned or frozen fruit or vegetable

1 medium-size vegetable or fruit (potato, apple, banana)

½ cup (125 mL) cooked vegetable

Meat & Alternatives

You need at least two servings per day.

Choose leaner meats, poultry and fish, as well as dried peas, beans and lentils more often.

Examples of one serving:

⅓ cup (100 g) tofu

1 cup (250 mL) baked beans

2 – 3 ounces (50 - 100 g) fish, meat or poultry

Step Two: How does your family measure up to the goals?
Now it is time to look at what your family actually eats, and how it compares to the recommendations in Canada's Food Guide To Healthy Eating.

Ideally, as a starting point, you should record what you and your family eat over two or three days. But if you don't have the time, use the chart on page 20 to write down what your family typically enjoys on daily eating occasions, or record one day's consumption.

Write in the number of servings from each food group that the meal represents. To help you out, see the menu plan example on page 19 of what the food record of one family looks like on one typical day.

Step Three: Making room for improvement
How do your family's current eating habits measure up? If you are typical, chances are there is room for some improvement in one or more food groups.

In the example given, the family was eating well, but could have added more grain products, fruits and vegetables and lower-fat dairy products. More emphasis could be placed on alternatives to meat, such as beans, lentils and other legumes.

Your challenge now is to find ways to make changes that will still fit with your family's food preferences.

Here are some suggestions for each food group:

Grain Products
• Whole grain muffins, like the lower-fat recipes found on pages 246–248 of this book, are great for breakfast, lunch or a snack.
• Keep a wide variety of whole grain cereals on hand.
• Look for buns and bagels with a higher whole grain content.
• Try out whole wheat pasta, brown rice, bulgur, quinoa and other new grains. There are 11 recipes using these on pages 82, 83, 89, 90, 126, 134, 148, 161, 193, 222, and 223.

Vegetables & Fruit
• Substitute whole fruits (fresh, canned or frozen) for fruit juices more often. While juices have lots of vitamins and minerals, they contain very little fibre.
• Include interesting, exotic and less familiar fruits in fruit salads as a dessert item. Serve with a low-fat yogurt or with the delicious angel food cake found on page 281.
• Serve bigger portions of vegetables that are well liked. Vegetables should take up more than $\frac{1}{3}$ of the plate. In fact, the recommendation is that the protein portion of the meal should make up only $\frac{1}{4}$ of the plate, with vegetables and grains making up $\frac{3}{4}$.

FIBRE
Strictly speaking, dietary fibre is not a nutrient but it does provide a host of benefits. They include:
• Regulating the bowels
• Helping to reduce the risk of certain types of cancer
• Helping to regulate blood sugar
• Playing a role in lowering blood cholesterol

Fibre is found only in foods of vegetable origin, especially in whole grain foods, bran, vegetables, fruit and legumes, such as dried beans, peas and lentils.

Adults should aim for a daily fibre intake of 25-35 grams.

Milk Products
- Use lower-fat individual yogurts and lower-fat cheese in lunches or as snacks.
- Serve milk (skim, 1% or 2%) at more meals.
- To reduce fat, replace ice cream with lower-fat frozen yogurt and substitute low-fat yogurt for sour cream or mayonnaise in dips.
- Try 1% cottage cheese or light ricotta and partly-skimmed mozzarella in lasagna and other Italian dishes. See the recipes on pages 58, 104 and 122 for more great lower-fat dishes.

Meat & Alternatives
- Add more bean, lentil and other legume recipes to your dinner menus. Chili is always a favourite. Check out the recipes on pages 34, 37, 48, 51, 54, 67, 86, 105, 116, 118, 124, 128, 129, 130, 134, 198, 200.
- Use seafood in tomato-based pasta sauces or with rice, as in the recipe on page 107.
- Try bean soups like the one on page 66 or add canned beans to canned soup.
- Serve baked beans as a vegetable with dinner or breakfast.
- Experiment with bean salads and add chickpeas and beans to regular salads more often.
- Serve stir-fries and other mixed dishes more often. That way, a small amount of meat, fish or poultry goes a long way.

Step Four: Rewrite the meal plan
Make any changes in your meal planning gradually, so that everyone has a chance to adjust to new tastes.

In planning meals, consider the other activities of the day. Keep weekday meals simple and save more elaborate meals for weekends. Some other hints:
- Prepare a shopping list as you write the meal plan.
- Make sure you include everything you need for any recipes.
- As you do your plan, compare your menus to the Menu Planning Checklist on page 21 to be sure you are meeting your nutrition goals.
- A pre-designed shopping list can help organize your shopping for you and see that regular-use items such as flour, seasonings, snack food, margarine, sugar, tea and coffee are included in your list. One you might like to follow is the Healthy Shopping Checklist on page 22.

HOW TO CHOOSE A HEALTHY MARGARINE
All margarines are not equal. Here's what to look for.
- Choose a soft, spreadable margarine sold in a tub, not the stick or brick type of margarine.
- Quality margarines are labelled with nutrition information for a 10 gram serving. If a margarine isn't labelled, don't buy it.
- Choose margarine based on its content of unsaturated fat. Look on the label under Nutrition Information.
- Add up the grams of polyunsaturates and monounsaturates. If the total is 6 grams or more of unsaturated fat for a 10 gram (2 teaspoons) serving, then it is a good choice for a regular margarine.
- A light margarine would contain 3 grams or more of unsaturated fat for a 10 gram serving.
- If a margarine meets these guidelines, do not be concerned about small amounts of palm, palm kernel or hydrogenated vegetable oil in the ingredients. They are needed to produce the product's texture.

Meal	Grain Products	Vegetables & Fruit	Milk Products	Meat & Alternatives	Other Foods
	You need *at least* 5 servings per day. *Choose whole grain and enriched products more often.*	You need *at least* 5 servings per day. *Choose dark green and orange vegetables and orange fruit more often.*	You need *at least* 2 servings per day. Children and adolescents need at least 3 servings per day. *Choose lower-fat milk products more often.*	You need *at least* 2 servings per day. *Choose leaner meats, poultry and fish, as well as dried peas, beans and lentils more often.*	Choose these foods in moderation.
Breakfast Orange juice Cereal with milk Coffee	cereal – 1 or 2 servings	fruit juice – 1 serving	milk – 1 serving	0	0
Lunch A sandwich (fish, meat or egg with lettuce on a Kaiser roll) Fruit juice	Kaiser roll – 2 servings	fruit juice – 1 serving	0	fish, meat or egg – 1 serving	mayonnaise
Dinner Pork chop with baked potato and green beans Frozen yogurt for dessert	0	potato and green beans – 2 servings	frozen yogurt – 1 serving	pork chop – 1 serving	margarine
Snacks Morning: a muffin Afternoon: banana Evening: chips	muffin – 2 servings	banana – 1 serving	0	0	chips
Areas for Improvement	• vary the breakfast cereals or add whole wheat toast to your breakfast • try whole wheat buns for variety • plan your dinner meals around grain products (e.g., rice, pasta more often) • watch out for fat content of commercial muffins	• try more fresh fruit with lunch or breakfast to increase the fibre • have raw veggies on hand for snacking or part of your lunch • substitute fruit salad for dessert	• add lower-fat cheese on a ham sandwich or substitute skim, 1% or 2% milk for juice at lunch • choose lower-fat yogurt for dessert or snacks • try lower fat cheeses and whole wheat crackers for snacks	• watch the fat and salt content of deli meats • try meat alternatives more often (e.g., chickpeas in salad, lentil soup or stew)	• limit added fats (e.g., mayonnaise) • instead of chips, try pretzels or air-popped popcorn

MENU PLANNING

Meal	Grain Products	Vegetables & Fruit	Milk Products	Meat & Alternatives	Other Foods
	You need *at least* 5 servings per day. *Choose whole grain and enriched products more often.*	You need *at least* 5 servings per day. *Choose dark green and orange vegetables and orange fruit more often.*	You need *at least* 2 servings per day. Children and adolescents need at least 3 servings per day. *Choose lower-fat milk products more often.*	You need *at least* 2 servings per day. *Choose leaner meats, poultry and fish, as well as dried peas, beans and lentils more often.*	Choose these foods in moderation.
Breakfast					
Lunch					
Dinner					
Snacks					
Areas for Improvement					

MENU PLANNING CHECKLIST

Evaluate your menu using this checklist.

My Menu Includes	Yes	No
1. A variety of foods from each of the 4 food groups	☐	☐
2. A minimum of:		
5 servings of Grain Products	☐	☐
5 servings of Vegetables and Fruit	☐	☐
The required servings of Milk Products	☐	☐

(dependent on age)
Children 4–9 years: 2–3 servings
Youth 10–16 years: 3–4 servings
Adults: 2–4 servings
Pregnant and breast feeding: 3–4 servings

	Yes	No
2–3 servings of Meat and Alternatives	☐	☐
3. A variety of colour, flavour and texture	☐	☐
4. Meats trimmed of fat	☐	☐
5. Beans, lentils, dried peas or beans	☐	☐
6. Whole grain products	☐	☐
7. Lower-fat dairy products (1%, 2% milk, light cheese)	☐	☐
8. Food choices that we enjoy and that fit within our budget and lifestyle	☐	☐

HEALTHY SHOPPING CHECKLIST

Going shopping? Plan ahead. Check and list the foods you need. Remember to choose foods for healthy eating. This means choosing: a wide variety of foods; whole grain products, vegetables and fruit for fibre; and products lower in fat and salt.

The Bakery ☐
Look for whole grain products: they provide fibre.
e.g., bread, buns/rolls

Baking Supplies ☐
e.g., flour, pancake/muffin mixes, dried fruit

Beverages ☐
e.g., coffee/tea, bottled water/pop

Breakfast Cereals ☐
Choose whole grain or high-fibre cereals that provide at least 4 grams of fibre per serving.

Canned and Jarred Foods ☐
Buy products with less salt.
e.g., canned vegetables, fruit, juice, spaghetti sauce, legumes, tuna (in water/broth), salmon, peanut butter/jam/honey

Cookies and Crackers ☐
Buy products with less salt and fat.
e.g., melba toast, fig cookies

The Dairy Case ☐
Choose lower-fat dairy products.
e.g., milk (skim, 1%, 2%), yogurt, cheese (include varieties with 20% or less fat), soft margarine, eggs

Fresh Produce ☐
Stock up on these. They contain fibre and are low in fat.
e.g., fresh vegetables, fresh fruit

Frozen Foods ☐
e.g., frozen vegetables (choose plain, no sauces), frozen fruit, frozen juice, frozen meat/fish (without breading or batter), meals/entrées (buy light or lean varieties), sherbet/frozen yogurt/ lower-fat dairy desserts (choose ice cream less often)

Meat Counter ☐
Select leaner meats, poultry and fish.

Deli-style Meats ☐
Buy lower-fat varieties.
e.g., sliced beef, turkey, roast beef, ham.

Oils and Condiments ☐
e.g., oil, salad dressings (choose low calorie/lower-fat dressings), relishes/mustards/ketchup/vinegar, spices/herbs

Packaged Products ☐
(Pasta/Rice/Legumes)
Buy more of these foods.
e.g., pasta (buy enriched), rice, legumes (split peas, lentils, kidney beans, chickpeas)

Snack Foods ☐
Go easy on high-fat foods in this section.
e.g., chips, cheesies.
Make healthy choices such as popcorn, pretzels.

Shopping

The most important nutrition decisions are made in the super-market. Some suggestions to help you make the most of your shopping trip:

• Never shop when you are hungry.

• Always use a list to guide your purchasing.

• Control the food choices in your home. If you buy a food item, chances are someone will eat it. If you don't buy it, they won't. Make your choices as healthy as possible.

• Set a weekly routine time for shopping, with quick stops in between for perishables such as milk, fruit, vegetables, fish and poultry.

• Shop more in the outside aisles of the supermarket, where the four food group foods are to be found — fresh produce, the dairy case, the meat counter and the bakery.

• Buy locally grown foods. They should be fresher and cheaper.

• Watch for store specials and plan meals around them.

READING LABELS

Nutrition labels can help you make healthy decisions in the market. There are three important areas that can help your decision-making:

The ingredient list

• This list must be on the label.

• The list reveals important information such as the presence of whole grains, whether the product is enriched with vitamins or minerals, the sources of salt/sodium, and the kinds of fat in the product.

• Ingredients are listed in descending order by weight, with the ingredient present in the largest amount listed first.

• The list can alert you to ingredients to which you might be allergic.

Nutrition information

• The nutritional profile of a product is optional on food labels.

• It will give you the facts on the nutrient content for a single serving. Watch out for variations in serving sizes, though. One ounce (30 g) of cereal can range from a cup (250 mL) to a ¼ cup (25 g) for granola. At breakfast, very few people stop eating at just ¼ cup (25 g) of granola.

- Nutrition information is given per serving, so it is important to know exactly what the serving size is. If you eat more or less than the stated serving size, remember to reduce or increase the calories, fat, fibre and sodium you actually consume.
- Look at the calories and fat, especially the saturated fat content, and the fibre content, too. Compare similar products to choose the healthiest.

Nutrition claims
- Nutrition claims are big, bold statements that can tell you at-a-glance the key nutrition features of a food.
- "Cholesterol free," "Low in saturated fats," "High source of dietary fibre" and "50% less salt" are some of the most common claims.
- These claims must be backed up with facts on the nutrient content that prove the claim is true.
- Beware of misleading claims. A product may be labelled "Cholesterol free," not mentioning that the product has never had any cholesterol in it. Many naturally lower-fat foods such as breads and pretzels have always been lower in fat and cholesterol free.
- A product may be labelled "lite" or "light" which can refer to its taste, texture or look, not just its calories, fat or sodium.

ACHIEVING A LOWER-FAT DIET
Serious about reducing the amount of fat you consume? Here are some things to keep in mind.
- Some foods, such as peanut butter and cream cheese, are naturally high-fat foods. Rather than eliminate them from your diet, balance them with lower-fat foods such as bread or bagels. Balance and moderation are still the guidelines.
- Look for lower-fat choices. With dairy products, look for skim, 1% or 2% milk or yogurt.
- Remove the visible fat around meat and skin from poultry either before you cook it or at the table. Watch out for the high-fat blends used to make sausages, deli meats and other meat products.
- As a rule, whole grain breads and cereals are higher in fibre and lower in fat, with the exception of many granola cereals.
- With the exception of avocado and olives, which are high in fat, fruits and vegetables are also low in fat and high in fibre.
- Nuts and seeds are high in fat but are also sources of nutrients. Consumed in moderation, they can be part of a healthy diet.

- Apart from fats and oils, other sources of fat (and sodium) in the diet are prepared products such as dessert items (cakes, pies, donuts, cookies); snack foods (chips, cheesies); and prepared main courses (lasagna, casseroles, meat-based dinners). Use them occasionally instead of routinely. Instead, opt for fruit or sorbets for dessert; lower-fat crackers, fruit and raw vegetables for snacks; and prepare your own main courses.

Recipes

Many nutrition-conscious cookbooks are available today with full nutritional analyses for each recipe. The Heart and Stroke Foundation has published several excellent ones using old family favourites that have been modified to reduce fat but still deliver flavour.

Nutrition information can be useful when you are planning your family's total diet. For example, serve a recipe that is higher in fat with a lower-fat dish, to balance the meal.

Look at your family recipes to see how you might minimize fat while maximizing taste. Some areas to consider:

- Replace mayonnaise and sour cream with low-fat yogurt, light mayonnaise, light or no-fat sour cream, or the yogurt cheese recipe on page 229.
- In some recipes you can use milk or evaporated skim milk in recipes calling for cream, although the taste will be altered.
- The amount of oil in a regular recipe (not one that is already low in fat) can be usually reduced by a third without ruining the dish. For example, the maximum amount of oil in a muffin recipe should be ¼ cup (50 mL).
- Many recipes turn out successfully if you use two egg whites instead of a whole egg. The white of an egg is fat free.
- Enjoy the recipes in this book. They are all lower in fat.

Eating out

Restaurant food can be a challenge if you are trying to eat healthily. But a few guidelines can keep you on track.

- Look for restaurants that participate in the HeartSmart Restaurant Program. They have menu items that meet the criteria for lower fat and sodium content. As well, most provide non-smoking areas. You can recognize these restaurants by the signs in the window and the stylized heart checkmark on the menu.
- For restaurant breakfasts, focus on cereal, fruit, yogurt or pancakes, without the butter topping.

- If you travel for extended periods of time, tackle breakfast by stocking the mini bar with juices, milk, cereal and lower-fat muffins.
- At lunch or dinner, order one course at a time when you have the time. It will prevent you from ordering more than you normally eat.
- If you are with a group who are all ordering appetizers, opt for a clear or tomato-based soup.
- If you choose a grilled meat, ask that it be broiled without added oil or butter. Many meats labelled "grilled" are brushed with butter or oil before cooking.
- Salads can be ordered with dressing on the side so that you control the amount of fat you add. Watch out for marinated salads or regular caesar salad.
- Look for lower-fat desserts such as fruits and homemade ices.
- Remember the "total diet" credo — balance your choices, look for variety and enjoy all foods in moderation.

Prepared with you in mind

This cookbook has been designed for healthy people who love good food and want to eat better in general. With that in mind, the book includes recipes you will cook every day and those you will reserve for dinner party occasions.

People with diabetes will find the recipes easy to incorporate into their personal diet plans, using the Canadian Diabetes Association Food Choice Values beginning on page 291.

Because they are low in fat, heart patients should enjoy the recipes, even if they sometimes have to further reduce the salt, fat and dietary cholesterol. Some tips on how to do this are included in the Appendices on page 285.

From breakfast through to night-time snacks, from tempting appetizers to luscious desserts, these recipes prove that great tasting food can be healthy food, too. Bon appetit!

HEALTHFUL COOKING FOR EVERY OCCASION

A lot has happened since the publication of *Simply HeartSmart Cooking*. More and more people have become interested in lowering the fat in their diet and eating healthfully. Recipes in mainstream magazines and cookbooks generally tend to be lower in fat. As well, many restaurants are featuring healthful dishes on their menus. When I was travelling to promote *Simply HeartSmart Cooking*, we held several events in restaurants and hotels where the chefs had to recreate recipes from the book. Sometimes they were so surprised that healthy food could taste so delicious that they added the recipes to their regular menus!

People everywhere are choosing a healthier lifestyle. And many realize that eating less fat and more legumes, grains and vegetables goes hand in hand with quitting smoking, exercising regularly and reducing stress.

Heartsmart choices can be a part of all your cooking, whether you are entertaining, cooking for kids or looking for quick-and-easy dishes. Here are some ideas that might help.

COOKING FOR KIDS

It can be a real challenge cooking for a family these days. Everyone seems to have different needs. One's a vegetarian, another is lactose intolerant, one has a food allergy — and that's not even taking into account the picky eaters!

I solve this problem by cooking in layers. For example, if you are making Grilled Chicken Sandwiches with Charmoula (page 240), the plain chicken can be served in the bun or beside it; the grilled vegetables can be put on top of the chicken or not; the bun can be spread with hummos or salsa; and vegetarians can leave out the chicken altogether.

Or you might decide to make Pasta with Tomato and Red Pepper Sauce (page 99). You can serve the pasta with or without the sauce; you can add grilled chicken or fish to the sauce at the end of the cooking for those who want a more substantial meal; or vegetarians can add cooked chickpeas and other vegetables. You are only cooking one dinner, but adapting it to each person's needs.

Here are some recipes that most kids will like:

Veggie Cheese Spread (page 41)

Hummos (page 48)

Lemony Lentil Soup (page 67)

Chicken Soup with Rice (page 69)

Caesar Salad with Creamy Roasted Garlic Dressing (page 79)

Rice Salsa Salad (page 84)

Spaghetti Salad with Roasted Garlic and Tomato Salsa (page 85) – omit the jalapeño

Chinese Chicken Salad (page 91)

Angelhair Pasta with Fresh and Cooked Tomato Sauce (page 98)

Pasta with Tomato and Red Pepper Sauce (page 99)

Sweet and Spicy Chicken Lo Mein (page 110) – omit chili paste

Soupy Chinese Noodles (page 112)

Stuffed Baked Potatoes with Stir-fried Vegetables (page 117)

Salmon Patties with Fresh Dill (page 142)

Barbecued Chicken Steaks (page 160)

Turkey Burgers with Old-fashioned Coleslaw (page 176)

Barbecued Butterflied Turkey Breast (page 180)

Beef and Broccoli with Baked Noodle Cake (page 182)

Lamb Chops with Cashew Nut Couscous (page 193) – serve the couscous plain

Buttermilk Mashed Potatoes (page 215)

Roasted "French-fried" Potatoes (page 217)

Summer Crêpes with Berry Berry Salad (page 230)

Lemon Polenta Waffles (page 234) – call them Sunshine Waffles!

Chicken Burritos with Cooked Tomato Salsa (page 238)

Tropical Smoothie (page 244)

Yogurt Fruit Shake (page 244)

Blueberry Bran Muffins (page 246)

Apple Spice Muffins (page 248)

Mini Berry Cornmeal Muffins (page 251)

Prince Edward Island Dinner Rolls (page 254)

Banana Bread (page 256)

Apple Strudel (page 264)

Caramelized Fruit Crisp (page 267)

Rosy Applesauce (page 271)

Baked Alaska (page 272)

Crispy Chocolate Cookies (page 282)

COOKING FOR VEGETARIANS

People are becoming vegetarians for a variety of reasons. Some are dedicated to preserving our planet. Others don't like killing animals. Some feel a meat-free diet will help them control their weight. Still others just feel better not eating meat.

And many people want to eat more meatless meals without becoming strict vegetarians.

There are also many different kinds of vegetarians. Many eat eggs and dairy products; many eat fish and chicken, and some will even eat meat once in a while. So before you change your menus because one family member or dinner guest has declared vegetarian status, be sure to get a detailed definition!

One way of handling the situation is to cook what you normally make, including extra vegetables and a protein-rich grain or legume dish; the vegetarian can simply omit the meat course.

Or, you can choose one of the meatless main courses. There are also many meatless spreads and dips in the Appetizers chapter, several meatless soups (substitute vegetable stock for chicken stock where necessary), pastas, salads, vegetable and side dishes, pancakes, crêpes and frittatas.

COOKING FOR TEENAGERS

Teenagers will enjoy the breakfast and brunch recipes, chicken dishes, pastas with tomato sauces, breads and desserts. Many teenagers are vegetarians (Generation V), so check out the meatless main courses, too.

In addition to the children's recipes, the teenagers I know especially like these dishes:

Smoked Salmon Sushi (page 46)

Chicken Soup with Rice (page 69)

Thai Chicken Noodle Soup (page 70)

Caesar Salad with Creamy Roasted Garlic Dressing (page 79)

Tabbouleh Salad with Fresh Herbs (page 83)

Spaghetti Salad with Roasted Garlic and Tomato Salsa (page 85)

Chopped Tuna Salad (page 88)

Chinese Chicken Salad (page 91)

Sweet and Spicy Chicken Lo Mein (page 110)

Portobello Mushroom Burgers with Roasted Garlic Mayonnaise (page 114)

Lentil and Mushroom Burgers (page 116)

Stuffed Baked Potatoes with Stir-fried Vegetables (page 117)

Fresh Herb and Vegetable Lasagna (page 122)

Pizza Salad with Roasted Garlic Hummos (page 130)

Salmon Patties with Fresh Dill (page 142)

Glazed Swordfish (page 143)

Teriyaki Swordfish Burgers with Sweet Pickled Ginger Salsa (page 144)

Oven-roasted Sea Bass (page 147)

Lightly Breaded Shrimp with Hot Garlic Sauce (page 154)

Stir-fried Scallops (page 156)

Beef and Broccoli with Baked Noodle Cake (page 182)

Grilled Steak Sandwiches with Barbecued Onion Sauce (page 184)

Lamb Chops with Cashew Nut Couscous (page 193)

Roasted "French-fried" Potatoes (page 217)

COOKING FOR THE LACTOSE-INTOLERANT

My husband has been lactose-intolerant for more than ten years, and although many people feel this is a huge change to deal with, I think it is easier to handle than many other problems. There are also different degrees of intolerance. Some people can't even bear to look at dairy products; others overcome their intolerance by taking Lactaid pills; still others can tolerate yogurt cheese — it seems that when you strain out the whey, much of the lactose goes with it! I've served Breakfast Brûlée (page 226) to lactose-intolerant people, and it's been extremely successful, but test this very gradually and carefully.

The recipes in this book work well for lactose-intolerant people, because most do not contain dairy products. Cheese can be left out of soups, pasta dishes and many appetizers. In recipes where cheese is used to hold things together, as in pizzas and quesadillas, a bean puree will sometimes do a similar job.

COOKING QUICK AND EASY DINNERS

No one seems to have the time to cook leisurely dinners these days. Some solve the problem by cooking make-ahead meals and freezing them. Or you can make a great dinner by serving a simple meal of soup and salad with good bread.

In this book there are many recipes that you can make quickly at the last minute. Here are some good quick dinner ideas:

Chicken Satays with Peanut Sauce (page 54)

Tortilla Soup (page 68)

Thai Chicken Noodle Soup (page 70)

Seafood Chowder (page 74)

Asian Grilled Steak Salad (page 92)

Vietnamese Chicken Noodle Salad (page 94)

Spaghetti with Roasted Tomato Sauce (page 96)

Broken Spaghetti with Fresh Salsa and Scallops (page 107)

Pasta with Swordfish and Olives (page 108)

Fettuccine with Chicken and Mixed Peppers (page 109)

Sweet and Spicy Chicken Lo Mein (page 110)

Pizza with Black Bean Salsa (page 128)

Pizza Salad with Roasted Garlic Hummos (page 130)

Spicy Singapore Noodles (page 132)

Glazed Swordfish (page 143)

Oven-roasted Sea Bass (page 147)

Stir-fried Scallops (page 156)

Steamed Fish with Spinach and Black Bean Sauce (page 158)

Barbecued Chicken Steaks (page 160)

Flattened Cumin-grilled Chicken Breasts with Garlic Couscous (page 161)

Chicken Adobo (page 174)

Turkey Burgers with Old-fashioned Coleslaw (page 176)

Turkey Paillards (page 177)

Lamb Chops with Cashew Nut Couscous (page 193)

COOKING FOR COMPANY

Even when more people began to eat healthfully, many tended to make heart-healthy meals for themselves, but they would revert back to their higher-fat recipes for entertaining. This was probably partly due to the fact that rich ingredients were considered "fancy," and high-priced restaurant meals were typically very rich. But now we have many sensational foods from around the world available to us, and it is much easier to make creative and delicious meals for guests using ingredients that are naturally low in fat, such as fresh herbs, exotic spices, specialty vinegars and hot chiles.

Here are some good dishes for entertaining. Some may take a little longer to make, but they are especially pretty and not at all difficult to prepare:

Wild Mushroom Bruschetta with Chèvre (page 44)

Smoked Salmon Sushi (page 46)

Asparagus Tarts with Chèvre (page 52)

Malka's Bouillabaisse (page 72)

Quinoa and Crab Salad with Cilantro Lime Dressing (page 89)

Trenne with Wild Mushrooms (page 101)

Salmon Baked in Parchment with Parsley Pesto (page 140)

Salmon Fillets in Rice Paper Wrappers (page 141)

Sea Bass with Couscous Crust and Tomato Olive Vinaigrette (page 148)

Lightly Breaded Shrimp with Hot Garlic Sauce (page 154)

Hunter-style Chicken with Wild Mushrooms (page 168)

Roast Turkey Breast with Spinach Stuffing (page 178)

Shishkebab-flavoured Butterflied Leg of Lamb (page 192)

Lamb Chops with Cashew Nut Couscous (page 193)

Osso Bucco (page 194)

Apple Strudel (page 264)

Baked Wild Rice Pudding Brûlée (page 266)

Baked Alaska (page 272)

Pavlova with Berries and Flowers (page 275)

Gingerbread Angel Cake (page 281)

ABOUT THE
NUTRIENT ANALYSIS

Nutrient analysis of the recipes was performed by Info Access (1988) Inc., Don Mills, Ontario using the Nutritional Accounting component of the CBORD Menu Management System.

- The nutrient database was the 1991 Canadian Nutrient File supplemented when necessary with documented data from reliable sources.
- The analysis was based on:
  - the imperial weights and measures,
  - the smaller number of servings (i.e., larger portion) when there was a range, and
  - the first ingredient listed when there was a choice of ingredients.
- Canola vegetable oil, 1% milk, homemade unsalted stocks, regular white rice (not parboiled) and unenriched pasta were used throughout.
- Optional ingredients and garnishes in unspecified amounts were not calculated.
- Specific measures of salt were included in the analyses but "salt to taste" was not.
- When previously prepared dried legumes, rice or pasta were called for they were assumed to have been prepared without salt.

NUTRIENT INFORMATION ON RECIPES:

- Nutrient values have been rounded to the nearest whole number. Non-zero values less than .5 are shown as "trace".
- Good and excellent sources of vitamins (A, C, thiamine, riboflavin, niacin, B_6, folacin, B_{12}) and minerals (calcium and iron) have been identified according to the criteria established for nutrition labelling (*Guide to Food Labelling and Advertising*, Agriculture and Agri-Food Canada, March 1996).

  A serving which supplies 15% of the Recommended Daily Intake (RDI) for a vitamin or mineral (30% for vitamin C) is a good source of that nutrient. An excellent source must supply 25% of the RDI (50% for vitamin C).
- A serving providing at least 2 g of dietary fibre is considered a moderate source. Servings providing 4 g and 6 g are high and very high sources respectively (*Guide to Food Labelling and Advertising*).

Roasted Squash Spread *(page 38)*
Beet and Potato Skordalia *(page 36)*
Red Pepper, Feta and Garlic Hummos *(page 34)*

Tortilla Rolls with Hummos and Grilled Eggplant *(page 48)*
Salad Rolls *(page 50)*
Smoked Salmon Sushi *(page 46)*

APPETIZERS

Red Pepper, Feta and Garlic Hummos

Creamy Salsa

Beet and Potato Skordalia

White Bean and Roasted Garlic Spread

Roasted Squash Spread

Roasted Eggplant Spread

Grilled Vegetables with Chèvre Dip

Veggie Cheese Spread

Smoked Trout Spread

Cooked Salad

Wild Mushroom Bruschetta with Chèvre

Roasted Garlic Pesto on Bruschetta

Smoked Salmon Sushi

Tortilla Rolls with Hummos and Grilled Eggplant

Salad Rolls

Smoked Cheese and Sweet Onion Quesadillas

Asparagus Tarts with Chèvre

Chicken Satays with Peanut Sauce

RED PEPPER, FETA AND GARLIC HUMMOS

See photo opposite page 32.

One night when I was having a wonderful dinner at a Greek restaurant, I was served about eight small bowls of different, delicious dips. As I always find it hard to stop cooking no matter where I am, I combined a few of the dips in yet another bowl and came up with this! Serve it with grilled pita bread.

There are many variations of hummos. Try the jalapeño and cilantro version in the sidebar, the more traditional recipe on page 48 or the roasted garlic hummos on page 130.

Makes about 2 cups/500 mL

1	19-oz/540 mL tin chickpeas, drained and rinsed	1
2	sweet red peppers, roasted (page 241), peeled, seeded and diced	2
2	cloves garlic, minced, or 1 head roasted garlic (page 131)	2
2 oz	feta cheese, crumbled	60 g
¼ tsp	hot red pepper sauce	1 mL
½ tsp	pepper	2 mL
	Salt to taste	

1. Place chickpeas in food processor and chop finely (until almost mashed).

2. Add red peppers and garlic. Process on/off until combined but not completely pureed.

3. Add feta cheese, hot pepper sauce and pepper and process on/off until evenly distributed. Taste and season with salt.

JALAPEÑO AND CILANTRO HUMMOS

In food processor or blender, combine 1 19-oz/540 mL tin drained chickpeas, 1 roasted head garlic (page 131), ¼ cup/50 mL lemon juice, 1 seeded and chopped jalapeño, ½ cup/125 mL chopped fresh cilantro and 1 tbsp/15 mL olive oil. Thin with a few spoonfuls of unflavoured yogurt or yogurt cheese (page 229) if necessary.

Makes about 2 cups/500 mL

PER TBSP (15 mL)

Calories	23
g carbohydrate	3
g fibre	1
g total fat	1
g saturated fat	trace
g protein	1
mg cholesterol	2
mg sodium	46
mg potassium	29

CREAMY SALSA

This is great served as a dip with baked tortilla chips (see sidebar); it also works well in burritos, fajitas and tacos. The salsa can be made without the yogurt, but add 2 tbsp/25 mL lime juice or lemon juice instead.

For other salsas, see page 85 (Roasted Garlic and Tomato Salsa), page 84 (Tomato Salsa) and page 107 (Fresh Tomato Salsa).

Makes about 2 cups/500 mL

3	fresh plum tomatoes, seeded and diced	3
1	jalapeño, diced	1
1	clove garlic, minced	1
3	green onions, chopped	3
½ cup	chopped fresh cilantro or parsley	125 mL
½ tsp	ground cumin	2 mL
¾ cup	yogurt cheese (page 229) or thick yogurt	175 mL
	Salt, pepper and hot red pepper sauce to taste	

1. In bowl, combine tomatoes, jalapeño, garlic, green onions, cilantro and cumin.

2. Stir in yogurt cheese. Taste and adjust seasonings with salt, pepper and hot pepper sauce.

PER TBSP (15 mL)

Calories	8
g carbohydrate	1
g fibre	trace
g total fat	trace
g saturated fat	trace
g protein	1
mg cholesterol	1
mg sodium	6
mg potassium	37

BEET AND POTATO SKORDALIA

See photo opposite page 32.

This is a delicious, brightly coloured variation of the famous Greek potato and garlic dip. The colour is almost shocking! Even people who don't like beets will love this dip, so don't tell your guests what is in it until after they've tasted some!
Serve this with grilled bread (pages 44 or 45) or pita bread.

Makes about 2 cups/500 mL

1 lb	beets (2 large)	500 g
2	baking potatoes (1 lb/500 g)	2
1	head garlic	1
¼ tsp	hot red pepper sauce	1 mL
1 tbsp	red wine vinegar	15 mL
	Salt and pepper to taste	

1. Trim beets but do not peel. Wrap in foil. Wrap potatoes in foil. Trim about ½ inch/1 cm off top of garlic and wrap garlic head in foil. Arrange foil packages on baking sheet and bake in preheated 400°F/200°C oven. Bake garlic for 45 minutes, potatoes for 1 hour and beets for 1½ hours. Check to see if vegetables are cooked by squeezing garlic and by piercing potatoes and beets.

2. Cool beets until you can handle them. Peel while they are still warm — the skins should just slip off. Scoop potatoes out of skins.

3. In bowl, mash beets with potatoes. Squeeze garlic out of skins and mash with potatoes and beets (mixture could also be pureed).

4. Stir in hot pepper sauce, vinegar, salt and pepper.

PER TBSP (15 mL)

Calories	12
g carbohydrate	3
g fibre	trace
g total fat	0
g saturated fat	0
g protein	trace
mg cholesterol	0
mg sodium	6
mg potassium	67

WHITE BEAN AND ROASTED GARLIC SPREAD

People are always so surprised when they taste a delicious bean dish like this one. Use chickpeas or black beans instead of kidney beans if you wish. You can also heat this mixture and serve it as a side dish.

If you start with dried beans, soak 1 cup/250 mL in cold water overnight in the refrigerator. Drain, add fresh cold water, bring to a boil and cook, covered, for one hour, or until very tender. You should have about 2 cups/500 mL cooked beans.

If the dip is too thick, thin it with a little low-fat yogurt or yogurt cheese (page 229). Serve with grilled bread (pages 44 or 45).

Makes about 1½ cups/375 mL

1	19-oz/540 mL tin white kidney beans, drained and rinsed	1
1	head roasted garlic (page 131), or 2 cloves raw garlic, minced	1
2 tbsp	lemon juice	25 mL
½ tsp	hot red pepper sauce	2 mL
½ tsp	ground cumin	2 mL
1 tbsp	olive oil	15 mL
½ tsp	pepper	2 mL
	Salt to taste	

1. Place beans in food processor. Squeeze garlic out of skins and add to beans. Blend.

2. Blend in lemon juice, hot pepper sauce, cumin, oil and pepper.

3. Taste and add salt or more lemon juice if necessary.

PER TBSP (15 mL)

Calories	26
g carbohydrate	4
g fibre	1
g total fat	1
g saturated fat	trace
g protein	1
mg cholesterol	0
mg sodium	53
mg potassium	45

ROASTED SQUASH SPREAD

See photo opposite page 32.

This is an unusual way to use up cooked squash. I discovered it by accident when I had leftover pureed vegetables and then, coincidentally, found it on many fancy restaurant tables as a little treat served with bread before dinner. I guess they had leftovers, too!

I like to use butternut squash because it is less watery than other winter squashes.

Makes about 2 cups / 500 mL

2 lb	butternut squash	1 kg
10	sprigs fresh rosemary, or ½ tsp/2 mL dried	10
1	head garlic	1
1 tbsp	balsamic vinegar	15 mL
1 tsp	brown sugar	5 mL
1 tsp	ground cumin	5 mL
½ tsp	pepper	2 mL
	Salt to taste	

1. Cut squash in half and scoop out seeds. Place rosemary in hollow and place squash, cut side down, on baking sheet lined with parchment paper.

2. Cut about ¼ inch/5 mm off top of garlic. Place cut side down on baking sheet beside squash.

3. Bake squash and garlic in preheated 375°F/190°C oven for 1 hour, or until garlic and squash are tender. Cool. Discard rosemary.

4. Scoop out squash into food processor (you should have about 2 cups/500 mL). Squeeze garlic out of skins into squash. Add vinegar, sugar, cumin and pepper and puree on/off until blended. Taste and season with salt if necessary.

PER TBSP (15 mL)	
Calories	13
g carbohydrate	3
g fibre	0
g total fat	0
g saturated fat	0
g protein	trace

Good: vitamin A

mg cholesterol	0
mg sodium	1
mg potassium	81

ROASTED EGGPLANT SPREAD

Rhonda Caplan, who works at the cooking school, often brings us wonderful treats that she has made at home for friends. This was one of our favourites, and we have adapted it into a great-tasting low-fat spread using yogurt cheese.

Rhonda says that if you want eggplant mixtures to be very white, do not use metal utensils or bowls when baking or mashing. And if you buy long, thin eggplants rather than the fat ones, there will be fewer seeds.

Serve this dip with pita bread or pita chips (page 35).

Makes about 2¹/₂ cups/625 mL

2	large eggplants, halved (3 lb/1.5 kg)	2
1	head roasted garlic (page 131), or 2 cloves raw garlic, minced	1
2 tbsp	lemon juice	25 mL
2 tbsp	yogurt cheese (page 229) or mayonnaise	25 mL
1 tsp	granulated sugar	5 mL
	Salt and pepper to taste	

1. Cut piece of parchment paper or waxed paper just to fit under eggplants on baking sheet. Place eggplants, cut side down, on paper. Place under broiler until skin is charred and eggplant is very tender, about 20 minutes.

2. Scoop eggplant out of skins into bowl. Squeeze roasted garlic out of skins into bowl and mash with eggplant.

3. Add lemon juice, yogurt cheese and sugar and blend in. Taste and add salt and pepper.

EGGPLANT

There are many types of eggplant. For grilling I prefer the thin Asian or Japanese eggplants, as they do not need to be peeled or salted (some recipes call for eggplants to be sprinkled with salt to extract liquid and bitterness). But for eggplant purees I like the larger eggplants, as they have more flesh. Look for shiny purple skin without any discoloration.

PER TBSP (15 mL)

Calories	10
g carbohydrate	2
g fibre	1
g total fat	trace
g saturated fat	0
g protein	trace
mg cholesterol	0
mg sodium	2
mg potassium	70

GRILLED VEGETABLES WITH CHÈVRE DIP

Serve this with grilled bread (pages 44 or 45) or focaccia for a wonderful appetizer, or as a salad. The dip can be used as a dressing on rice or potato salads, or you can serve the vegetables and dip in pita bread for a sensational sandwich. The vegetables can also be served on their own as a side dish.

If you cannot find all the vegetables, just use more of the ones you can find.

Makes 8 to 10 servings

Balsamic Glaze:

½ cup	balsamic vinegar	125 mL
1 tbsp	brown sugar	15 mL
1	clove garlic, minced	1
1 tbsp	chopped fresh rosemary, or ½ tsp/2 mL dried	15 mL

Grilled Vegetables:

1	bulb fennel, trimmed (page 211) and cut in thin wedges	1
1	red onion, cut in wedges	1
1 lb	thin eggplants (about 4), cut in 1-inch/2.5 cm chunks	500 g
½ lb	portobello mushrooms, cut in chunks	250 g
2	Belgian endives, cut lengthwise in quarters	2
½ lb	thick asparagus, trimmed	250 g
2 cups	cherry tomatoes	500 mL
	Sprigs fresh basil or parsley	

Chèvre Dip:

4 oz	chèvre (goat cheese)	125 g
¾ cup	yogurt cheese (page 229) or thick yogurt	175 mL
1	head roasted garlic (page 131), or 2 cloves raw garlic, minced	1
1 tbsp	balsamic vinegar	15 mL
1 tsp	pepper	5 mL

GOAT CHEESE

There are as many kinds of cheese made from goat's milk as there are made from cow's milk. Most recipes that call for chèvre, however, refer to the soft, creamy variety. The taste becomes milder when the cheese is combined with other ingredients, or when it is warmed.

PER SERVING

Calories	140
g carbohydrate	21
g fibre	5
g total fat	5
g saturated fat	2
g protein	7

Excellent: folacin
Good: vitamin C; niacin; riboflavin; vitamin B$_6$

mg cholesterol	12
mg sodium	113
mg potassium	672

1. To make glaze, in small saucepan, combine vinegar, sugar, minced garlic and rosemary. Bring to a boil. Cook for about 5 minutes, or until slightly thickened.

2. Brush fennel, red onion, eggplant and mushroom pieces with glaze. Grill for 5 to 15 minutes, or until well browned. Brush Belgian endive and asparagus with glaze. Grill just until browned, about 5 minutes. Watch vegetables closely, turning often.

3. Arrange vegetables on serving platter. Garnish with cherry tomatoes and sprigs of fresh basil.

4. To make dip, in food processor, combine chèvre and yogurt cheese. Squeeze garlic out of skins and add to cheese. Add vinegar and pepper. Puree until smooth. Taste and adjust seasonings if necessary. (You should have about 1 cup/250 mL dip.)

5. Place dip in bowl and serve with vegetables.

VEGGIE CHEESE SPREAD

This spread is crunchy and flavourful. Use it on bagels, as a sandwich filling or as a vegetable dip.

Makes about 2 cups/500 mL

¼ cup	finely chopped carrots	50 mL
¼ cup	finely chopped green onions	50 mL
¼ cup	finely chopped celery	50 mL
¼ cup	finely chopped sweet red pepper, patted dry	50 mL
1	small clove garlic, minced	1
1½ cups	yogurt cheese (page 229)	375 mL
	Salt and pepper to taste	

1. In bowl, combine carrots, green onions, celery, red pepper, garlic and yogurt cheese. Taste and season with salt and pepper.

PER TBSP (15 mL)

Calories	12
g carbohydrate	1
g fibre	0
g total fat	trace
g saturated fat	trace
g protein	1
mg cholesterol	1
mg sodium	11
mg potassium	45

SMOKED TROUT SPREAD

This is delicious spread on bagels for a weekend breakfast, stuffed into mini pitas for hors d'oeuvres or served on rounds of French bread as an appetizer. Smoked salmon or whitefish can be used instead of the trout.

Makes about 2 cups / 500 mL

8 oz	filleted and boned smoked trout (1½ or 2 small whole trout)	250 g
1 cup	yogurt cheese (page 229) or light ricotta cheese, well drained	250 mL
1 tbsp	grated white horseradish	15 mL
2 tbsp	lemon juice	25 mL
2 tbsp	chopped fresh dill	25 mL
2 tbsp	chopped fresh chives or green onions	25 mL
½ tsp	pepper	2 mL
	Salt to taste	

1. Remove and discard as many bones from trout as possible. Break up fillets and chop in food processor or with knife.

2. Blend in yogurt cheese, horseradish and lemon juice.

3. Stir in dill, chives and pepper. Taste and season with salt if necessary.

PER TBSP (15 mL)

Calories	16
g carbohydrate	1
g fibre	0
g total fat	1
g saturated fat	trace
g protein	2

Good: vitamin B_{12}

mg cholesterol	2
mg sodium	63
mg potassium	39

COOKED SALAD

Rhonda Caplan, the main recipe tester at the cooking school and the person who brought us the Roasted Eggplant Spread (page 39), is also responsible for this wonderful recipe. She is from Montreal and brings us many Montreal food ideas. This "cooked" salad is really a thick tomato dip. It has its roots in Moroccan cooking, which is very popular in Montreal.

You can serve this as a dip with pita chips (page 35) or vegetable sticks, but it also makes a great pasta sauce and a terrific spread for sandwiches. If you are in a hurry, omit the roasting and peeling of the red peppers.

Although we usually make this with canned plum tomatoes, ripe fresh tomatoes taste sensational when they are in season!

Makes about 5 cups/1.25 L

4	sweet red peppers	4
2 tsp	olive oil	10 mL
12	cloves garlic, finely chopped	12
4	jalapeños, seeded and finely chopped	4
3 lb	fresh plum tomatoes, peeled, seeded and chopped, or 3 28-oz/796 mL tins plum tomatoes, drained and chopped	1.5 kg
	Salt to taste	

1. Cut peppers in half and remove seeds. Arrange peppers, cut side down, on baking sheet. Broil until skins turn black. Cool. Peel and dice peppers and reserve.

2. Heat oil in large, deep non-stick skillet. Add garlic and jalapeños and cook gently until soft and fragrant but do not brown.

3. Add tomatoes and cook, stirring often, on medium heat, until mixture is very thick and sauce-like, about 20 minutes.

4. Add reserved peppers and salt. Continue to cook gently for 10 to 15 minutes, stirring occasionally to prevent sticking. Taste and adjust seasonings if necessary. I like it chunky, but it can also be pureed.

PER TBSP (15 mL)

Calories	6
g carbohydrate	1
g fibre	trace
g total fat	trace
g saturated fat	0
g protein	trace
mg cholesterol	0
mg sodium	1
mg potassium	44

WILD MUSHROOM BRUSCHETTA WITH CHÈVRE

Bruschetta, or grilled bread, has become extremely popular. You can use different breads, different toppings, or combine toppings as in this recipe. If you cannot find wild mushrooms (page 115) or if they are too expensive, simply use regular mushrooms, caramelized onions (page 212) or salsa.

Makes 20 pieces

2 tsp	olive oil	10 mL
2	shallots, finely chopped, or 1 small onion	2
2	cloves garlic, finely chopped	2
1 lb	wild mushrooms, sliced	500 g
2 tsp	chopped fresh thyme, or ½ tsp/2 mL dried	10 mL
1 tsp	pepper, divided	5 mL
	Salt to taste	
2 tbsp	chopped fresh parsley	25 mL
3 oz	chèvre (goat cheese)	90 g
2 tbsp	yogurt cheese (page 229) or light ricotta cheese, well drained	25 mL
1	clove garlic, minced	1
20	slices crusty French stick (2 inches/5 cm in diameter and ½ inch/1 cm thick)	20
20	small sprigs fresh basil or parsley	20

1. Heat olive oil in large, deep non–stick skillet. Add shallots and chopped garlic. Cook gently for 2 minutes.

2. Add mushrooms, thyme and ½ tsp/2 mL pepper. When mushrooms begin to render liquid, increase heat and cook for 5 to 10 minutes until liquid evaporates and mushrooms are cooked. Taste and add salt. Stir in parsley.

3. In bowl or food processor, blend chèvre, yogurt cheese, minced garlic and remaining ½ tsp/2 mL pepper. Add a little more yogurt if necessary to make mixture spreadable (you should have about ½ cup/125 mL).

4. Grill bread lightly on both sides until crusty on the outside and chewy on the inside. Spread with cheese mixture (1 tsp/ 5 mL per slice). Top with mushrooms and garnish with basil.

SHALLOTS
Shallots have a very special flavour, not unlike a combination of sweet onion with a little garlic. Some cooks confuse them with scallions, the American name for green onions. Shallots look like a small bulb and pack a lot of flavour for their size. If you can't find them and a recipe calls for raw shallots, substitute green onions; if a recipe calls for a cooked shallot, you can substitute a small onion plus a small clove of garlic.

PER PIECE

Calories	52
g carbohydrate	7
g fibre	1
g total fat	2
g saturated fat	1
g protein	2
mg cholesterol	3
mg sodium	79
mg potassium	80

ROASTED GARLIC PESTO ON BRUSCHETTA

It is very hard to produce a rich-tasting pesto sauce without a lot of olive oil, but using pureed roasted garlic as a base will also give you a sauce that is rich in taste and texture.

Pesto has many uses. It makes a great garnish for soups or a sauce for grilled lamb chops, fish or chicken. You can stir it into pasta, rice or salad dressings or use it as a flavour boost for other sauces. It even makes a good sandwich spread. Add 2 tbsp/25 mL grated Parmesan cheese if you wish.

Makes 32 pieces

2 cups	packed fresh basil	500 mL
1 cup	packed fresh parsley	250 mL
2 tbsp	pine nuts, toasted (see sidebar)	25 mL
2 tbsp	olive oil	25 mL
2	heads roasted garlic (page 131)	2
	Salt and pepper to taste	
3 tbsp	hot water	45 mL
32	slices crusty French stick (2 inches/5 cm in diameter and ½ inch/1 cm thick)	32

1. Place basil and parsley in food processor or blender and chop finely.

2. Add pine nuts and chop coarsely.

3. Blend in olive oil. Squeeze garlic out of skins and blend in. Taste and season with salt and pepper. Blend in hot water.

4. Grill bread lightly on both sides until crusty on the outside and chewy on the inside. Spread bread with pesto and serve.

PINE NUTS

Pine nuts are used in Italian and Middle Eastern cooking, but they are also very common in Chinese dishes. They are high in fat, so toast them before using — the flavour will be stronger, and you won't need to use as many. To toast nuts, place on a baking sheet and bake in preheated 350°F/180°C oven for about 5 minutes, or until lightly browned.

Keep pine nuts in the freezer if you are not using them right away.

PER PIECE

Calories	42
g carbohydrate	6
g fibre	trace
g total fat	2
g saturated fat	trace
g protein	1
mg cholesterol	0
mg sodium	55
mg potassium	41

SMOKED SALMON SUSHI

See photo opposite page 33.

Cooked shrimp, smoked salmon, smoked trout or eel, crab and avocado are just a few of the traditional ingredients you can use instead of raw fish. Sudari mats, available at Japanese specialty stores, will help you roll the sushi, but if you don't have one, just use a clean tea towel.

Freshly made sushi, of course, is the best, but I have also made these a day ahead of time. Keep them refrigerated if you are making them more than one hour ahead, and slice just before serving if possible. For dipping, use soy sauce mixed with a little wasabi.

Nori is the compressed sea vegetable that is used as a wrapper in sushi. Try to find the toasted variety — it is worth the extra expense. Keep any unused nori in the freezer. Like wasabi, it can be found at most Asian food stores and some health food stores.

Normally I use seasoned and unseasoned rice vinegar interchangeably, but in sushi I like seasoned vinegar for the traditional taste.

Makes 32 pieces

1½ cups	short-grain rice, preferably Japanese	375 mL
1¾ cups	cold water	425 mL
¼ cup	seasoned rice vinegar	50 mL
4	large sheets toasted nori (8 x 7 inches/20 x 18 cm)	4
1 tbsp	wasabi, or 2 tbsp/25 mL honeycup mustard	15 mL
3 oz	smoked salmon, cut in strips	90 g
¼	English cucumber, unpeeled and cut in strips 8 inches/20 cm long	¼
8	long sprigs dill	8
8	fresh chives or thin strips green onion	8

HOMESTYLE SUSHI
Simply combine all sushi ingredients together and serve as a "salad." Toasted sesame seeds, pickled ginger root and bits of fish and vegetables can also be added.

PER PIECE

Calories	42
g carbohydrate	8
g fibre	trace
g total fat	trace
g saturated fat	0
g protein	2
mg cholesterol	1
mg sodium	92
mg potassium	39

1. Rinse rice under cold water until water runs clear. Place in heavy saucepan with cold water. Cover tightly and allow to rest for 15 minutes. Bring to boil and cook over high heat for 4 minutes while lid jumps up and down and rice bubbles and foams. Reduce heat to medium and cook for 8 to 10 minutes. Remove from heat and allow rice to rest for 15 minutes to steam. Do not remove lid at any time.

2. When rice is ready, place in bowl and toss gently while sprinkling with vinegar. Divide rice into 4 equal portions — about 1 cup/250 mL each.

3. Place one sheet of nori, rough side up, on sudari mat or damp tea towel. Top with one portion of rice. Dampen hands with cold water and spread rice all the way to edges on three sides. Leave about ½ inch/1 cm nori uncovered at one end.

4. Combine wasabi with tiny bit of water to make a paste and let rest, covered, for 2 minutes. Then spread down centre of rice.

5. Top wasabi with one or two strips of salmon, cucumber, dill and chives. Roll up using mat to help and press firmly at top to seal (dampen edge of nori if necessary to help seal). Repeat with remaining ingredients to form 4 rolls.

6. Using sharp, wet knife, cut each roll into 8 pieces and arrange on serving platter.

TORTILLA ROLLS WITH HUMMOS AND GRILLED EGGPLANT

See photo opposite page 33.

This is a great idea for an appetizer, but these rolls can also be served whole as sandwiches. Instead of the hummos you can use white bean spread (page 37) or eggplant spread (page 39); try fillings like caramelized onions (page 212) or sauteed wild mushrooms (page 62). The filling can be as simple or as complex as you wish. (The hummos can also be served on its own as a dip.)

If you make these rolls ahead of time, wrap them in plastic wrap and refrigerate for a few hours or overnight — that way they will be even easier to slice.

Makes 32 pieces

1 lb	thin eggplants (about 4)	500 g
3	sweet red peppers	3
½ cup	shredded fresh basil or chopped parsley	125 mL

Hummos:

1	19-oz/540 mL tin chickpeas, drained and rinsed	1
3 tbsp	lemon juice	45 mL
1 tbsp	sesame oil	15 mL
2	cloves garlic, minced	2
½ tsp	ground cumin	2 mL
½ tsp	hot red pepper sauce	2 mL
½ tsp	pepper	2 mL
3 tbsp	low-fat yogurt or yogurt cheese (page 229)	45 mL
4	10-inch/25 cm flour tortillas	4

PER PIECE

Calories	50
g carbohydrate	9
g fibre	1
g total fat	1
g saturated fat	trace
g protein	2

Good: vitamin C

mg cholesterol	0
mg sodium	55
mg potassium	81

1. Cut eggplants lengthwise into ¼-inch/5 mm slices. Grill until browned on both sides.

2. Grill peppers until blackened on all sides. Cool, remove skin and seeds and cut into strips.

3. To prepare hummos, in food processor, combine chickpeas, lemon juice, sesame oil, garlic, cumin, hot pepper sauce and pepper. Add enough yogurt to make hummos spreadable. Taste and adjust seasonings if necessary.

4. Spread hummos over the 4 tortillas. Arrange strips of eggplant and peppers over two-thirds of each tortilla. Leaving an edge at top without vegetables, roll up tortillas tightly. Wrap individually in plastic wrap and refrigerate.

5. Slice rolls on diagonal to serve (the cook gets to eat the ragged ends of the rolls!).

SALAD ROLLS

See photo opposite page 33.

I first tasted these at the Granville Market in Vancouver and was thrilled with the clean, fresh taste. They are a perfect low-fat appetizer. Instead of chicken you can use strips of tofu, shrimp or barbecued pork or duck.

These rolls should be very delicate, so if you have too many vegetables, just eat the extra. Serve them with Thai dipping sauce (page 207), peanut sauce (page 54) or sweet and hot Thai chili sauce (page 94).

Makes 16 rolls

2 oz	thin rice vermicelli	60 g
2 tbsp	rice vinegar or cider vinegar	25 mL
2 tbsp	finely chopped fresh cilantro or parsley	25 mL
16	8-inch/20 cm rice paper wrappers	16
16	small leaves leaf lettuce	16
1	carrot, cut in 16 4-inch/10 cm matchstick pieces	1
1	stalk celery, cut in 16 4-inch/10 cm matchstick pieces	1
¼	English cucumber, cut in strips	¼
1	sweet red pepper, seeded and cut in strips	1
½ lb	cooked chicken, cut in strips	250 g
16	sprigs fresh mint or basil	16
32	sprigs fresh cilantro or parsley	32
32	fresh chives or green onion slivers	32

1. Place noodles in large bowl and cover with hot tap water. Allow to soak for 15 minutes. Drain well. Toss noodles with rice vinegar and chopped cilantro. Reserve.

2. Soak rice paper wrappers in hot water for a few seconds until they soften. Arrange in single layer on damp tea towels.

3. Fold down top third of wrappers. Arrange piece of lettuce about one-third of way from bottom so it protrudes above flat top. Arrange carrot, celery, cucumber, red pepper and chicken on top of lettuce, also protruding. Add noodles. Top with sprig of mint, 2 sprigs cilantro and 2 chives.

4. Fold up bottom third over filling. Roll up wrappers tightly from either side. Wrapper should stick to itself to seal.

PER ROLL

Calories	56
g carbohydrate	6
g fibre	1
g total fat	1
g saturated fat	trace
g protein	5

Good: vitamin A; vitamin C

mg cholesterol	13
mg sodium	18
mg potassium	121

SMOKED CHEESE AND SWEET ONION QUESADILLAS

This combination of tastes and textures is sensational, but I often make quesadillas just with cheese (like grilled cheese sandwiches) and then use a dip to spice them up. That way, picky kids and adults alike will love them.

These can be cut into wedges and served as an appetizer, or you can serve them on top of a salad for an interesting brunch dish. Or you can leave them whole (like a pizza) for a light meal.

Makes 24 wedges

2 tsp	olive oil	10 mL
2	sweet onions (Vidalia or Spanish), chopped	2
½ tsp	pepper	2 mL
1½ cups	grated part-skim smoked mozzarella cheese or light Monterey Jack cheese (½ lb/250 g)	375 mL
1 cup	cooked chickpeas, coarsely chopped	250 mL
6	10-inch/25 cm flour tortillas	6

1. Heat oil in large non-stick skillet. Add onions and pepper. Cook on medium-high heat, without stirring, until onions start to brown. Stir and keep cooking until onions brown well. Reduce heat and cook gently until onions are sweet and any liquid has completely evaporated. (If onions start to stick, add a few spoonfuls of water and cook until it evaporates.)

2. Assemble quesadillas by laying tortillas on work surface in a single layer. Spread onions on half of each tortilla. Top with chickpeas and cheese. Fold tortillas in half and press edges together firmly.

3. Grill tortillas for a few minutes per side until cheese starts to melt and tortillas are brown. Tortillas can also be cooked in non-stick or lightly oiled skillet or baked in preheated 400°F/200°C oven for 10 minutes until crusty and lightly browned. Allow to rest for a few minutes before cutting into wedges.

SWEET ONIONS

Although all onions are sweet once they have been cooked, some varieties are really sweet even when raw. Vidalia, Maui and Spanish onions can even be too sweet for some recipes (as in some soups), but they are delicious used in salads, quesadillas, relishes, pizzas and sandwiches.

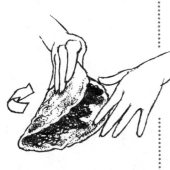

PER WEDGE

Calories	92
g carbohydrate	13
g fibre	1
g total fat	3
g saturated fat	1
g protein	4
mg cholesterol	4
mg sodium	92
mg potassium	89

ASPARAGUS TARTS WITH CHÈVRE

See photo opposite page 64.

The idea for these fanciful spring tarts came from Buffalo Mountain Lodge in Banff. They make a wonderful appetizer before a special dinner party. You can also fill them with caramelized onions (page 212) and Gorgonzola or sauteed wild mushrooms and mashed potatoes.

Makes 8 servings

3 tbsp	unsalted butter, melted, or olive oil	45 mL
3 tbsp	water	45 mL
8	sheets phyllo pastry	8
½ cup	dry breadcrumbs	125 mL

Filling:

1 lb	asparagus	500 g
2 tsp	olive oil	10 mL
2	leeks, trimmed and sliced	2
2	cloves garlic, finely chopped	2
3	shallots or 1 small onion, finely chopped	3
1 tbsp	chopped fresh thyme, or ½ tsp/2 mL dried	15 mL
1 tsp	chopped fresh rosemary, or pinch dried	5 mL
	Salt and pepper to taste	
3 oz	chèvre (goat cheese), crumbled	90 g
1	bunch fresh chives or slivered green onions, cut in 4-inch/10 cm pieces	1

DESSERT PHYLLO CUPS

A wonderful dessert can be made in a similar manner to these tarts. Use melted butter or unflavoured vegetable oil for brushing, and dust the phyllo with granulated sugar instead of breadcrumbs when you are assembling the cups. Bake the unfilled cups for 15 to 18 minutes, until crisp. Cool and remove from pans. Fill with fruit sorbet and top with fresh berries. Or you can fill the cups with caramelized fruit or compotes. Sprinkle with icing sugar before serving.

PER SERVING

Calories	197
g carbohydrate	24
g fibre	2
g total fat	9
g saturated fat	4
g protein	6

Excellent: folacin

mg cholesterol	19
mg sodium	253
mg potassium	154

1. In small bowl, combine butter and water.

2. Working with one sheet of phyllo at a time (cover rest with plastic wrap or damp tea towel), brush phyllo with butter mixture and sprinkle with breadcrumbs. Cut into 6 squares. Place squares on top of each other at irregular angles and press into bottom of muffin cup with edges sticking up. Repeat with remaining phyllo.

3. To make filling, trim asparagus and peel about 2 inches/5 cm up from bottom of stalks. Bring large skillet of water to boil. Add asparagus and cook for 3 to 4 minutes. Trim off 2-inch/5 cm tips and reserve. Cut stalks into ½-inch/1 cm slices.

4. Heat oil in large, deep non-stick skillet. Add leeks, garlic and shallots. Cook gently until vegetables are very tender (add a few spoonfuls of water if they start to stick). Add chopped asparagus, thyme, rosemary, salt and pepper.

5. Divide mixture among phyllo shells. Top with cheese. Arrange asparagus tips so they stick out of filling.

6. Bake in preheated 375°F/190°C oven for 20 minutes, or until golden brown. Garnish with chives inserted into filling.

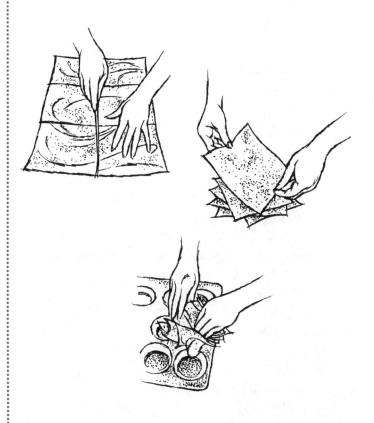

CHICKEN SATAYS WITH PEANUT SAUCE

This recipe is also good made with pork or lamb. Serve it as an appetizer or as a main course with stir-fried vegetables and rice. It is delicious with or without the sauce.

Using chickpeas in the peanut sauce is a great solution for a normally high-fat sauce, and the chickpeas are a perfect foil for the peanut butter. The sauce also makes a good vegetable dip, or you can toss it with linguine.

Makes 16 skewers

1 lb	boneless, skinless chicken breasts	500 g
1 tsp	curry powder	5 mL
1	clove garlic, minced	1
1 tbsp	soy sauce	15 mL
1 tbsp	lemon juice	15 mL
1 tbsp	honey	15 mL
1 tbsp	water	15 mL

Peanut Sauce:

½ cup	cooked chickpeas	125 mL
1 tbsp	smooth peanut butter	15 mL
2 tbsp	rice wine	25 mL
2 tbsp	honey	25 mL
2 tbsp	soy sauce	25 mL
2 tbsp	water	25 mL
dash	hot red pepper sauce	dash

1. Cut chicken into 4 x 1-inch/10 x 2.5 cm strips (you should have about 16 strips).

2. To make marinade, in large bowl, combine curry powder, garlic, soy sauce, lemon juice, honey and water. Add chicken strips and combine. Marinate in refrigerator for 10 to 60 minutes.

3. To make sauce, in food processor or blender, combine chickpeas, peanut butter, rice wine, honey, soy sauce, water and hot pepper sauce. Taste and adjust seasonings if necessary.

4. Thread chicken on skewers. Grill on medium-high heat for 4 to 5 minutes per side, or until chicken is cooked through. Serve with peanut sauce drizzled on top or as dip.

SKEWERS
Bamboo or wooden skewers should be soaked in cold water for about 30 minutes before using to reduce the chance of burning. I also arrange the food so that most of the wood is covered, or avoid placing the exposed wood on the hottest part of the grill. Metal skewers get very hot, but they are reusable. I like to use double-pronged skewers so the food does not roll around when you turn it. Or simply use two skewers at a time as shown above.

PER SKEWER

Calories	60
g carbohydrate	5
g fibre	trace
g total fat	1
g saturated fat	trace
g protein	7

Good: niacin

mg cholesterol	18
mg sodium	164
mg potassium	86

SOUPS

Winter Root Vegetable Soup

Fresh Herb Soup with Ricotta Croutons

Fresh Tomato Soup with Pesto Cream

Calconnan Soup

Butternut Squash Soup with Wild Mushroom Sauté

Corn Chowder with Herb Cheese

Curried Squash Soup

White Bean and Spinach Soup

Lemony Lentil Soup

Tortilla Soup

Chicken Soup with Rice

Thai Chicken Noodle Soup

Malka's Bouillabaisse

Seafood Chowder

Spicy Gazpacho

Cold Cucumber Tzatziki Soup

WINTER ROOT VEGETABLE SOUP

See photo opposite page 65.

During the promotion for Simply HeartSmart Cooking, *I had the wonderful opportunity to meet many new people and see parts of my country that I had never seen before. The Rocky Mountains really captured my heart and my tastebuds. This recipe comes from Cilantro's, a cosy cottage restaurant on the premises of Buffalo Mountain Lodge in Banff, Alberta (where I am now lucky enough to teach the occasional cooking class). Grant Coughlin, Cilantro's chef, cooked this soup there one winter night, and I have been making it at home ever since.*

The beets will add a stunning red colour, but precooking them will prevent the taste and colour from overpowering the soup. If you wish, you can add a spoonful of yogurt cheese (page 229) for a garnish, as for a beet borscht.

Makes 6 servings

1 lb	beets (3 medium)	500 g
2 tsp	olive oil	10 mL
1	large onion, cut in 1-inch/2.5 cm chunks	1
2	cloves garlic, finely chopped	2
2	carrots, cut in 1-inch/2.5 cm chunks	2
2	parsnips, cut in 1-inch/2.5 cm chunks	2
½ lb	rutabaga, peeled and cut in 1-inch/2.5 cm chunks (1½ cups/375 mL)	250 g
2	small turnips, peeled and cut in 1-inch/2.5 cm chunks	2
6 cups	homemade chicken stock (page 57), or 1 10-oz/284 mL tin chicken broth plus water	1.5 L
1	sprig fresh rosemary, or ½ tsp/2 mL dried	1
	Salt and pepper to taste	
6	large sprigs fresh parsley, or small handful fresh chives, cut in 2-inch/5 cm lengths	6

SOUP STOCKS

Salt-free, fat-free homemade stocks are the best, but if you do not have homemade stock, there are substitutes:

• Frozen stock is usually salt free, with the fat removed. It is generally quite expensive, so dilute it with water to make it go farther.

• Canned broth, boullion cubes and powdered soup bases usually contain more salt than necessary; they can also contain MSG, fat and food colouring.

• For canned broth, refrigerate the can before opening — the fat will solidify on the surface so you can remove it before using. I always dilute canned broth more than the directions recommend; simply freeze any extra. Buy lower-salt, lower-fat broths if possible.

PER SERVING

Calories	154
g carbohydrate	24
g fibre	6
g total fat	3
g saturated fat	1
g protein	8

Excellent: vitamin A; niacin; folacin
Good: vitamin C, vitamin B_6

mg cholesterol	1
mg sodium	118
mg potassium	834

1. Peel beets and cut into 1-inch/2.5 cm chunks. Cook in boiling water for 20 minutes, or until almost tender. Drain and reserve.

2. Meanwhile, heat oil in large saucepan or Dutch oven. Add onion and garlic. Cook on low heat for a few minutes.

3. Add carrots, parsnips, rutabaga and turnips. Cook for a few minutes longer.

4. Add stock, rosemary, salt and pepper. Bring to boil. Reduce heat and simmer for 15 minutes, or until vegetables are almost tender.

5. Add beets and cook for about 10 minutes longer. Taste and adjust seasonings if necessary. Garnish each serving with a sprig of parsley or chive sticks (or chop parsley coarsely and sprinkle on top).

- For bouillon cubes and powdered soup bases, dilute them with lots of water, and look for lower-salt, lower-fat brands.
- Water can be a good substitute for stock when there are many other flavourful ingredients in the recipe.

HOMEMADE STOCKS

Homemade Chicken Stock

Cut 4 lb/2 kg chicken into pieces and remove any visible fat (leave on skin for flavour). Place chicken in large pot and add enough cold water to cover by about 2 inches/5 cm. Bring to boil and skim off any scum. Add 2 onions, 2 carrots, 2 stalks celery and 2 leeks (all cut in chunks). Return to boil and skim again if necessary. Add 1 bay leaf, ½ tsp/2 mL dried thyme, 6 whole peppercorns and small handful fresh parsley. Reduce heat and simmer, uncovered, for 1½ hours. (If necessary, add water to keep chicken covered.) Strain stock and chill. Skim off surface fat before freezing.

Makes about 3 qt/3 L

Homemade Vegetable Stock

In large pot, combine 1 onion, 2 carrots, 2 stalks celery, 1 leek, 1 potato, 2 tomatoes and ¼ lb/125 g mushrooms (all cut in chunks). Add 3 qt/3 L cold water, 1 bay leaf, ½ tsp/2 mL dried thyme, handful fresh parsley, 4 peeled cloves garlic and 6 peppercorns. Bring to boil and remove any scum. Cover and simmer gently for 1 hour. Strain stock and freeze.

Makes about 3 qt/3 L

Homemade Roasted Vegetable Stock

Brush bottom of roasting pan with olive oil. Place in 450°F/230°C oven while oven is preheating. Coarsely chop 2 onions, 2 carrots, 2 stalks celery and 2 leeks. Add to pan along with ¼ lb/125 g quartered mushrooms and toss together. Sprinkle with 1 tbsp/15 mL granulated sugar and roast for 40 to 50 minutes, or until browned. Place vegetables in large pot. Add 1 cup/250 mL water to roasting pan and scrape brown bits off pan. Add to vegetables along with 4 qt/4 L cold water, or enough to cover vegetables, and 1 bay leaf. Bring to boil. Skim off scum. Cover and simmer for 2 hours. Strain stock and freeze.

Makes about 2 qt/2 L

Homemade Fish Stock

Place 3 lb/1.5 kg fish bones, tails and heads in large pot (use only lean, white-fleshed fish). Add 2 onions, 2 carrots, 2 stalks celery and 1 leek (all cut in chunks). Add small handful fresh parsley, 1 bay leaf, ½ tsp/2 mL dried thyme, 6 whole peppercorns and 1 cup/250 mL dry white wine or water. Cover with 3 qt/3 L cold water. Bring to boil and skim off any scum. Reduce heat and simmer gently for 30 minutes. Strain before using. Freeze any leftover stock.

Makes about 3 qt/3 L

FRESH HERB SOUP
WITH RICOTTA CROUTONS

When a recipe calls for herbs in large quantities (as in pesto or a herb soup like this one), you know they are being used as more than just a seasoning. Therefore, dried herbs would not be acceptable as a substitute. But if you can't find all the herbs listed, just use more of any that you can find, such as parsley, dill, green onions or even chopped spinach. (You can also simply leave out the herbs for a great version of leek and potato soup!)

The ricotta croutons also make a wonderful appetizer or salad garnish.

Italian parsley

Makes 6 servings

2 tsp	olive oil	10 mL
2	leeks, trimmed and chopped	2
2	cloves garlic, finely chopped	2
3	large potatoes, peeled and diced (1½ lb/750 g)	3
5 cups	homemade chicken stock (page 57), approx., or 1 10-oz/ 284 mL tin chicken broth plus water	1.25 L
2 cups	chopped fresh herbs (combination of chives, parsley, basil, cilantro, tarragon, dill)	500 mL
	Salt and pepper to taste	

Ricotta Croutons:

6	thin slices French bread (2 inches/5 cm in diameter)	6
1	clove garlic, halved	1
⅓ cup	light ricotta cheese, well drained	75 mL
2 tbsp	chopped fresh herbs (reserved from soup)	25 mL
1 tbsp	finely chopped black olives	15 mL
1	small clove garlic, minced	1
	Small handful fresh chives, cut in 2-inch/5 cm lengths	

PER SERVING

Calories	172
g carbohydrate	26
g fibre	2
g total fat	4
g saturated fat	1
g protein	8

Excellent: niacin
Good: vitamin B$_6$

mg cholesterol	5
mg sodium	102
mg potassium	566

1. Heat oil in large saucepan or Dutch oven. Add leeks and garlic and cook on low heat until fragrant, about 5 minutes.

2. Add potatoes and 4 cups/1 L stock. Bring to boil. Reduce heat and simmer for 20 minutes.

3. Add herbs (reserving 2 tbsp/25 mL for croutons). Cook for 5 minutes.

4. Puree soup in blender or food processor. Add more liquid if soup is too thick. Taste and season with salt and pepper if necessary.

5. Meanwhile, to make croutons, place bread on baking sheet and rub with cut side of garlic. Bake in preheated 400°F/200°C oven for about 5 minutes, or until lightly browned.

6. In small bowl, combine ricotta, herbs, olives and minced garlic. Spread on bread.

7. Ladle soup into bowls and place croutons on each serving. Scatter chives on top.

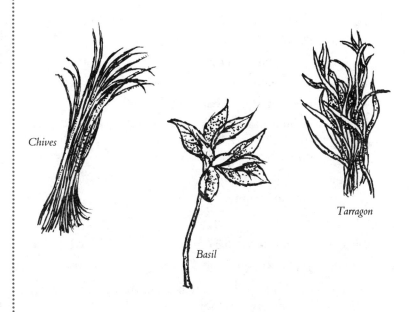

Chives

Basil

Tarragon

FRESH TOMATO SOUP WITH PESTO CREAM

If you use an old-fashioned food mill to puree the tomatoes, the skin and seeds will be strained out as you puree. If you use a blender or food processor, you can leave the bits of skin and seeds in or strain them out through a sieve. Or you can peel and seed the tomatoes before adding them to the soup.

Most of the time I prefer to cook with plum tomatoes (sometimes called Roma), as I think they have more pulp in proportion to seeds, and they seem to have better flavour, even when tomatoes are not in season. The sun-dried tomatoes add a more intense taste to the soup, and if you can find smoked sun-dried tomatoes, the flavour will be even more intriguing! If your sun-dried tomatoes are packed in oil, be sure to rinse them well before using.

Makes 6 servings

2 tsp	olive oil	10 mL
1	clove garlic, finely chopped	1
1	onion, finely chopped	1
¼ cup	chopped sun-dried tomatoes	50 mL
4 lb	ripe tomatoes, coarsely chopped	2 kg
1 cup	homemade chicken stock (page 57), or 1 10-oz/284 mL tin chicken broth plus water	250 mL
1 tsp	granulated sugar	5 mL
	Salt and pepper to taste	

Pesto Cream:

2 tbsp	pesto (see sidebar)	25 mL
⅓ cup	yogurt cheese (page 229)	75 mL

1. Heat oil in large saucepan or Dutch oven. Add garlic and onion and cook on low heat for about 5 minutes, or until tender and fragrant.

2. Add sun-dried tomatoes, fresh tomatoes, stock and sugar. Bring to boil. Reduce heat and simmer for about 15 minutes.

3. Puree soup in food mill, food processor or blender. Return to heat and season with salt and pepper to taste.

4. Combine pesto with yogurt cheese. Ladle soup into bowls and swirl a spoonful of pesto cream into each serving.

PESTO SAUCE

In food processor, chop 2 peeled cloves garlic. Add 2 cups/500 mL packed fresh basil leaves and 1 tbsp/15 mL toasted pine nuts (page 45). Chop. Add ¼ cup/50 mL V8 juice or tomato juice and ½ tsp/2 mL pepper and puree.

Makes about ½ cup/125 mL

PER SERVING

Calories	110
g carbohydrate	18
g fibre	4
g total fat	3
g saturated fat	1
g protein	6

Excellent: vitamin A; vitamin C
Good: thiamine; niacin

mg cholesterol	2
mg sodium	106
mg potassium	824

CALCONNAN SOUP

Calconnan is actually a famous Irish mashed potato dish that incorporates cabbage and green onions. The same flavours translate into a marvellous, robust soup.

Makes 6 to 8 servings

2 tsp	olive oil	10 mL
2	leeks, trimmed and chopped	2
4 cups	chopped cabbage (1 lb/500 g)	1 L
3	large potatoes (1½ lb/750 g), peeled and diced	3
4 cups	homemade chicken stock (page 57), or 1 10-oz/284 mL tin chicken broth plus water	1 L
½ cup	milk	125 mL
	Salt and pepper to taste	
6	green onions, chopped	6

1. Heat oil in large saucepan or Dutch oven. Add leeks and cook on low heat just until wilted.

2. Add cabbage and combine well. Cook for a few minutes.

3. Add potatoes and stock. Bring to boil, reduce heat and simmer for 20 minutes, or until potatoes are very tender.

4. With potato masher, gently mash some of the potatoes so soup thickens. Stir in milk until soup is the consistency you like. Taste and season with salt and pepper. Add green onions and cook for 1 minute longer.

PER SERVING

Calories	149
g carbohydrate	25
g fibre	3
g total fat	3
g saturated fat	1
g protein	6

Good: vitamin C; niacin; vitamin B_6; folacin

mg cholesterol	2
mg sodium	51
mg potassium	615

BUTTERNUT SQUASH SOUP WITH WILD MUSHROOM SAUTÉ

Just one strip of bacon will add a wonderful smoky flavour to this soup, but you can use 2 tsp/10 mL olive oil if you prefer.

The soup is good on its own without the mushroom garnish; the mushroom sauté is great served on toast as an appetizer or over grilled chicken, veal chops or steak. If you cannot find fresh portobello mushrooms, use regular mushrooms instead.

Makes 8 servings

1	strip bacon, in one piece	1
1	onion, chopped	1
2	cloves garlic, finely chopped	2
1	sweet potato, peeled and diced (¾ lb/375 g)	1
6 cups	butternut squash, peeled and diced (2 lb/1 kg)	1.5 L
6 cups	homemade chicken stock (page 57), or 1 10-oz/284 mL tin chicken broth plus water	1 kg
	Salt and pepper to taste	

Wild Mushroom Sauté:

1 tbsp	olive oil	15 mL
3	cloves garlic, finely chopped	3
¾ lb	portobello mushrooms, sliced	375 g
1 tbsp	chopped fresh rosemary, or ¼ tsp/1 mL dried	15 mL
1 tbsp	chopped fresh thyme, or ¼ tsp/1 mL dried	15 mL
2 tbsp	chopped fresh parsley	25 mL
	Salt and pepper to taste	
	Small handful fresh chives	

SOUP GARNISHES

- popcorn
- salsas
- yogurt cheese (page 229)
- crushed baked tortilla chips or pita chips (page 35)
- grilled chicken or shellfish strips
- small amount of grated cheese
- crispy cereal
- blanched vegetables
- fresh herbs
- dusting of spices
- roasted garlic cloves (page 131)
- croutons (page 74)

PER SERVING

Calories	157
g carbohydrate	25
g fibre	5
g total fat	4
g saturated fat	1
g protein	6

Excellent: vitamin A; niacin
Good: vitamin C; thiamine; vitamin B$_6$; iron

mg cholesterol	2
mg sodium	34
mg potassium	710

1. In large saucepan or Dutch oven, cook bacon on low heat until crispy.

2. Add onion and garlic and cook gently until fragrant and wilted.

3. Add sweet potato, squash and stock and bring to boil. Reduce heat and simmer for 30 minutes, or until vegetables are very tender. Remove bacon and discard.

4. Puree soup and return to heat. Add more stock or water if soup is too thick. Season with salt and pepper to taste.

5. Meanwhile, to prepare mushroom sauté, heat oil in large non-stick skillet. Add garlic and cook gently until fragrant but not brown. Add mushrooms and cook for a few minutes until wilted. Add rosemary and thyme and cook until any liquid has evaporated. Add parsley, salt and pepper.

6. Serve soup in bowls and spoon some mushrooms on each serving. Cut chives into long lengths and scatter over soup.

SQUASH VARIETIES

Summer squash like zucchini have thin, edible skins. Winter squash comes in a number of delicious varieties, including acorn, hubbard and butternut. I like the buttery, firm texture of butternut, but any winter squash can usually be substituted.

Winter squash are easier to cook if you bake them before removing the flesh. Slice the squash in half, scoop out the seeds and bake cut side down on a parchment paper-lined baking sheet. After baking, scoop out the flesh and mash or puree.

CORN CHOWDER WITH HERB CHEESE

Although the soup will still be very good if it is made with frozen corn, adding the cobs gives this soup a sweet-flavoured richness. Add milk if you wish, or if the soup seems too thick.

Makes 4 to 6 servings

2 tsp	olive oil	10 mL
1	clove garlic, finely chopped	1
1	small onion, chopped	1
6	ears corn, or 4 cups/1 L corn niblets	6
1	potato, peeled and diced	1
4 cups	homemade chicken stock (page 57), or 1 10-oz/284 mL tin chicken broth plus water	1 L
	Salt and pepper to taste	
½ cup	milk, optional	125 mL
⅓ cup	light herb cheese, homemade (see sidebar) or commercial	75 mL
⅓ cup	coarsely chopped fresh chives or green onions	75 mL

1. Heat oil in large saucepan or Dutch oven. Add garlic and onion and cook on low heat for 5 minutes.

2. Meanwhile, cut corn off cobs and reserve. To saucepan, add corn cobs, potato, stock, salt and pepper. Bring to boil, reduce heat and simmer for 15 minutes, or until potato is almost tender.

3. Add corn to soup, reserving about ⅓ cup/75 mL for garnish. Cook soup 5 minutes longer.

4. Remove cobs from soup and discard. Puree soup. Add milk if you wish. Taste and adjust seasonings if necessary.

5. To serve, place spoonful of herb cheese in bottom of soup bowls. Ladle soup over cheese. Scatter chives and reserved raw corn on top.

LIGHT HERB CHEESE
Combine 1 cup/250 mL firm yogurt cheese (page 229) with 2 minced cloves garlic, 1 tbsp/15 mL each chopped fresh parsley, chives or green onions and tarragon or dill (if using dried herbs, use about ¼ tsp/1 mL of each). Season to taste with salt, pepper and hot red pepper sauce.

Makes about 1 cup/250 mL

PER SERVING

Calories	307
g carbohydrate	55
g fibre	7
g total fat	7
g saturated fat	1
g protein	14

Excellent: thiamine; niacin; folacin
Good: vitamin C; riboflavin; vitamin B_6; vitamin B_{12}

mg cholesterol	3
mg sodium	82
mg potassium	859

Asparagus Tarts with Chèvre
(page 52)

Winter Root Vegetable Soup *(page 56)*
Cheddar Sage Biscuits *(page 252)*

CURRIED SQUASH SOUP

Shelley Tanaka has been the editor of my cookbooks for more than ten years. One of the biggest compliments she pays me is that she often cooks my recipes as she is editing them, saying that she just can't resist. Last year I visited her at her wonderful country kitchen near Napanee, and she gave me the inspiration for this yummy soup.

I like to use winter squash (such as butternut) in this soup, but you can use zucchini or other summer squash instead if you prefer.

Makes 6 servings

2 tsp	olive oil	10 mL
2	leeks, trimmed and chopped	2
2	cloves garlic, finely chopped	2
1 tsp	curry powder	5 mL
1	large carrot, diced	1
1	large potato, peeled and diced	1
4 cups	diced squash (1½ lb/750 g)	1 L
4 cups	homemade chicken stock (page 57), or 1 10-oz/284 mL tin chicken broth plus water	1 L
	Salt and pepper to taste	
2 tbsp	toasted sliced almonds (page 193)	25 mL

1. Heat oil in large saucepan or Dutch oven. Add leeks and garlic. Cook over low heat until wilted and tender.

2. Add curry powder. Stirring constantly, cook for 30 to 60 seconds.

3. Add carrot, potato, squash and stock. Bring to boil. Reduce heat and cook gently for 30 minutes, or until vegetables are tender.

4. Puree soup. Season with salt and pepper to taste. Serve sprinkled with sliced almonds.

PER SERVING

Calories	144
g carbohydrate	24
g fibre	4
g total fat	4
g saturated fat	1
g protein	6

Excellent: vitamin A
Good: thiamine; niacin; vitamin B$_6$

mg cholesterol	1
mg sodium	41
mg potassium	676

WHITE BEAN AND SPINACH SOUP

This hearty soup can be served as an appetizer or as a main course. If you are using your own cooked beans instead of canned, use 2 cups/500 mL.

Makes 6 servings

2 tsp	olive oil	10 mL
1	onion, chopped	1
2	cloves garlic, finely chopped	2
pinch	hot red pepper flakes	pinch
1	19-oz/540 mL tin white kidney beans, drained and rinsed	1
5 cups	homemade chicken stock (page 57), or 1 10-oz/284 mL tin chicken broth plus water	1.25 L
½ cup	small pasta (macaroni, wheels, stars)	125 mL
¾ lb	fresh spinach, trimmed and chopped	375 g
1	tomato, halved, seeded and diced	1
	Salt and pepper to taste	
2 tbsp	finely chopped fresh parsley	25 mL

1. Heat oil in large saucepan or Dutch oven. Add onion, garlic and hot pepper flakes. Cook on low heat until tender.

2. Add beans and stock and bring to boil. Reduce heat, cover and simmer for 10 minutes.

3. Puree soup and return to heat. Add pasta and cook for 5 to 10 minutes, or until tender. Soup will thicken.

4. Add spinach and cook just until wilted, 2 to 3 minutes.

5. Add tomato. Taste soup and season with salt and pepper if necessary. Add additional stock or water if soup is too thick. Sprinkle with parsley before serving.

FREEZING SOUPS

Most soups freeze well, so I like to make more than I need and freeze some for another time. Place soup in plastic or glass containers, leaving about ½ inch/1 cm headspace to allow for expansion in the freezing process. Defrost in the refrigerator overnight, or in the microwave according to the manufacturer's instructions.

PER SERVING

Calories	177
g carbohydrate	25
g fibre	8
g total fat	3
g saturated fat	1
g protein	12

Excellent: vitamin A; niacin; folacin
Good: riboflavin; iron

mg cholesterol	1
mg sodium	270
mg potassium	637

LEMONY LENTIL SOUP

The Jerusalem has been one of my favourite restaurants in Toronto for more than twenty-five years. Their food is full of flavour and reasonably priced. This is my rendition of their fabulous lentil soup.

I use the tiny red lentils in soups because they cook quickly and thicken almost as if they have been pureed.

Makes 6 servings

2 tsp	olive oil	10 mL
1	onion, chopped	1
2	cloves garlic, finely chopped	2
pinch	hot red pepper flakes	pinch
1 tsp	ground cumin	5 mL
1½ cups	red lentils, rinsed and picked over	375 mL
6 cups	homemade chicken stock (page 57), or 1 10-oz/284 mL tin chicken broth plus water	1.5 L
	Salt and pepper to taste	
2 tbsp	lemon juice	25 mL
2 tbsp	finely chopped fresh cilantro or parsley	25 mL

1. Heat oil in large saucepan or Dutch oven. Add onion, garlic and hot pepper flakes and cook on low heat for 3 to 5 minutes, until fragrant.

2. Add cumin and cook for 30 seconds. Stir in lentils and combine well.

3. Add stock, salt and pepper and bring to boil. Reduce heat, cover and simmer until lentils are tender and soup is beginning to thicken, about 25 to 30 minutes.

4. Soup can be pureed, partially pureed or left thick but coarse. Add extra stock or water to thin if necessary. Add lemon juice and taste and adjust seasonings if necessary. Serve sprinkled with cilantro.

PER SERVING

Calories	225
g carbohydrate	31
g fibre	7
g total fat	4
g saturated fat	1
g protein	18

Excellent: niacin; folacin; iron
Good: thiamine; vitamin B$_6$

mg cholesterol	1
mg sodium	37
mg potassium	758

TORTILLA SOUP

Traditionally, this soup is served by placing the garnishes in each serving bowl and ladling the hot soup over the top, but you could also just put everything right in the soup (except the cheese and tortillas, which are sprinkled on top).

If you cannot find corn tortillas, sprinkle a few crushed baked tortilla chips (page 35) on each serving.

Makes 6 servings

2 tsp	olive oil	10 mL
1	onion, chopped	1
2	cloves garlic, finely chopped	2
1 tsp	ground cumin	5 mL
6 cups	homemade chicken stock (page 57), or 1 10-oz/284 mL tin chicken broth plus water	1.5 L
2 tbsp	lime juice	25 mL
	Salt and pepper to taste	
2	corn tortillas, cut in small wedges or triangles	2
1 cup	fresh or frozen corn niblets	250 mL
1½ cups	diced smoked or cooked chicken or turkey breast	375 mL
½ cup	chopped fresh cilantro or parsley	125 mL
1	jalapeño, seeded and diced, optional	1
2	tomatoes, seeded and diced	2
½ cup	grated Monterey Jack cheese, optional	125 mL

1. Heat oil in large saucepan or Dutch oven. Add onion and garlic and cook on low heat until tender. Add cumin and cook for about 30 seconds, until fragrant.

2. Add chicken stock. Bring to boil. Reduce heat and simmer for 15 minutes. Add lime juice. Taste and season with salt and pepper.

3. Meanwhile, arrange tortilla wedges on baking sheet in single layer. Bake in preheated 400°F/200°C oven for about 8 minutes, or until lightly browned and crisp.

4. Place a little corn, chicken, cilantro, jalapeño and tomatoes in each bowl. Ladle soup over garnishes. Sprinkle with grated cheese and tortilla wedges. Serve immediately.

PER SERVING

Calories	176
g carbohydrate	16
g fibre	2
g total fat	5
g saturated fat	1
g protein	18

Excellent: niacin
Good: vitamin B$_6$; vitamin B$_{12}$

mg cholesterol	25
mg sodium	77
mg potassium	512

Chicken Soup with Rice

When my husband was camp doctor at Camp Tamakwa in Algonquin Park, I found being the doctor's wife one of the best "jobs" I have ever had! The food, cooked by Jean-Marc Dubois of Landed Loon, a catering company in Huntsville, Ontario, was better than any camp food I could remember.

This soup was one of our favourites. It is a great way to use up leftover rice and chicken, and although it tastes rich and creamy, it is actually quite light and healthful.

Makes 6 servings

1 tbsp	vegetable oil	15 mL
1	onion, chopped	1
1	stalk celery, chopped	1
1	carrot, chopped	1
2 tbsp	all-purpose flour	25 mL
2 cups	homemade chicken stock (page 57), or 1 10-oz/284 mL tin chicken broth plus water	500 mL
2 cups	milk	500 mL
pinch	dried sage	pinch
pinch	dried thyme	pinch
pinch	dried savory	pinch
1 tsp	Worcestershire sauce	5 mL
1 cup	diced cooked chicken breast	250 mL
1 cup	cooked rice	250 mL
	Salt and pepper to taste	

1. Heat oil in large saucepan or Dutch oven. Add onion, celery and carrot. Cook on low heat for a few minutes until tender but not brown.

2. Sprinkle flour over vegetables and cook gently for 3 to 4 minutes. Add chicken stock and milk. Bring to boil.

3. Add sage, thyme, savory and Worcestershire. Reduce heat and simmer for 10 minutes.

4. Add chicken and rice. Cook for 10 minutes. Taste and season with salt and pepper. (The soup will thicken on standing. Thin it with additional milk or water when reheating.)

THAI CHICKEN NOODLE SOUP

This soup has a bright, fresh flavour. If you want to serve it as a main course, use twice the amount of chicken. You can also marinate the chicken in 2 tbsp/25 mL oyster sauce and grill it for 5 minutes per side before slicing and adding it to the soup.

Lemon grass has an aromatic lemon flavour. The centre of the stalk should be moist and easy to chop. If it is dry and coarse, add it to the soup in large pieces and remove before serving. If you cannot find lemon grass, use 1 tsp/5 mL grated lemon peel.

Makes 6 servings

¼ lb	thin rice vermicelli or angelhair pasta	125 g
1 tsp	vegetable oil	5 mL
1 tbsp	finely chopped lemon grass	15 mL
1 tsp	finely grated lime peel	5 mL
1 tsp	finely chopped fresh ginger root	5 mL
pinch	hot red pepper flakes	pinch
6 cups	homemade chicken stock (page 57), or 1 10-oz/284 mL tin chicken broth plus water	1.5 L
½ lb	boneless, skinless chicken breasts, thinly sliced	250 g
1	carrot, grated	1
1	sweet red pepper, diced	1
1 tbsp	Thai fish sauce or soy sauce	15 mL
½ tsp	hot chili paste	2 mL
¼ cup	lime juice	50 mL
	Salt to taste	
¼ cup	coarsely chopped fresh cilantro or parsley	50 mL

SOUPS AS MAIN COURSES

Many soups make great main courses. Serve them in large bowls with homemade biscuits or muffins and a salad. If you want the soup to be a little more substantial, garnish with strips of grilled meat, chicken or seafood; you can also add cooked beans, thin slices of cheese or tofu for meatless protein.

PER SERVING

Calories	172
g carbohydrate	19
g fibre	1
g total fat	3
g saturated fat	1
g protein	16

Excellent: vitamin A; vitamin C; niacin
Good: vitamin B$_6$; vitamin B$_{12}$

mg cholesterol	23
mg sodium	326
mg potassium	395

1. Place rice noodles in bowl and cover with warm water. Allow to stand for 15 minutes. Drain well and reserve. (If you are using angelhair pasta, cook in boiling water until tender.)

2. Heat oil in large saucepan or Dutch oven. Add lemon grass, lime peel, ginger and hot pepper flakes and cook on low heat for about 30 seconds, or until fragrant.

3. Add chicken stock and bring to boil.

4. Add chicken, carrot, red pepper, fish sauce and chili paste. Reduce heat and simmer for 5 minutes. Add drained noodles and cook for 2 minutes longer, or until heated through.

5. Stir in lime juice, salt and cilantro. Taste and adjust seasonings if necessary.

FRESH GINGER

Fresh ginger root is a wonderful flavouring ingredient used in many recipes. Look for firm roots with tight skin. I usually peel it before using it (unless it is to be removed from the dish before serving or is being used in a marinade).

To chop fresh ginger, slice it very thinly, place slices on top of each other and slice again in the other direction and then once more. For minced ginger, keep chopping until very fine. Or you can chop or mince the ginger in a food processor, using the on/off technique.

Store fresh ginger root at room temperature where the air can circulate around it. You can also peel it, cut it into chunks and store it in rice wine, brandy or vodka.

MALKA'S BOUILLABAISSE

My good friend Malka Marom is a talented singer, broadcaster and author.

When I had this dish at her home, she told me that the secret of great food is good ingredients, good friends, good wine, good love and all sorts of other wonderful things. I have adapted the original recipe by using considerably less of the rich ingredients, but find it is just as delicious — as long as you use good ingredients and eat it with good friends!

Serve this with a salad and lots of extra bread.

Makes 8 large servings

1 cup	dry white wine or water	250 mL
1 lb	clams, cleaned (about 16)	500 g
1 lb	mussels, cleaned (about 16)	500 g
1 tbsp	olive oil	15 mL
3	leeks, trimmed and thinly sliced	3
1	onion, chopped	1
2 tbsp	all-purpose flour	25 mL
1	28-oz/796 mL tin plum tomatoes, with juices, pureed or broken up	1
3	fresh tomatoes, chopped	3
¼ cup	chopped fresh thyme, or 1 tsp/5 mL dried	50 mL
2	bay leaves	2
3 cups	homemade fish stock (page 57) or water	750 mL
1 cup	dry white wine, homemade fish stock or water	250 mL
¼ cup	chopped fresh parsley, divided	50 mL
	Salt and pepper to taste	
1 tbsp	saffron threads	15 mL
¾ lb	cleaned shrimp (see diagram)	375 g
2 lb	fresh firm-fleshed white fish fillets, skin removed (halibut, sea bass, cod), cut in 3-inch/7.5 cm chunks	1 kg
1	12-inch/30 cm loaf French bread, cut in chunks	1

SAFFRON

Saffron is the most expensive spice. The dried stigmas of the crocus flower must be gathered by hand, which increases the labour cost significantly. Saffron adds a wonderful colour and flavour to foods (usually rice, breads, sauces and soups), but if it is used to excess it tends to taste medicinal. Try to buy saffron threads; ground saffron is sometimes blended with the less expensive turmeric.

PER SERVING

Calories	361
g carbohydrate	31
g fibre	3
g total fat	6
g saturated fat	1
g protein	42

Excellent: thiamine; niacin; vitamin B$_6$; folacin; vitamin B$_{12}$; iron
Good: vitamin A; vitamin C; riboflavin

mg cholesterol	129
mg sodium	524
mg potassium	1185

1. In Dutch oven, bring 1 cup/250 mL wine to boil. Add clams. Cover and cook for 3 minutes. Add mussels and cover. Continue to cook for 3 to 5 minutes, or until mussels open. Strain and reserve juices, mussels and clams in the shells (discard any clams or mussels that do not open).

2. Heat oil in Dutch oven. Add leeks and onion. Cook gently, covered, until very tender, about 10 minutes. Stir in flour and cook for a few minutes, stirring.

3. Add canned tomatoes, fresh tomatoes, thyme, bay leaves, stock, 1 cup/250 mL wine and half the parsley. Bring to boil and cook for 25 minutes. Season with salt and pepper.

4. Crush saffron with mortar and pestle or back of spoon. Add to soup and cook for about 5 minutes.

5. Add shrimp and fish. Cook for 5 minutes. Add reserved clams, mussels and juices and cook for another 5 minutes, but do not overcook!

6. Serve in large bowls sprinkled with remaining parsley. Serve with bread.

SEAFOOD CHOWDER

This chunky chowder can be served in small portions as an appetizer or in larger portions as a main course.

Makes 4 to 6 servings

1 tbsp	vegetable oil	15 mL
1	onion, chopped	1
2 tbsp	all-purpose flour	25 mL
2	large potatoes, peeled and diced (1 lb/500 g)	2
2 cups	homemade chicken stock (page 57), or 1 10-oz/284 mL tin chicken broth plus water	500 mL
¼ tsp	dried thyme	1 mL
½ cup	milk	125 mL
½ lb	thick white-fleshed fish fillets, cut in 2-inch/5 cm chunks	250 g
½ lb	scallops, cleaned and halved	250 g
½ lb	shrimp, cleaned and halved	250 g
	Salt and pepper to taste	
1 cup	croutons (see sidebar)	250 mL
2 tbsp	finely chopped fresh parsley	25 mL

1. Heat oil in large saucepan or Dutch oven. Add onion and cook gently for 5 minutes, or until tender and fragrant.

2. Sprinkle onion with flour and cook, stirring, for 2 to 3 minutes.

3. Add potatoes, stock and thyme. Bring to boil. Reduce heat and simmer for 20 minutes, or until potatoes are very tender.

4. With potato masher, mash about half the potatoes in soup, leaving some still chunky. Soup should be quite thick. Add milk and heat thoroughly.

5. Add fish, scallops and shrimp. Bring to boil. Soup will thin out as juices in seafood are released.

6. Taste and add salt and pepper if necessary. If soup is too thick, add a little more milk. Serve sprinkled with croutons and parsley.

HOMEMADE CROUTONS

Make croutons from leftover bread of all kinds (full-grain breads make fabulous croutons). Cut bread into cubes and place on a baking sheet. Bake at 325°F/160°C until dried out, about 30 minutes. You can also toss bread cubes with a little grated cheese, herbs, spices, vinegar or garlic before baking.

PER SERVING

Calories	356
g carbohydrate	36
g fibre	2
g total fat	7
g saturated fat	1
g protein	36

Excellent: niacin; vitamin B_6; vitamin B_{12}
Good: thiamine; folacin; iron

mg cholesterol	117
mg sodium	324
mg potassium	909

SPICY GAZPACHO

Gazpacho is really a salad in a bowl. It should be cool and refreshing, and I like it spicy.

Makes 6 servings

3	large ripe tomatoes, coarsely chopped	3
1	sweet green pepper, coarsely chopped	1
1	sweet red pepper, coarsely chopped	1
1	stalk celery, coarsely chopped	1
1	English cucumber, peeled and coarsely chopped	1
3	green onions, coarsely chopped	3
2	cloves garlic, minced	2
1 tbsp	olive oil	15 mL
1 tbsp	Worcestershire sauce	15 mL
½ tsp	hot red pepper sauce	2 mL
1 tbsp	sherry vinegar or balsamic vinegar	15 mL
1½ cups	V8 juice or tomato juice	375 mL
1 cup	water	250 mL
	Salt and pepper to taste	

Garnish:

1	tomato, diced	1
1 cup	diced English cucumber	250 mL
2 tbsp	chopped fresh chives or green onions	25 mL
2 tbsp	chopped fresh parsley	25 mL
2 tbsp	shredded fresh basil or chopped parsley	25 mL
1½ cups	croutons (page 74)	375 mL

1. In blender or food processor, combine tomatoes, green pepper, red pepper, celery, cucumber, green onions and garlic. Chop finely.

2. Add olive oil, Worcestershire, hot pepper sauce, vinegar, V8 juice, water, salt and pepper. Puree until smooth. Taste and adjust seasonings with salt and pepper, vinegar and hot sauce.

3. For garnish, in small bowl, combine tomato, cucumber, chives, parsley and basil. Sprinkle on soup. Add croutons and serve.

PER SERVING

Calories	133
g carbohydrate	24
g fibre	4
g total fat	3
g saturated fat	1
g protein	4

Excellent: vitamin A; vitamin C; folacin
Good: thiamine; vitamin B_6

mg cholesterol	0
mg sodium	368
mg potassium	627

COLD CUCUMBER TZATZIKI SOUP

Before I learned to make a thick, rich and creamy tzatziki using yogurt cheese (page 229) instead of plain yogurt, my tzatziki would always be watery. So I would just turn it into a soup like this. With a new name and served in a bowl, everyone loved it!

Makes 6 to 8 servings

2	English cucumbers, peeled, chopped or grated (3 cups/750 mL)	2
3 cups	unflavoured low-fat yogurt	750 mL
1 cup	cold water	250 mL
2	cloves garlic, minced	2
½ cup	chopped fresh dill	125 mL
2 tbsp	chopped fresh mint	25 mL
½ tsp	hot red pepper sauce	2 mL
½ tsp	pepper	2 mL
	Salt to taste	
1 cup	crushed pita chips (page 35)	250 mL

1. In large bowl, combine cucumber, yogurt, water, garlic, dill, mint, hot pepper sauce, pepper and salt. If you are not serving soup right away, refrigerate until just before serving.

2. Before serving, stir in extra water if necessary so that soup is the consistency you wish (the longer the soup sits, the more watery it will become). Taste and adjust seasonings if necessary. Serve sprinkled with crushed pita chips and/or additional fresh herbs.

PER SERVING

Calories	123
g carbohydrate	18
g fibre	1
g total fat	2
g saturated fat	1
g protein	8

Excellent: vitamin B_{12}
Good: riboflavin; folacin; calcium

mg cholesterol	7
mg sodium	128
mg potassium	479

SALADS

Grilled Corn Salad

Caesar Salad with Creamy Roasted Garlic Dressing

Carrot Salad with Moroccan Dressing

Baked Beets with Mustard Horseradish Dressing

Wheat Berry Salad

Tabbouleh Salad with Fresh Herbs

Rice Salsa Salad

Spaghetti Salad with Roasted Garlic and Tomato Salsa

White Bean and Chopped Shrimp Salad

Chopped Tuna Salad

Quinoa and Crab Salad with Cilantro Lime Dressing

Wild Salad with Cranberry Vinaigrette

Chinese Chicken Salad

Asian Grilled Steak Salad

Vietnamese Chicken Noodle Salad

GRILLED CORN SALAD

This recipe is a real winner, and it's the reason I now seldom cook for parties of more than thirty people. I once made it for a wedding party of seventy-five. I got such a good price for a huge bag of six dozen ears that I decided to make even more than I really needed. But it started to rain just as I began grilling. It took my husband, Ray, and I hours to cook all the corn, and we were soaked. It's a good thing we loved the friends we were cooking for — and that they loved the salad!

Chipotles are dried, smoked jalapeños. They are very hot, so use them cautiously. If you can't find them, substitute a jalapeño or sweet and hot Thai sauce (page 94).

Makes 6 to 8 servings

8	ears corn, husked	8
1	red onion	1
2	sweet red peppers	2
½ cup	chopped fresh cilantro or parsley	125 mL
¼ cup	chopped fresh chives or green onions	50 mL
⅓ cup	rice vinegar or cider vinegar	75 mL
1 tbsp	orange juice concentrate	15 mL
1	clove garlic, minced	1
1½ tsp	minced chipotle chile	7 mL
1 tsp	salt	5 mL
½ tsp	pepper	2 mL
2 tbsp	olive oil	25 mL

1. Barbecue corn directly on grill. Turn and cook until corn is dotted with brown.

2. Slice onion into ½-inch/1 cm rings and grill on both sides until cooked and browned. Dice.

3. Place peppers on barbecue and grill until blackened on all sides. Cool, peel and discard ribs and seeds. Dice.

4. Cut off niblets by breaking cobs in half and standing cut end on cutting board (page 88). Cut off niblets from top to bottom.

5. In large bowl, combine corn, onion, red pepper, cilantro and chives.

6. In small bowl, combine vinegar, orange juice concentrate, garlic, chipotle, salt and pepper. Whisk in olive oil. Toss vegetables with dressing. Taste and adjust seasonings.

PER SERVING

Calories	258
g carbohydrate	51
g fibre	8
g total fat	7
g saturated fat	1
g protein	7

Excellent: vitamin C; thiamine; folacin
Good: vitamin A; niacin; vitamin B$_6$

mg cholesterol	0
mg sodium	413
mg potassium	598

CAESAR SALAD WITH CREAMY ROASTED GARLIC DRESSING

Caesar salad is as popular as ever, and this lower-fat version is sensational. I avoid raw eggs by using roasted garlic to achieve a creamy effect. The dressing also makes a perfect dip for vegetables, chicken fingers or shrimp.

For a main course, top the salad with grilled chicken or shrimp.

Makes 6 servings

Creamy Roasted Garlic Dressing:

1	head roasted garlic (page 131)	1
1 tsp	anchovy paste, or 2 minced anchovies, optional	5 mL
1 tsp	Dijon mustard	5 mL
1 tsp	Worcestershire sauce	5 mL
2 tbsp	red wine vinegar	25 mL
2 tbsp	olive oil	25 mL
⅓ cup	low-fat yogurt	75 mL
¼ cup	grated Parmesan cheese	50 mL
	Salt and pepper to taste	

Salad:

3	1-inch/2.5 cm slices crusty whole wheat or white bread, cut in 1-inch/2.5 cm cubes (2 cups/500 mL)	3
1	large head Romaine lettuce, cut or broken in 1-inch/2.5 cm pieces (10 cups/2.5 L)	1
2	tomatoes, cut in wedges	2

1. To make dressing, in food processor or blender, blend together roasted garlic, anchovy paste, mustard, Worcestershire, vinegar, oil, yogurt and Parmesan. Taste and season with salt and pepper. Refrigerate until ready to use.

2. To make croutons, spread bread cubes on baking sheet. Bake at 375°F/190°C for 10 to 12 minutes, or until crunchy. Stir once or twice during baking time.

3. Just before serving, toss lettuce with desired amount of dressing and top with croutons. Garnish with tomatoes.

PER SERVING

Calories	126
g carbohydrate	12
g fibre	3
g total fat	7
g saturated fat	2
g protein	6

Excellent: vitamin A; vitamin C; folacin

mg cholesterol	4
mg sodium	173
mg potassium	449

CARROT SALAD WITH MOROCCAN DRESSING

Serve this as a salad or side dish. It is so flavourful that it tastes great with any plain roast or grilled entree.

Makes 6 to 8 servings

2 lb	carrots	1 kg
⅓ cup	orange juice	75 mL
2 tbsp	lemon juice	25 mL
1 tbsp	honey	15 mL
1 tsp	paprika	5 mL
1 tsp	ground cumin	5 mL
pinch	cinnamon	pinch
2 tbsp	chopped fresh mint or parsley	25 mL
2 tbsp	chopped fresh cilantro or parsley	25 mL
1 tsp	sesame oil	5 mL
1 tsp	toasted sesame seeds (see sidebar)	5 mL
	Salt and pepper to taste	

1. Cut carrots on diagonal into ½-inch/1 cm slices. Bring pot of water to boil. Add carrots and cook for about 4 minutes. Drain, rinse with cold water and pat dry.

2. In large bowl, combine orange juice, lemon juice, honey, paprika, cumin and cinnamon. Add carrots and toss. Sprinkle with mint, cilantro, sesame oil and sesame seeds. Taste and season with salt and pepper.

TOASTING SESAME SEEDS
Sesame seeds will have twice the flavour if you toast them before using. Place them in a dry skillet and shake over medium-high heat until lightly toasted. They can also be spread on a baking sheet and baked at 350°F/180°C for a couple of minutes, but they cook quickly, so be sure to watch them carefully!

PER SERVING

Calories	87
g carbohydrate	18
g fibre	4
g total fat	1
g saturated fat	trace
g protein	2

Excellent: vitamin A
Good: vitamin B$_6$

mg cholesterol	0
mg sodium	85
mg potassium	337

Baked Beets with Mustard Horseradish Dressing

If you think you don't like beets, keep trying them — one day you're sure to discover that they are absolutely delicious. For a special treat, if you have a local organic market, look for heirloom varieties such as Golden or Candy Cane.

When beets are baked, they retain more flavour and colour than they do when they are boiled; the skins will slip off easily while they are still warm.

Makes 6 servings

2 lb	beets (6 medium)	1 kg
1 tbsp	Dijon mustard	15 mL
1	clove garlic, minced	1
1 tbsp	grated white horseradish	15 mL
3 tbsp	white wine vinegar	45 mL
¼ tsp	pepper	1 mL
	Salt to taste	
½ cup	chives, cut in 4-inch/10 cm pieces	125 mL

1. Leave skins, root ends and a bit of stems on beets. Wrap beets in a single layer in foil (make sure beets are all about the same size, or wrap same-sized beets in separate packages and bake the larger ones for a longer time). Bake in preheated 400°F/200°C oven for 1 to 2 hours, or until beets are very tender (test by piercing beets through foil with a knife). Open foil packages and let beets cool just until they can be handled.

2. Trim beets and slip off skins. Slice beets or cut into wedges.

3. To make dressing, in small bowl, whisk together mustard, garlic, horseradish, vinegar and pepper. Add salt to taste.

4. Drizzle dressing over sliced beets. Sprinkle with chives. Serve at room temperature.

PER SERVING

Calories	42
g carbohydrate	9
g fibre	3
g total fat	trace
g saturated fat	0
g protein	2

Excellent: folacin

mg cholesterol	0
mg sodium	90
mg potassium	388

WHEAT BERRY SALAD

See photo opposite page 96.

Wheat berries are soft wheat kernels that are chewy, crunchy and tender all at the same time. They can be used in pilafs, or salads, or in hamburgers or meatloaf as a filler. If you have time, soak them overnight in cold water — this will shorten the cooking time, but only slightly.

Makes 6 servings

1 cup	wheat berries	250 mL
½ lb	green or yellow beans	250 g
1 cup	cherry tomatoes, quartered	250 mL

Dressing:

3 tbsp	rice vinegar or cider vinegar	45 mL
2	cloves garlic, minced	2
1 tbsp	olive oil	15 mL
¼ cup	chopped fresh cilantro or parsley	50 mL
¼ cup	chopped fresh chives or green onions	50 mL
	Salt and pepper to taste	

1. Place wheat berries in saucepan and cover with cold water by about 4 inches/10 cm. Bring to boil and simmer gently for 1 to 1½ hours until tender. Drain well (berries should be chewy but tender) and place in large bowl.

2. Bring pot of water to boil. Add beans and cook for 4 to 5 minutes. Drain and chill in cold water. Pat dry and slice into ½ inch/1 cm pieces.

3. Add beans and tomatoes to wheat berries and combine.

4. For dressing, whisk together vinegar, garlic and oil. Stir in cilantro and chives. Toss salad with dressing. Taste and season with salt and pepper if necessary.

SALSA VINAIGRETTE
Spoon this over grilled fish or chicken, or use it as a salad dressing. Combine 1 ripe seeded and diced tomato with 1 tbsp/15 mL finely diced red onion, 1 minced clove garlic, 2 tbsp/25 mL minced cucumber, 2 tbsp/25 mL minced zucchini and 2 tbsp/25 mL minced red pepper. Add 2 tbsp/25 mL sherry vinegar, 2 tbsp/25 mL olive oil, 2 tbsp/25 mL chopped fresh cilantro or parsley and 2 tbsp/25 mL chopped fresh chives or green onions.

Makes about ½ cup/125 mL

PER SERVING

Calories	143
g carbohydrate	27
g fibre	5
g total fat	3
g saturated fat	trace
g protein	5
mg cholesterol	0
mg sodium	4
mg potassium	272

See photo opposite page 96.

TABBOULEH SALAD WITH FRESH HERBS

This version of tabbouleh, made with lots of parsley, is like the traditional version. If you can't find fresh mint, simply omit it; do not substitute dried.

This salad can also be made with couscous, rice or quinoa (page 89). It makes a great side dish or appetizer.

Makes 6 to 8 servings

¾ cup	fine or medium bulgur	175 mL
¾ cup	boiling water	175 mL
2	tomatoes, diced	2
1	small English cucumber, diced	1
3	green onions, chopped	3
4 cups	chopped fresh parsley (4 bunches)	1 L
½ cup	chopped fresh mint	125 mL
⅓ cup	lemon juice	75 mL
2 tbsp	olive oil	25 mL
1	clove garlic, minced	1
½ tsp	salt	2 mL
½ tsp	pepper	2 mL

1. Place bulgur in 8-inch/1.5 L square baking dish. Cover with boiling water. Cover dish tightly with foil. Let sit for 30 minutes. Fluff.

2. In large bowl, combine bulgur, tomatoes, cucumber, green onions, parsley and mint.

3. To make dressing, in small bowl, whisk together lemon juice, oil, garlic, salt and pepper. Toss with salad. Taste and adjust seasonings if necessary.

CUCUMBERS

I prefer to use English cucumbers as they are not waxed and I can use the skins if I wish. They also have fewer seeds. If you are adding cucumbers to a salad dressing, it is a good idea to salt them first and then rinse and drain off the excess liquid so the dressing will not be too watery.

PER SERVING

Calories	135
g carbohydrate	21
g fibre	6
g total fat	5
g saturated fat	1
g protein	4

Excellent: vitamin A; vitamin C; folacin; iron

mg cholesterol	0
mg sodium	220
mg potassium	462

RICE SALSA SALAD

See photo opposite page 96.

This is such a simple idea, and yet it tastes so good. Homemade salsa gives the best results, but store-bought salsa would also work. When tomatoes are not at their best, buy fresh plum tomatoes (they usually have more flavour) or use canned plum tomatoes.

This salsa is also good on bruschetta (pages 44 or 45), grilled meats or fish.

Makes 4 to 5 servings

1 cup	basmati or other fragrant rice	250 mL

Tomato Salsa:

1	clove garlic, minced	1
1	small jalapeño, seeded and finely chopped	1
½ cup	chopped fresh cilantro or parsley	125 mL
1 tbsp	olive oil	15 mL
4	tomatoes, seeded and diced (1 lb/500 g)	4
1 tbsp	chopped black olives	15 mL
	Salt and pepper to taste	

1. Place rice in sieve and rinse under cold running water until water runs clear.

2. Bring large pot of water to boil. Add rice and cook for 10 to 12 minutes, or until tender. Drain and rinse with cold water.

3. Meanwhile, prepare salsa by whisking together garlic, jalapeño and cilantro. Beat in olive oil. Stir in tomatoes and olives. Taste and season with salt and pepper.

4. In large bowl, combine rice and salsa.

POTATO SALAD

Cook 2 lb/1 kg potatoes and cut into cubes. Combine with about ½ to ¾ cup/ 125 to 175 mL Creamy Roasted Garlic Dressing (page 79), Creamy Salsa (page 35), Chèvre Dip (page 40) or Pesto Cream (page 60). (You can also use any of these dressings on roasted potatoes or cooked mashed potatoes.)

Makes 4 to 6 servings

PER SERVING

Calories	226
g carbohydrate	42
g fibre	2
g total fat	4
g saturated fat	1
g protein	5

Good: vitamin C

mg cholesterol	0
mg sodium	30
mg potassium	325

SPAGHETTI SALAD WITH ROASTED GARLIC AND TOMATO SALSA

This is an easy and delicious dish. You can serve it warm or at room temperature (if you make it ahead and refrigerate it, bring the salad to room temperature before serving). It is best made when tomatoes are in season; out of season I always use plum tomatoes, as they seem to be fairly good all year.

If you do not have roasted garlic, substitute 3 minced cloves of garlic. A few diced roasted red or yellow peppers would be great in this salad, too.

Makes 8 servings

Roasted Garlic and Tomato Salsa:

3 tbsp	olive oil	45 mL
2	heads roasted garlic (page 131)	2
3 tbsp	balsamic vinegar	45 mL
¼ tsp	hot red pepper flakes, optional	1 mL
½ tsp	pepper	2 mL
½ tsp	salt	2 mL
1 lb	ripe tomatoes (4 to 6), seeded and diced	500 g
½ cup	shredded fresh basil or chopped parsley	125 mL
¼ cup	chopped fresh parsley	50 mL
¼ cup	chopped fresh chives or green onions	50 mL
1 lb	spaghetti	500 g

1. Place olive oil in large serving bowl. Squeeze garlic into oil and combine with whisk until almost completely pureed. Add vinegar, hot pepper flakes, pepper and salt.

2. Add tomatoes, basil, parsley and chives. Let salsa marinate while preparing pasta.

3. Bring large pot of water to boil. Add pasta and cook until tender but firm. Drain, rinse with cold water and drain well.

4. Add pasta to large bowl and toss well. Taste and adjust seasonings if necessary.

PER SERVING

Calories	281
g carbohydrate	47
g fibre	3
g total fat	7
g saturated fat	1
g protein	8
mg cholesterol	0
mg sodium	151
mg potassium	218

White Bean and Chopped Shrimp Salad

Use any beans in place of the white kidney beans (you can also use a 19-oz/540 mL tin of beans). Canned or grilled tuna can be substituted for the shrimp.

Makes 6 servings

1 cup	dry white kidney beans	250 mL
1 tbsp	olive oil	15 mL
1	clove garlic, minced	1
½ tsp	salt	2 mL
½ tsp	pepper	2 mL
¼ tsp	hot red pepper flakes	1 mL
1 tbsp	chopped fresh rosemary, or ½ tsp/2 mL dried	15 mL
1 lb	cleaned shrimp (page 73)	500 g
1	large red onion, cut in ½-inch/1 cm slices	1
1	head radicchio or Boston lettuce, coarsely chopped (2 cups/500 mL)	1
1	bunch arugula or watercress, chopped (2 cups/500 mL)	1
2	tomatoes, seeded and diced	2
¼ cup	chopped fresh parsley	50 mL

Dressing:

3 tbsp	lemon juice	45 mL
2	cloves garlic, minced	2
½ tsp	salt	2 mL
¼ tsp	pepper	1 mL
3 tbsp	olive oil	45 mL

SALAD GARNISHES
- croutons (page 74)
- tortilla chips (page 35)
- fresh herbs
- edible flowers (page 275)
- ricotta croutons (page 58)
- small amount of finely chopped toasted nuts
- crunchy cereals
- dried cherries or cranberries
- small amount of grated or crumbled light cheese
- diced cold frittata or omelette
- chickpeas
- Parmesan cheese crisps (page 118)

PER SERVING

Calories	315
g carbohydrate	30
g fibre	10
g total fat	11
g saturated fat	2
g protein	25

Excellent: niacin; folacin; vitamin B_{12}; iron
Good: vitamin C; thiamine; vitamin B_6

mg cholesterol	115
mg sodium	517
mg potassium	815

1. Soak white beans in lots of cold water for about 3 hours at room temperature, or overnight in refrigerator. Drain.

2. Place beans in large pot and cover with cold water. Bring to boil. Skim off any scum that rises to surface, reduce heat and simmer gently until beans are thoroughly cooked, about 1 hour. Drain well.

3. To make marinade, in large bowl, combine 1 tbsp/15 mL olive oil, 1 minced clove garlic, salt, pepper, hot pepper flakes and rosemary.

4. Pat shrimp dry. Toss with marinade and marinate in refrigerator until ready to cook.

5. Barbecue or broil shrimp just until cooked. Dice. Barbecue or broil onion until browned. Dice.

6. In large bowl, combine beans, shrimp, onion, radicchio, arugula, tomatoes and parsley.

7. For dressing, in small bowl, whisk together lemon juice, garlic, salt, pepper and olive oil. Toss with salad.

LOWER-FAT SALAD DRESSINGS

Salad dressings that contain oil usually have a high percentage of calories from fat, because most of the calories are in the oil. When the dressing is added to a salad, however, the total fat percentage usually comes down. But you can also reduce the oil in dressings by using mild vinegars, such as balsamic, raspberry or other fruit vinegars, rice vinegar and sherry vinegar. Use olive oil (you'll need less than if you use unflavoured oil), and add flavour with fresh herbs and spices. Or you can use a puree of vegetables, orange juice, buttermilk, yogurt or yogurt cheese (page 229) in place of some of the oil.

Salads can be delicious without an oil-based dressing. Try sprinkling salads with a little rice vinegar or balsamic vinegar; lemon juice, orange juice or pineapple juice; yogurt or yogurt cheese (page 229), salsa, pureed roasted tomatoes (page 96), pureed roasted red peppers (page 241), leftover soup (at room temperature) or tomato sauce.

Here are two excellent lower-fat salad dressings:

Tomato Balsamic Dressing
In food processor or blender, puree 2 cloves garlic, 2 seeded tomatoes, 2 tbsp/25 mL balsamic vinegar, 2 tbsp/25 mL red wine vinegar and 2 tbsp/25 mL olive oil. Taste and season with salt and pepper.
Makes about 1/3 cup/75 mL

Roasted Garlic and Balsamic Dressing
Squeeze garlic from 1 head roasted garlic (page 131) into bowl. Whisk in 2 tbsp/25 mL balsamic vinegar, 2 tbsp/25 mL orange juice, 1 tbsp/15 mL olive oil, 1/2 tsp/2 mL salt and 1/4 cup/50 mL chopped fresh basil or parsley.
Makes about 1/3 cup/75 mL

CHOPPED TUNA SALAD

Tuna salad is an all-time favourite. This chopped version is easy to eat, and every mouthful contains lots of different textures and tastes.

Makes 4 to 6 servings

1 lb	asparagus, cooked and diced	500 g
1½ lb	potatoes, cooked and diced	750 g
2	ears corn, cooked or raw (1½ cups/375 mL niblets)	2
2	7-oz/198 g tins white tuna (water-packed), drained and flaked	2
4 cups	coarsely chopped ruby-tipped lettuce or Boston lettuce (1 lb/500 g)	1 L
⅓ cup	shredded fresh basil or chopped parsley	75 mL
4	green onions, chopped	4

Dressing:

1	clove garlic, minced	1
½ tsp	salt	2 mL
½ tsp	pepper	2 mL
3 tbsp	balsamic vinegar	45 mL
2 tbsp	olive oil	25 mL

1. In large bowl, combine asparagus and potatoes. Cut corn off cobs and add to large bowl.

2. Add tuna, lettuce, basil and green onions to large bowl.

3. To make dressing, in small bowl, combine garlic, salt, pepper and vinegar. Whisk in oil. Toss salad with dressing. Taste and adjust seasonings if necessary.

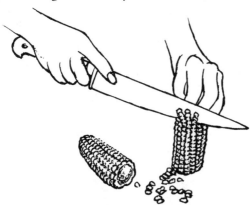

CORN
Frozen or raw corn cut off the cobs is delicious in salads. The raw corn tastes very crunchy. Cobs of corn can also be grilled directly on the barbecue until they brown (page 78).

PER SERVING

Calories	391
g carbohydrate	51
g fibre	7
g total fat	10
g saturated fat	2
g protein	29

Excellent: vitamin C; thiamine; niacin; iron; vitamin B_6; folacin; vitamin B_{12}
Good: vitamin A; riboflavin

mg cholesterol	33
mg sodium	628
mg potassium	1259

QUINOA AND CRAB SALAD WITH CILANTRO LIME DRESSING

Don't hesitate to use cooked shrimp or chicken in place of the crab in this recipe. Cooked couscous, bulgur or rice could be used instead of quinoa.

Makes 6 to 8 servings

2 cups	quinoa	500 mL
1 lb	cooked snow crab meat	500 g
½ cup	chopped fresh cilantro or parsley	125 mL
¼ cup	chopped fresh chives or green onions	50 mL

Cilantro Lime Dressing:

2	jalapeños, minced	2
1	clove garlic, minced	1
½ tsp	salt	2 mL
½ tsp	pepper	2 mL
⅓ cup	lime juice or lemon juice	75 mL
2 tbsp	honey	25 mL
1½ tbsp	Thai fish sauce or soy sauce	20 mL
1 tbsp	olive oil	15 mL
1 tbsp	sesame oil	15 mL
1	bunch watercress or parsley	1

1. Rinse quinoa well in large sieve. Bring large pot of water to boil. Add quinoa and cook for 12 to 15 minutes until just tender. Drain, rinse with cold water and gently press or squeeze dry. Place in large bowl.

2. Pick over crab meat and squeeze out any excess liquid. Combine with quinoa, cilantro and chives.

3. To make dressing, in small bowl, whisk together jalapeños, garlic, salt, pepper, lime juice, honey, fish sauce, olive oil and sesame oil. Toss gently with quinoa. Taste and adjust seasonings if necessary.

4. Pack mixture into serving-sized moulds (e.g., breakfast cereal bowls or empty small tuna tins). Unmould onto serving dishes and surround with watercress.

QUINOA

Quinoa is a delicious, protein-rich grain that can be found at health food stores or bulk food stores. It needs to be thoroughly washed before cooking, as it has a slightly bitter covering that should be rinsed away. You can also toast the washed quinoa to add a nutty taste — add it to a dry skillet and cook, stirring, until it colours slightly.

PER SERVING

Calories	371
g carbohydrate	47
g fibre	3
g total fat	9
g saturated fat	1
g protein	27

Excellent: riboflavin; niacin; folacin; vitamin B_{12}; iron
Good: vitamin A; vitamin C; thiamine; vitamin B_6

mg cholesterol	54
mg sodium	1129
mg potassium	671

WILD SALAD WITH CRANBERRY VINAIGRETTE

This wild salad can be served as a main course or as part of a buffet. Smoked trout or barbecued chicken can be substituted for the smoked chicken.

Makes 6 to 8 servings

1 cup	wehani brown rice or wild rice	250 mL
2 cups	diced smoked chicken or turkey	500 mL
1 cup	fresh or frozen corn niblets	250 mL
1	raw or roasted sweet red pepper, diced	1
¼ cup	dried cranberries	50 mL
2 tbsp	chopped fresh tarragon, or ½ tsp/2 mL dried	25 mL

Cranberry Vinaigrette:

1	small shallot, or 2 green onions, finely chopped	1
1	clove garlic, minced	1
2 tbsp	cranberry juice concentrate	25 mL
1 tbsp	red wine vinegar	15 mL
1 tbsp	maple syrup or honey	15 mL
1 tsp	Dijon mustard	5 mL
½ tsp	salt	2 mL
¼ tsp	pepper	1 mL
2 tbsp	olive oil	25 mL
	Salt and pepper to taste	
1	bunch watercress or parsley	1

1. Place rice in strainer and rinse well. Bring large pot of water to boil. Add rice and cook, uncovered, for 25 to 35 minutes, or until tender and grains puff. Drain well and place in large bowl.

2. Add chicken, corn, red pepper, cranberries and tarragon. Toss.

3. Soak shallot in ice water for 15 minutes (do not bother soaking if you prefer a stronger flavour). Drain well and pat dry.

4. In small bowl, whisk together shallot, garlic, cranberry juice concentrate, vinegar, maple syrup, mustard, salt and pepper. Whisk in oil.

5. Toss salad gently with dressing. Arrange watercress on platter and spoon salad on top.

WEHANI RICE
Wehani rice is a delicious type of brown rice that resembles wild rice in taste, appearance and texture. Cook in plenty of boiling water for about 25 to 35 minutes until tender and the grains puff and look like rice. It can be used in any recipe that calls for brown rice or wild rice. Look for it in health food stores, bulk food stores and specialty stores.

PER SERVING

Calories	298
g carbohydrate	42
g fibre	4
g total fat	9
g saturated fat	2
g protein	14

Excellent: vitamin C
Good: vitamin A; vitamin B$_6$

mg cholesterol	35
mg sodium	251
mg potassium	392

CHINESE CHICKEN SALAD

The peanut dressing in this salad also makes a great dipping sauce for vegetables, salad rolls or satays.

You can use poached, roasted, smoked or barbecued chicken or turkey in this recipe.

Makes 6 to 8 servings

½ lb	linguine	250 g
1	large head iceberg lettuce, chopped (8 cups/2 L)	1
½ cup	chopped fresh cilantro or parsley	125 mL
¼ cup	chopped fresh chives or green onions	50 mL
2 cups	shredded or diced cooked chicken breast (1 lb/500 g raw)	500 mL
2	carrots, grated	2
1	English cucumber, diced	1

Peanut Dressing:

1 tbsp	peanut butter	15 mL
½ cup	cooked chickpeas	125 mL
2 tbsp	soy sauce	25 mL
1 tbsp	honey or molasses	15 mL
½ tsp	hot chili paste, optional	2 mL
	Salt and pepper to taste	

1. Bring large pot of water to boil. Add linguine and cook until tender but firm. Drain and rinse. Reserve.

2. In large bowl, combine lettuce, cilantro, chives, chicken, carrots, cucumber and noodles.

3. To make dressing, in food processor or blender, combine peanut butter, chickpeas, soy sauce, honey and chili paste. Taste and season with salt and pepper if necessary.

4. Toss salad with dressing.

5. Allow salad to marinate for 1 to 2 hours. Do not worry if lettuce gets soggy, but if you want crunchy lettuce, add it just before serving.

PER SERVING

Calories	298
g carbohydrate	42
g fibre	4
g total fat	4
g saturated fat	1
g protein	23

Excellent: vitamin A; niacin; vitamin B$_6$; folacin
Good: iron

mg cholesterol	40
mg sodium	344
mg potassium	529

ASIAN GRILLED STEAK SALAD

See photo opposite page 97.

This is a stunning and delicious main course salad. The dressing, which contains no fat at all, also makes a wonderful dipping sauce for shrimp, salad rolls and satays. This salad could also be made with shrimp or boneless, skinless chicken breasts.

Makes 6 servings

½	bunch cilantro, including roots, stems and leaves	½
2	cloves garlic, chopped	2
1 tbsp	chopped fresh ginger root	15 mL
1 tsp	hot chili paste	5 mL
2 tbsp	hoisin sauce	25 mL
2 tbsp	soy sauce	25 mL
2 tbsp	lemon juice	25 mL
1 lb	flank steak	500 g

Citrus Dipping Sauce:

⅓ cup	granulated sugar	75 mL
⅓ cup	water	75 mL
2 tbsp	rice vinegar or cider vinegar	25 mL
2 tbsp	orange juice	25 mL
1 tbsp	lemon juice	15 mL
1 tbsp	soy sauce	15 mL
1	clove garlic, minced	1
½ tsp	hot chili paste	2 mL
1	small carrot, grated or chopped (⅓ cup/75 mL)	1

Salad:

10 cups	mixed salad greens	2.5 L
1	large English cucumber, thinly sliced	1
½ cup	coarsely chopped fresh cilantro or parsley	125 mL
¼ cup	chopped fresh mint	50 mL
¼ cup	chopped fresh chives or green onions	50 mL

INGREDIENTS FOR ASIAN COOKING

Ingredients like oyster sauce, hoisin sauce and black bean sauce are becoming easier and easier to find in local supermarkets. If not, you can usually find them in Asian grocery stores; in a pinch, ask the chef at your local Asian restaurant if you can buy a small quantity of hard-to-find items. I like to use Koon Chun hoisin sauce and the Lee Kum Kee brand of oyster sauce and black bean sauce.

PER SERVING

Calories	210
g carbohydrate	20
g fibre	2
g total fat	6
g saturated fat	2
g protein	20

Excellent: vitamin A; niacin; folacin; vitamin B$_{12}$
Good: vitamin C; riboflavin; iron; vitamin B$_6$

mg cholesterol	29
mg sodium	404
mg potassium	734

1. For marinade, in food processor or blender, puree whole cilantro, chopped garlic, ginger, chili paste, hoisin, soy sauce and lemon juice.

2. Trim any fat from steak. Coat steak with marinade and marinate for 3 hours or overnight in refrigerator.

3. Grill flank steak for 4 to 5 minutes per side, or until cooked medium-rare. Cool for at least 10 minutes. Slice thinly on diagonal.

4. Meanwhile, to prepare sauce, combine sugar and water in small saucepan and heat until sugar dissolves. Add rice vinegar, orange juice, lemon juice, soy sauce, garlic, chili paste and carrot. Taste and adjust seasonings if necessary. Cool.

5. To serve, arrange salad greens on flat dish. Arrange cucumber on top and sprinkle with chopped cilantro, mint and chives. Place steak slices on top and drizzle with sauce.

VIETNAMESE CHICKEN NOODLE SALAD

This salad also tastes great made with lamb or shrimp.

Makes 6 servings

½ lb	thin rice vermicelli or spaghettini	250 g
1 lb	boneless, skinless chicken breasts	500 g
2 tbsp	hoisin sauce	25 mL
1	English cucumber, quartered lengthwise and thinly sliced	1
1	carrot, grated	1
1	sweet red pepper, thinly sliced	1
3	green onions, thinly sliced	3
½ cup	chopped fresh cilantro or parsley	125 mL

Lemon Sesame Dressing:

1	clove garlic, minced	1
1 tsp	minced fresh ginger root	5 mL
3 tbsp	Thai fish sauce or soy sauce	45 mL
3 tbsp	granulated sugar	45 mL
3 tbsp	lemon juice	45 mL
3 tbsp	water	45 mL
1 tbsp	sweet and hot Thai sauce (see sidebar), or ½ tsp/2 mL hot chili paste	15 mL
1 tbsp	sesame oil	15 mL

1. Place rice noodles in large bowl and cover with boiling water. Allow to soak for 15 minutes. Drain and rinse with cold water. Drain well and place in large serving bowl. (If you are using spaghettini, cook in boiling water until tender, drain, rinse and place in bowl.)

2. Meanwhile, coat chicken with hoisin sauce and cook in non-stick skillet, or bake in preheated 350°F/180°C oven for 20 to 25 minutes until just cooked through. Slice thinly.

3. In bowl, toss together chicken, cucumber, carrot and red pepper. Place on top of noodles. Sprinkle with green onions and cilantro.

4. To prepare dressing, whisk together garlic, ginger, fish sauce, sugar, lemon juice, water, Thai sauce and sesame oil. Drizzle over salad. Toss gently when serving.

SWEET AND HOT THAI CHILI SAUCE
Caprial Pence introduced us to this Thai condiment when she taught at the school. It contains red chiles, sugar, garlic, vinegar and salt. Use it on its own or in Asian-flavoured sauces, dips and marinades. You can find it at Asian markets; I use the Mae Ploy brand.

PER SERVING

Calories	308
g carbohydrate	44
g fibre	2
g total fat	4
g saturated fat	1
g protein	22

Excellent: vitamin A; vitamin C; niacin; vitamin B$_6$

mg cholesterol	47
mg sodium	982
mg potassium	405

PASTAS

Spaghetti with Roasted Tomato Sauce

Linguine with Hot Garlic Tomato Sauce

Angelhair Pasta with Fresh and Cooked Tomato Sauce

Pasta with Tomato and Red Pepper Sauce

Penne with Tomatoes and Arugula

Trenne with Wild Mushrooms

Pasta with Roasted Cauliflower

Bow Ties with Spring Vegetables

Penne with Eggplant, Peppers and Ricotta

Spaghetti Rustica

Spaghetti and Seafood Casserole

Broken Spaghetti with Fresh Salsa and Scallops

Pasta with Swordfish and Olives

Fettuccine with Chicken and Mixed Peppers

Sweet and Spicy Chicken Lo Mein

Soupy Chinese Noodles

SPAGHETTI WITH ROASTED TOMATO SAUCE

This is a very easy and delicious sauce with a lot of flavour. Not only that — it is a good source of fibre and contains practically no fat! If you don't like things too spicy, omit the jalapeño.

Makes 6 servings

Roasted Tomato Sauce:

2 lb	ripe plum tomatoes, quartered	1 kg
1	onion, peeled and quartered	1
1	jalapeño, whole	1
1	head garlic	1
1 lb	whole wheat or regular spaghetti	500 g
½ cup	chopped fresh basil or cilantro	125 mL
	Salt and pepper to taste	

1. Line baking sheet with parchment paper or foil. Arrange tomatoes, onion and jalapeño on baking sheet. Cut top off garlic head and place cut side down on foil. Roast in preheated 425°F/220°C oven for 45 to 50 minutes, or until lightly browned. (If garlic and/or onion are tender before this, remove them ahead of time and reserve.)

2. Squeeze garlic out of skins into food processor or blender. Add tomatoes, onion and jalapeño and puree. If you have made this sauce ahead of time, reheat thoroughly.

3. Meanwhile, bring large pot of water to boil. Add spaghetti and cook until tender but firm. Drain well and toss with vegetable puree and basil. Taste and season with salt and pepper.

COOKING PASTA

Freshly made pasta takes only about 1 minute to cook. Pasta from pasta shops (that has been made ahead) usually takes about 6 minutes to cook. Dried commercial pasta takes 8 to 12 minutes to cook, depending on the manufacturer, the size and how long the pasta has been sitting on the shelf. No matter what kind of pasta you are cooking, never rely only on a timer to determine whether it is ready — always taste it.

PER SERVING

Calories	306
g carbohydrate	66
g fibre	11
g total fat	2
g saturated fat	trace
g protein	13

Excellent: thiamine
Good: vitamin A; vitamin C; niacin; vitamin B$_6$; iron

mg cholesterol	0
mg sodium	20
mg potassium	464

Rice Salsa Salad *(page 84)*
Wheat Berry Salad *(page 82)*
Tabbouleh Salad with Fresh Herbs *(page 83)*

Asian Grilled Steak Salad
(page 92)

LINGUINE WITH HOT GARLIC TOMATO SAUCE

This is a delicious and strongly flavoured tomato sauce, but if you like things mild and gentle, use less garlic and fewer hot pepper flakes.

Makes 4 to 6 servings

2 tbsp	olive oil	25 mL
1 lb	tomatoes, sliced ½ inch/1 cm thick (3 medium)	500 g
6	cloves garlic, finely chopped	6
½ tsp	hot red pepper flakes	2 mL
½ cup	tomato juice	125 mL
	Salt and pepper to taste	
¼ cup	chopped fresh parsley	50 mL
¾ lb	linguine	375 g

1. Heat oil in large, deep non-stick skillet. Arrange tomato slices in single layer in skillet. Cook on high heat, turn and sprinkle with garlic and hot pepper flakes (use 2 skillets if necessary and then combine cooked tomatoes in larger skillet).

2. Pour tomato juice over tomatoes and sprinkle with salt, pepper and parsley. Bring to boil. Reduce heat and simmer for 5 minutes, until sauce thickens slightly.

3. Meanwhile, bring large pot of water to boil. Add linguine and cook until tender but firm. Drain well and add to skillet. Toss with tomatoes. Taste and adjust seasonings if necessary.

PER SERVING

Calories	410
g carbohydrate	71
g fibre	5
g total fat	9
g saturated fat	1
g protein	12

Good: vitamin A; vitamin C; niacin; folacin; iron

mg cholesterol	0
mg sodium	120
mg potassium	407

ANGELHAIR PASTA WITH FRESH AND COOKED TOMATO SAUCE

This sauce has a wonderful texture with pieces of fresh tomato in the pureed cooked sauce. Instead of canned tomatoes, you can use 1½ lb/750 g peeled, seeded and chopped fresh tomatoes to make the cooked sauce.

Makes 4 to 6 servings

1 tbsp	olive oil	15 mL
1	small onion, chopped	1
3	cloves garlic, finely chopped	3
pinch	hot red pepper flakes	pinch
1	28-oz/796 mL tin plum tomatoes, with juices, chopped	1
¾ lb	angelhair pasta	375 g
4	fresh plum tomatoes, seeded and diced	4
3 tbsp	chopped fresh parsley	45 mL
¼ cup	grated Parmesan cheese	50 mL
	Salt and pepper to taste	

1. Heat olive oil in large, deep non-stick skillet. Add onion and garlic and cook gently until tender.

2. Add hot pepper flakes and canned tomatoes. Bring to boil and cook, uncovered, until thick. (Sauce can be made ahead to this point.)

3. Meanwhile, bring large pot of water to boil. Add pasta and cook until tender but firm.

4. Add fresh tomatoes to sauce just to heat. Drain pasta well and add to skillet with parsley. Toss over low heat until pasta is well coated with sauce.

5. Sprinkle pasta with cheese and toss well. Taste and season with salt and pepper.

PASTA POTS
Pasta pots are all the rage right now, with good reason. They have a built-in colander that allows you to lift the pasta out of the cooking water to drain it. The pots are also great for cooking vegetables like potatoes, and for making chicken stock; just pull out the bones, meat and vegetables, and you won't even have to strain the stock.

PER SERVING

Calories	436
g carbohydrate	77
g fibre	7
g total fat	7
g saturated fat	2
g protein	16

Excellent: vitamin C; niacin
Good: vitamin A; vitamin B$_6$; folacin; calcium; iron

mg cholesterol	5
mg sodium	452
mg potassium	687

PASTA WITH TOMATO AND RED PEPPER SAUCE

Some people add sugar to their tomato sauce, but I like to use a sweet vegetable like red pepper instead. It adds a wonderful flavour and great texture.

As variations, you can add 1 cup/250 mL cooked or smoked chicken or turkey to the sauce, or you can add 1 cup/250 mL ricotta cheese at the end for a "creamy" version. Instead of using fresh basil, try topping each serving with 1 tbsp/15 mL pesto (page 60).

Makes 6 to 8 servings

1 tbsp	olive oil	15 mL
1	onion, chopped	1
2	cloves garlic, finely chopped	2
pinch	hot red pepper flakes	pinch
1½ lb	fresh tomatoes, peeled, seeded and chopped (6 to 8 plum tomatoes), or 1 28-oz/796 mL tin plum tomatoes, with juices, chopped	750 g
4	sweet red peppers, roasted (page 241), peeled and chopped	4
	Salt and pepper to taste	
1 lb	pasta	500 g
¼ cup	grated Parmesan cheese, optional	50 mL
¼ cup	shredded fresh basil or chopped parsley	50 mL

1. Heat oil in large, deep non-stick skillet. Add onion, garlic and hot pepper flakes. Cook gently until tender and fragrant.

2. Add tomatoes and peppers. Cook until tomatoes cook down and become juice, about 5 to 10 minutes. Add salt and pepper to taste.

3. Meanwhile, bring large pot of water to boil. Add pasta and cook until tender but firm. Drain well and add to skillet with sauce. Toss well with cheese and basil. Taste and adjust seasonings if necessary.

PER SERVING

Calories	348
g carbohydrate	67
g fibre	6
g total fat	4
g saturated fat	1
g protein	11

Excellent: vitamin A; vitamin C;
Good: niacin; vitamin B$_6$; folacin

mg cholesterol	0
mg sodium	12
mg potassium	416

PENNE WITH TOMATOES AND ARUGULA

See photo opposite page 128.

When I made this pasta on the CFTO show Eye on Toronto *the crew ate it so quickly that I had to go home and make more for myself because I didn't get any! And while it is true that the CFTO staff will eat almost anything, this pasta did disappear very, very fast.*

Arugula is a delicious spicy green. If it is not available, use endive, Swiss chard leaves or even fresh spinach.

Makes 4 to 6 servings

1 tbsp	olive oil	15 mL
4	cloves garlic, finely chopped	4
pinch	hot red pepper flakes	pinch
1	28-oz/796 mL tin plum tomatoes, drained and chopped (1½ cups/375 mL)	1
2	bunches arugula, trimmed and chopped (4 cups/1 L)	2
¾ lb	penne	375 g
	Salt and pepper to taste	

1. Heat olive oil in large, deep non-stick skillet. Add garlic and hot pepper flakes and cook gently for a few minutes but do not brown.

2. Add tomatoes to skillet. Bring to boil. Reduce heat and cook for 5 minutes.

3. Add arugula and cook just until it wilts.

4. Meanwhile, bring large pot of water to boil. Add penne and cook until tender but firm. Drain well and add to skillet with sauce. Toss gently over low heat until everything is hot and sauce clings to noodles. Taste and season with salt and pepper.

PERFECT PASTA

Never add oil to the pasta-cooking water unless a recipe specifically tells you to (and why!). The oil will prevent the pasta from absorbing the sauce properly. If there is enough water in the pot, the pasta won't stick. Rinsing pasta before serving also prevents the sauce from coating it well; only rinse pasta if you are cooking it in advance and want to prevent the pieces from sticking, as when you are cooking lasagna or cannelloni.

PER SERVING

Calories	394
g carbohydrate	73
g fibre	5
g total fat	6
g saturated fat	1
g protein	14

Excellent: folacin
Good: vitamin A; niacin; vitamin B$_6$; calcium

mg cholesterol	0
mg sodium	238
mg potassium	636

TRENNE WITH WILD MUSHROOMS

Trenne is a triangular variation of penne, but using either is fine. Any kind of fresh wild mushrooms can be used (page 115); if you can't find them or they are too expensive, simply use regular cultivated mushrooms.

Makes 6 servings

2 tbsp	olive oil	25 mL
4	cloves garlic, finely chopped	4
pinch	hot red pepper flakes	pinch
1 lb	wild mushrooms, sliced	500 g
1 tbsp	chopped fresh thyme, or $\frac{1}{4}$ tsp/1 mL dried	15 mL
1 tsp	chopped fresh rosemary, or pinch dried	5 mL
$1\frac{1}{2}$ cups	fresh or frozen corn niblets (2 cobs)	375 mL
$\frac{3}{4}$ cup	homemade vegetable stock (page 57) or chicken stock	175 mL
1	bunch arugula or spinach, trimmed and chopped (2 cups/500 mL)	1
	Salt and pepper to taste	
1 lb	trenne or penne	500 g
$\frac{1}{4}$ cup	grated Parmesan cheese, optional	50 mL

1. Heat oil in large, deep non-stick skillet. Add garlic and hot pepper flakes and cook on low heat until very fragrant.

2. Add mushrooms. Raise heat and cook until any juices have evaporated, about 5 minutes.

3. Add thyme, rosemary, corn and stock and bring to boil. Stir in chopped arugula, salt and pepper.

4. Meanwhile, bring large pot of water to boil. Add pasta and cook until tender but firm. Drain well and add to mushroom mixture. Toss gently. Taste and adjust seasonings if necessary. Sprinkle with Parmesan cheese before serving.

PER SERVING

Calories	390
g carbohydrate	71
g fibre	6
g total fat	7
g saturated fat	1
g protein	13

Excellent: niacin; folacin
Good: riboflavin; iron

mg cholesterol	0
mg sodium	21
mg potassium	452

PASTA WITH ROASTED CAULIFLOWER

When vegetables are roasted, their flavour and texture intensify and their sugars caramelize into a sweet, brown essence. This dish makes a great vegetarian main course. You can also add four fresh plum tomatoes; cut them into quarters and roast them with the cauliflower.

Makes 4 to 6 servings

1	large head cauliflower (2 lb/1 kg)	1
2 tbsp	olive oil, divided	25 mL
½ tsp	salt	2 mL
½ lb	penne or other medium pasta	250 g
2 tbsp	red wine vinegar or balsamic vinegar	25 mL
1	clove garlic, minced	1
	Salt and pepper to taste	
2	sweet red peppers, roasted (page 241), peeled and diced	2
2 tbsp	chopped black olives	25 mL
¼ cup	shredded fresh basil or chopped parsley	50 mL

1. Trim cauliflower and break into florets. In large bowl, toss cauliflower with 1 tbsp/15 mL olive oil and ½ tsp/2 mL salt. Arrange in single layer on baking sheet.

2. Roast cauliflower in preheated 400°F/200°C oven for 25 to 30 minutes, or until cooked through and lightly browned. Stir occasionally.

3. Meanwhile, bring large pot of water to boil. Add pasta and cook until tender but firm. Drain well.

4. In small bowl, whisk together vinegar, garlic, salt and pepper. Whisk in remaining 1 tbsp/15 mL oil.

5. Toss dressing with cauliflower, peppers, olives, basil and pasta. Taste and adjust seasonings if necessary. Serve at room temperature.

HOW TO SERVE PASTA HOT
- Use a large pot for making the sauce. When the pasta is ready, drain it well, add it to the sauce and toss over low heat for a few minutes before serving.
- If you are using a serving dish, place it over the boiling pasta to heat.
- Heat the dinner plates.

PER SERVING

Calories	334
g carbohydrate	55
g fibre	7
g total fat	9
g saturated fat	1
g protein	11

Excellent: vitamin C; vitamin B$_6$; folacin
Good: vitamin A; niacin

mg cholesterol	0
mg sodium	336
mg potassium	706

BOW TIES WITH SPRING VEGETABLES

This recipe was inspired by a trip to the organic market on Easter weekend. David Cohlmeyer of Cookstown Greens in Cookstown, Ontario, only had tender young leeks left, but they were spectacular in this wonderful pasta dish.

Makes 8 servings

1 lb	asparagus, trimmed and cut in 1½-inch/4 cm lengths	500 g
1 tbsp	olive oil	15 mL
3	leeks, trimmed and thickly sliced	3
2	cloves garlic, finely chopped	2
1	bulb fennel, trimmed and cut in 1½-inch/4 cm strips (1 lb/500 g), or 2 stalks celery, cut in strips	1
1	sweet red pepper, cut in strips	1
1 cup	fresh or frozen peas	250 mL
¾ lb	bow tie pasta	375 g
¼ cup	shredded fresh basil or chopped chives	50 mL
¼ cup	grated Parmesan cheese, optional	50 mL
	Salt and pepper to taste	

1. Bring pot of water to boil. Add asparagus and cook for 2 minutes. Rinse with cold water and pat dry. Reserve.

2. Heat oil in large, deep non-stick skillet. Add leeks and garlic and cook on low heat for a few minutes. Add a little water if vegetables start to stick at any time.

3. Add fennel and red pepper to skillet and cook gently for 5 to 10 minutes, until tender. Add asparagus and peas and heat thoroughly.

4. Meanwhile, bring large pot of water to boil. Add pasta and cook until tender but firm. Drain well and toss with sauce. Add basil and cheese and combine well. Taste and season with salt and pepper if necessary.

PENNE WITH EGGPLANT, PEPPERS AND RICOTTA

Eggplant has a rich, meaty texture and it adds a lot of body to a pasta sauce. If you use the long, thin Japanese eggplants, you don't have to peel or salt them to get rid of any bitterness, as they are already sweet and tender. The eggplant can also be sliced and grilled before dicing, if you prefer.

Makes 6 servings

2 tbsp	olive oil	25 mL
1½ lb	Japanese eggplants, cut in ¾-inch/2 cm chunks (5 eggplants)	750 g
3	cloves garlic, finely chopped	3
1 tbsp	chopped fresh rosemary, or ½ tsp/2 mL dried	15 mL
¼ tsp	hot red pepper flakes	1 mL
3	sweet red peppers, preferably peeled, cut in ¾-inch/2 cm chunks	3
⅓ cup	dry white wine or water	75 mL
¾ lb	penne	375 g
½ lb	light ricotta cheese, well drained and broken up	250 g
¼ cup	grated Parmesan cheese	50 mL
¼ cup	shredded fresh basil or chopped parsley	50 mL
	Salt and pepper to taste	

1. Heat oil in large, deep non-stick skillet. Add eggplant and cook, stirring, until browned, about 10 minutes.

2. Add garlic, rosemary and hot pepper flakes. Cook for about 2 minutes.

3. Add red peppers and cook until wilted. Add wine.

4. Meanwhile, bring large pot of water to boil. Add penne and cook until tender but firm. Drain well and add to skillet. Stir in ricotta, Parmesan and basil. Season with salt and pepper to taste.

COOKING PASTA AHEAD

Although pasta tastes best when it is cooked at the last minute, you can cook it ahead, the way many restaurants do. When the pasta is cooked, chill it in cold water, drain well and toss with 1 tbsp/15 mL oil per 1 lb/500 g of pasta. Reheat it in boiling water or directly in the sauce just before serving.

PER SERVING

Calories	367
g carbohydrate	56
g fibre	6
g total fat	9
g saturated fat	3
g protein	15

Excellent: vitamin A; vitamin C
Good: niacin; vitamin B$_6$; folacin; calcium

mg cholesterol	15
mg sodium	131
mg potassium	476

SPAGHETTI RUSTICA

I love the taste of rapini. It has a slightly bitter edge and is actually a cross between broccoli and turnip greens. Its bitterness is mellowed when it is served in a pasta dish, so this recipe is a great way to introduce people to the green.

If you cannot find wild mushrooms (page 115), just use regular white mushrooms.

Makes 6 to 8 servings

1 tbsp	olive oil	15 mL
4	cloves garlic, finely chopped	4
pinch	hot red pepper flakes	pinch
¼ lb	fresh wild mushrooms, sliced	125 g
1 cup	cooked red kidney beans	250 mL
	Salt and pepper to taste	
1 lb	spaghetti	500 g
1	bunch rapini or broccoli, trimmed and chopped (1 lb/500 g)	1
¼ cup	pitted black olives, chopped	50 mL
¼ cup	chopped fresh parsley	50 mL

1. Heat oil in large, deep non-stick skillet. Add garlic and hot pepper flakes and cook on low heat until tender and fragrant.

2. Add mushrooms and cook until wilted. Add beans, salt and pepper and cook a few minutes longer.

3. Meanwhile, bring large pot of water to boil. Add spaghetti and cook for 5 minutes. Add rapini and cook 5 minutes longer. Drain well, reserving ½ cup/125 mL pasta cooking water.

4. Add reserved water and olives to skillet. Heat thoroughly. Toss with drained pasta, rapini and parsley.

PER SERVING

Calories	375
g carbohydrate	68
g fibre	8
g total fat	5
g saturated fat	1
g protein	15

Excellent: folacin; iron
Good: vitamin A; vitamin C; niacin; calcium

mg cholesterol	0
mg sodium	61
mg potassium	603

SPAGHETTI AND SEAFOOD CASSEROLE

This is a great one-pot meal. You can vary the pasta, fish or seasonings depending on what you have on hand.

Makes 8 servings

1 tbsp	olive oil	15 mL
¾ lb	sea bass or halibut fillets, skin removed, cut in 2-inch/5 cm cubes	375 g
¾ lb	salmon fillets, skin removed, cut in 2-inch/5 cm cubes	375 g
1	onion, finely chopped	1
4	cloves garlic, finely chopped	4
¼ tsp	hot red pepper flakes	1 mL
1	28-oz/796 mL tin plum tomatoes, with juices, pureed or broken up	1
1 lb	spaghetti or linguine, broken in 2-inch/5 cm pieces	500 g
4 cups	homemade fish stock (page 57), vegetable stock or water	1 L
½ lb	cleaned shrimp (page 73)	250 g
½ lb	mussels, cleaned	250 g
	Salt and pepper to taste	
2 tbsp	chopped fresh parsley	25 mL

1. Heat oil in large, deep non-stick skillet or Dutch oven. Add sea bass and salmon and brown lightly for a few minutes. Remove.

2. Add onion, garlic and hot pepper flakes to skillet. Cook gently for a few minutes, until softened.

3. Add tomatoes and bring to boil. Cook until sauce has thickened and reduced slightly.

4. Add pasta and stir well. Add stock and bring to boil. Bury fish, shrimp and mussels in liquid. Cover and cook gently for 15 minutes, or until pasta is tender.

5. Discard any mussels that have not opened. Season with salt and pepper. Sprinkle with parsley.

PER SERVING

Calories	404
g carbohydrate	49
g fibre	4
g total fat	8
g saturated fat	1
g protein	33

Excellent: niacin; vitamin B_6; vitamin B_{12}
Good: thiamine; riboflavin; folacin; iron

mg cholesterol	84
mg sodium	283
mg potassium	737

See photo opposite page 129.

BROKEN SPAGHETTI WITH FRESH SALSA AND SCALLOPS

This salsa is so delicious that it can be made without the scallops for a vegetarian pasta dish. You can reduce the olive oil to 2 tsp/10 mL, but I use a bit more because of the flavour that it adds to the dish.

I love using up the ends of different-shaped noodles in one pasta dish. Be sure that the pasta shapes are approximately the same size so they will take the same amount of time to cook. Or you can use broken spaghetti, as I do here. The short pieces are easier to eat!

BROKEN SPAGHETTI

Break up spaghetti into small bits the way professional chefs do. Wrap the spaghetti in a tea towel. Hold one end of the towel in each hand and run the length of the towel down the edge of your counter.

Makes 6 servings

Fresh Tomato Salsa:

4	fresh plum tomatoes, seeded and diced	4
2	sweet red peppers, roasted (page 241), peeled and diced	2
1	jalapeño, seeded and diced	1
2	cloves garlic, minced	2
⅓ cup	chopped fresh cilantro or parsley	75 mL
⅓ cup	chopped fresh chives or green onions	75 mL
1 lb	scallops, cleaned and halved	500 g
	Salt and pepper to taste	
2 tbsp	olive oil	25 mL
¾ lb	spaghetti, broken in 2-inch/5 cm lengths (see sidebar)	375 g

1. To make salsa, in bowl, combine tomatoes, red peppers, jalapeño, garlic, cilantro and chives.

2. Pat scallops dry. Season with salt and pepper.

3. Heat oil in large, deep non-stick skillet. Add scallops and brown on high heat.

4. Meanwhile, bring large pot of water to boil. Add spaghetti and cook until tender but firm. Drain well. Add cooked spaghetti and salsa to scallops. Toss until thoroughly heated (do not overcook). Taste and adjust seasonings if necessary.

PER SERVING

Calories	339
g carbohydrate	49
g fibre	4
g total fat	6
g saturated fat	1
g protein	21

Excellent: vitamin C; niacin; vitamin B$_{12}$
Good: vitamin A

mg cholesterol	25
mg sodium	128
mg potassium	458

PASTA WITH SWORDFISH AND OLIVES

This dish, a lower-fat adaptation of a delicious Giuliano Bugialli recipe, is easy and flavourful. It could also be made with fresh tuna, halibut, cod or any thick, meaty-textured fish. You could also grill the swordfish separately, cut it into cubes and add it to the sauce at the end for a smoky, grilled taste.

Makes 6 to 8 servings

1 tbsp	olive oil	15 mL
4	cloves garlic, finely chopped	4
1	onion, finely chopped	1
¼ tsp	hot red pepper flakes	1 mL
1	carrot, diced	1
1	stalk celery, diced	1
1	28-oz/796 mL tin plum tomatoes, with juices, pureed or broken up	1
3 tbsp	green or black olives, pitted and coarsely chopped	45 mL
2 tbsp	capers	25 mL
1½ lb	swordfish, cut in 1½-inch/4 cm chunks	750 g
1 lb	penne	500 g
¼ cup	chopped fresh parsley	50 mL
¼ cup	shredded fresh basil or chopped parsley	50 mL
	Salt and pepper to taste	

1. Heat oil in large, deep non-stick skillet. Add garlic, onion and hot pepper flakes. Cook gently for a few minutes.

2. Add carrot and celery and cook for 5 minutes longer. If vegetables begin to stick or burn, add a little water.

3. Add tomatoes and bring to boil. Lower heat and simmer for 10 minutes, until reduced and slightly thickened. Add olives, capers and swordfish and cook gently for 5 to 7 minutes, until fish is just cooked through.

4. Meanwhile, bring large pot of water to boil. Add pasta and cook until tender but firm. Drain well and toss with sauce, parsley and basil. Taste and season with salt and pepper if necessary.

PER SERVING

Calories	487
g carbohydrate	66
g fibre	6
g total fat	9
g saturated fat	2
g protein	34

Excellent: vitamin A; niacin; vitamin B_6; vitamin B_{12}
Good: vitamin C; folacin; iron

mg cholesterol	44
mg sodium	476
mg potassium	793

FETTUCCINE WITH CHICKEN AND MIXED PEPPERS

This is a colourful, quick and easy pasta dish. It can also be made with smoked chicken.

Makes 6 servings

1 tbsp	olive oil	15 mL
1	onion, thinly sliced	1
2	cloves garlic, finely chopped	2
pinch	hot red pepper flakes	pinch
¾ lb	chicken breast, cut in thin strips	375 g
1	sweet red pepper, cut in thin strips	1
1	sweet green pepper, cut in thin strips	1
1	sweet yellow pepper, cut in thin strips	1
1	28-oz/796 mL tin plum tomatoes, drained and pureed or broken up	1
	Salt and pepper to taste	
¾ lb	fettuccine	375 g
¼ cup	shredded fresh basil or chopped parsley	50 mL

1. Heat oil in large, deep non-stick skillet. Add onion, garlic and hot pepper flakes and cook on low heat for 5 to 8 minutes, until fragrant and tender.

2. Add chicken and cook just until lightly browned on all sides.

3. Add peppers and cook for 5 minutes, just until peppers begin to wilt.

4. Add tomatoes, salt and pepper. Bring to boil. Reduce heat and simmer gently for 5 to 8 minutes.

5. Meanwhile, bring large pot of water to boil. Add fettuccine and cook until tender but firm. Drain well and toss with sauce and basil. Taste and adjust seasonings if necessary.

PER SERVING

Calories	335
g carbohydrate	52
g fibre	5
g total fat	4
g saturated fat	1
g protein	22

Excellent: vitamin C; niacin; vitamin B$_6$
Good: vitamin A

mg cholesterol	33
mg sodium	184
mg potassium	530

SWEET AND SPICY CHICKEN LO MEIN

This is one of my favourite one-dish dinners. It can be prepared with turkey breast, flank steak, lamb or pork strips. You can also make a vegetarian version by using strips of firm tofu in place of the meat, and water instead of chicken stock. If you are using up leftover cooked meat, add it at the end with the noodles just to reheat.

Makes 6 servings

1 lb	linguine or Chinese noodles	500 g
1 lb	boneless, skinless chicken breast, thinly sliced	500 g
1 tbsp	soy sauce	15 mL
1 tbsp	cornstarch	15 mL

Sauce:

1 cup	homemade chicken stock (page 57) or water	250 mL
⅓ cup	rice vinegar	75 mL
3 tbsp	soy sauce	45 mL
2 tbsp	rice wine	25 mL
3 tbsp	brown sugar	45 mL
2 tbsp	molasses	25 mL
1 tbsp	sesame oil	15 mL
1 tbsp	cornstarch	15 mL

To Cook:

1 tbsp	vegetable oil	15 mL
3	cloves garlic, finely chopped	3
1 tbsp	chopped fresh ginger root	15 mL
5	green onions, chopped	5
1 tsp	hot chili paste	5 mL
1	leek or small onion, trimmed and thinly sliced	1
1	carrot, grated	1
1	sweet red pepper, thinly sliced	1
¼ lb	snow peas, sliced	125 g
¼ cup	chopped fresh cilantro or parsley	50 mL

LOW-FAT COOKING
If you want to cook vegetables like garlic and onions in a small amount of oil, use very low heat and try covering the skillet. If things are still browning too quickly, simply add a few spoonfuls of water to cool down the pan and slow down the cooking. Keep cooking until the water evaporates.

PER SERVING

Calories	508
g carbohydrate	79
g fibre	5
g total fat	7
g saturated fat	1
g protein	30

Excellent: vitamin A; vitamin C; niacin; vitamin B$_6$
Good: folacin; iron

mg cholesterol	44
mg sodium	631
mg potassium	570

1. Bring large pot of water to boil. Add Chinese noodles and cook for 2 minutes. (If you are using regular linguine, cook until tender but firm.) Rinse with cold water and drain well.

2. Meanwhile, in bowl, combine chicken with soy sauce and cornstarch. Reserve.

3. To make sauce, combine all sauce ingredients in bowl and reserve.

4. Just before serving, heat vegetable oil in wok or large, deep non-stick skillet. Add chicken and stir-fry just until it loses its raw appearance.

5. Add garlic, ginger, green onions and chili paste. Stir-fry for 1 minute. Add leek, carrot and red pepper. Cook for 3 to 4 minutes, just until vegetables wilt.

6. Stir up sauce and add to skillet. Bring to boil. Cook for 1 minute. Add snow peas and noodles. Toss well to reheat. Add cilantro. Taste and adjust seasonings if necessary.

PASTA SHAPES

Pasta comes in many different shapes. Although there are no longer any hard and fast rules, traditionally there is a reason for choosing one shape over another in a particular recipe. For example, tubular pasta is good for catching all the little treats that are found in a sauce full of chopped ingredients. Pastas like rigatoni are used with chunky vegetable, seafood or chicken sauces so that you can stab a piece of pasta and a chunk of something else at the same time. Long, thin pasta is used for smooth sauces or sauces with tiny pieces in them (big chunks would fall off when you are twirling the strands). Tiny pasta is used in soups so that it will fit on the spoon.

If you want to use different pasta shapes in one dish (kids especially love this), just make sure you are using shapes that all take the same amount of time to cook.

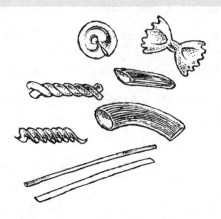

SOUPY CHINESE NOODLES

This is a satisfying and delicious meal in a bowl. If you do
not have leftover cooked chicken, use ¼ lb/125 g diced raw
chicken and add it with the garlic and ginger. You can use
turkey, shrimp or scallops instead of chicken. You can also
use cooked linguine noodles instead of the rice vermicelli.

If you like cilantro, sprinkle a few spoonfuls on the soup just
before serving.

Makes 6 servings

½ lb	rice vermicelli	250 g
2 tsp	sesame oil	10 mL
2 tsp	vegetable oil	10 mL
1 tbsp	chopped fresh ginger root	15 mL
1	small clove garlic, finely chopped	1
6 cups	homemade chicken stock (page 57), or 1 10-oz/284 mL tin chicken broth plus water	1.5 L
1 tbsp	soy sauce	15 mL
1 tbsp	rice wine	15 mL
½ tsp	hot chili paste	2 mL
2 cups	diced cooked chicken (1 whole boneless chicken breast)	500 mL
1	carrot, grated	1
½ lb	fresh spinach, chopped	250 g
6	green onions, chopped	6
	Salt and pepper to taste	

RICE VERMICELLI
Vermicelli actually refers
to any size of rice noodle,
both very thin and wide.
The noodles can be cooked
by soaking them in warm
water for 15 to 20 minutes.
Reheat them in a sauce or
soup or use them cold in
recipes such as salad rolls.

1. Soak rice vermicelli in hot water for 15 minutes. Drain, rinse
   and toss with sesame oil. Reserve.

2. In large saucepan or Dutch oven, heat vegetable oil. Add
   ginger and garlic and cook gently until fragrant.

3. Add stock, soy sauce, rice wine and hot chili paste and bring
   to a boil. Reduce heat and simmer for 5 minutes.

4. Add chicken, carrot and reserved noodles. Heat thoroughly.

5. Add spinach and green onions. Cook for 2 or 3 minutes.
   Season with salt and pepper to taste.

PER SERVING

Calories	303
g carbohydrate	35
g fibre	2
g total fat	7
g saturated fat	1
g protein	24

Excellent: vitamin A; niacin;
vitamin B$_6$; folacin
Good: riboflavin; vitamin B$_{12}$;
iron

mg cholesterol	40
mg sodium	991
mg potassium	627

Meatless Main Courses

Portobello Mushroom Burgers with Roasted Garlic Mayonnaise

Lentil and Mushroom Burgers

Stuffed Baked Potatoes with Stir-fried Vegetables

Risotto with Tomatoes and Beans

Rice Baked with Spinach, Feta and Dill

Polenta with Roasted Ratatouille

Fresh Herb and Vegetable Lasagna

Baked Beans in Brewmaster's Barbecue Sauce

Couscous Soup with Vegetables and Charmoula

Pizza with Black Bean Salsa

Lentil and Wild Rice Salad with Feta

Pizza Salad with Roasted Garlic Hummos

Spicy Singapore Noodles

Chickpea and Couscous Salad

Tofu and Onions Braised in Asian Barbecue Sauce with Noodles

Spicy Tofu with Eggplant and Mushrooms

Fried Rice with Grilled Tofu

PORTOBELLO MUSHROOM BURGERS WITH ROASTED GARLIC MAYONNAISE

Portobello mushrooms have a wonderful meaty taste and texture, and some of them are as big as burgers!

Instead of the garlic mayonnaise, you could use any of the dips or spreads in the Appetizers chapter. Serve the burgers with Roasted "French-fried" Potatoes (page 217) and coleslaw (page 176).

Makes 4 servings

1 tbsp	olive oil	15 mL
2 tbsp	lemon juice	25 mL
2	cloves garlic, minced	2
1 tbsp	chopped fresh rosemary, or ½ tsp/2 mL dried	15 mL
½ tsp	salt	2 mL
½ tsp	pepper	2 mL
4	large (4-inch/10 cm) portobello mushrooms	4
1	large red onion, cut in 4 slices	1
2	sweet red peppers	2
12	leaves fresh basil or small lettuce leaves	12
4	Kaiser rolls or hamburger buns	4

Roasted Garlic Mayonnaise:

1	head roasted garlic (page 131)	1
⅓ cup	yogurt cheese (page 229)	75 mL
2 tbsp	mayonnaise	25 mL
1 tbsp	lemon juice	15 mL
¼ tsp	pepper	1 mL
	Salt to taste	

PER SERVING

Calories	399
g carbohydrate	62
g fibre	7
g total fat	13
g saturated fat	2
g protein	13

Excellent: vitamin C; thiamine; riboflavin; niacin; vitamin B$_6$; folacin; iron
Good: vitamin A

mg cholesterol	8
mg sodium	730
mg potassium	860

1. In large bowl, combine olive oil, lemon juice, minced garlic, rosemary, salt and pepper.

2. Cut stems off mushrooms and reserve for another use. Marinate mushroom caps and onion slices in olive oil mixture.

3. Grill peppers on all sides until blackened. Cool, peel, discard stems, seeds and ribs. Cut peppers into large pieces.

4. Grill mushrooms until browned on both sides and cooked through. Grill onions.

5. To make mayonnaise, squeeze garlic out of skins into blender or food processor (or squeeze into bowl and mash with fork). Blend in yogurt cheese, mayonnaise, lemon juice and pepper. Taste and season with salt if necessary.

6. Assemble sandwiches by placing mushroom on bottom half of buns. Top with grilled onion, pieces of pepper and basil leaves. Smear top half of bun with garlic mayonnaise. Serve burgers hot or cold.

WILD MUSHROOMS

More and more varieties of fresh mushrooms are becoming available. Usually you can buy fresh portobello, cremini (small portobellos that are less expensive than the larger version), shiitake and oyster mushrooms; sometimes morels, chanterelles and enoki can be found, too. They can be quite expensive, but they add a lot of flavour to a special dish.

The stems of some wild mushrooms (e.g., shiitake) are too tough to use in some recipes; freeze them and use in stocks. The stems of other mushrooms, such as portobello, are flavourful and tender. If a recipe calls only for the caps, use the stems in rice dishes, stuffings, soups or sauces.

Dried wild mushrooms are concentrated in flavour and are used in small quantities. To reconstitute them, place in a bowl and cover with hot water. Allow to rest for 30 minutes, until softened. Strain liquid and use it in the recipe, or save for soups or sauces. Rinse mushrooms and chop.

LENTIL AND MUSHROOM BURGERS

*Veggie burgers are all the rage. Try this homemade version —
it's one of the best I've tasted. You can serve the burgers in
hamburger buns with the traditional toppings, but I love
them topped with red pepper sauce and served in Kaiser
buns. Although ⅓ cup/75 mL raw lentils makes about
1 cup/250 mL cooked, and 3 tbsp/45 mL dry couscous
makes about ½ cup/125 mL cooked, I usually make more,
use what I need and then freeze the rest (measured, in
packages) to use another time.*

Makes 4 servings

2 tsp	vegetable oil	10 mL
1	small onion, finely chopped	1
2	cloves garlic, finely chopped	2
¼ lb	chopped mushrooms (2 cups/500 mL)	125 g
1 cup	cooked lentils	250 mL
½ cup	cooked couscous, bulgur or barley	125 mL
¼ cup	fresh whole wheat or white breadcrumbs	50 mL
1 tsp	Dijon mustard	5 mL
1 tbsp	soy sauce	15 mL
½ tsp	pepper	2 mL
1 tbsp	vegetable oil	15 mL
4	Kaiser rolls or hamburger buns	4

1. Heat 2 tsp/10 mL oil in large non-stick skillet. Add onion
   and garlic and cook until lightly brown and fragrant. Add
   mushrooms. When mushrooms have begun to render their
   juices, increase heat and cook until all liquid has evaporated.

2. In food processor, combine mushroom mixture with lentils,
   couscous, breadcrumbs, mustard, soy sauce and pepper. Blend
   just until mixture starts to stick together.

3. Shape mixture into 4 patties about ½ inch/1 cm thick.
   Refrigerate for at least 1 hour.

4. Heat remaining 1 tbsp/15 mL oil in large non-stick skillet,
   or brush baking sheet with oil. Cook burgers for about
   5 minutes per side in skillet or 15 minutes per side in preheated
   375°F/190°C oven, or until crusty and cooked through.

LENTILS
The tiny red lentils
(sometimes called pink or
orange) are usually used in
soups, as they tend to break
down and become pureed all
on their own when cooked.
But if you want the lentils
to keep their shape, as in
salads, stews, casseroles and
rice dishes, use the green
(sometimes called brown)
lentils. I especially like the
tiny ones (sometimes called
French lentils) for their clean
taste and texture.

PER SERVING

Calories	352
g carbohydrate	57
g fibre	5
g total fat	8
g saturated fat	1
g protein	13

Excellent: niacin; folacin; iron
Good: thiamine

mg cholesterol	2
mg sodium	633
mg potassium	375

STUFFED BAKED POTATOES WITH STIR-FRIED VEGETABLES

When my stepdaughter, Fara, went backpacking in Europe, she came home with some great meatless dinner ideas. She said baked potatoes were stuffed with many different fillings, from tuna salad (page 88) to her favourite — stir-fried vegetables. If you want to add some protein to this, include chickpeas or diced extra-firm tofu in the stir-fry, or sprinkle grated Swiss or Cheddar cheese on top and broil just until melted.

Makes 4 servings

2	large baking potatoes (8 oz/250 g each)	2
2 tsp	vegetable oil	10 mL
1	small onion, diced	1
2	cloves garlic, finely chopped	2
1	yellow or green zucchini, diced	1
1	sweet red pepper, diced	1
8	stalks asparagus, trimmed and diced	8
½ cup	homemade vegetable stock (page 57) or water	125 mL
dash	hot red pepper sauce	dash
	Salt and pepper to taste	
1 tbsp	chopped fresh tarragon (or 1 tsp/5 mL dried)	15 mL

1. Prick potatoes with fork in a few places and place on baking sheet. Bake in preheated 425°F/220°C oven for 1 hour, or until crisp on outside and tender inside.

2. Meanwhile, heat oil in large non-stick skillet or wok on medium-high heat. Add onion and garlic and cook for about 30 seconds. Add zucchini, red pepper and asparagus and stir-fry for a few minutes, or until tender.

3. Combine stock and hot pepper sauce. Add to skillet and cook until liquid has almost completely evaporated. Season with salt, pepper and tarragon. Remove from heat.

4. Cut baked potatoes in half lengthwise. Fluff up some of inside and spoon about 1 cup/250 mL vegetables on each half.

WORCESTERSHIRE SAUCE

Worcestershire sauce contains anchovies. Vegetarians might want to look for white Worcestershire, although it is still hard to find. Or you can simply add more of the other seasonings listed in a recipe.

PER SERVING

Calories	132
g carbohydrate	26
g fibre	4
g total fat	3
g saturated fat	trace
g protein	3

Excellent: vitamin C
Good: vitamin B$_6$; folacin

mg cholesterol	0
mg sodium	16
mg potassium	535

RISOTTO WITH TOMATOES AND BEANS

Although many people say you have to use a lot of butter or oil to make a good risotto, I think the rice is so creamy anyway that in some cases you hardly miss the extra fat.

This is a very hearty risotto that makes an excellent meatless main course. Serve it with a salad.

Makes 6 to 8 servings

1 tbsp	olive oil	15 mL
1	onion, finely chopped	1
3	cloves garlic, finely chopped	3
½ tsp	hot red pepper flakes, or to taste	2 mL
2 cups	short-grain Italian rice	500 mL
1	28-oz/796 mL tin plum tomatoes, with juices, pureed or broken up (3 cups/750 mL), hot	1
4 cups	homemade vegetable stock (page 57) or water, hot	1 L
2 cups	cooked navy beans or white kidney beans	500 mL
	Salt and pepper to taste	
¼ cup	chopped fresh parsley	50 mL
½ cup	grated Parmesan cheese	125 mL

1. Heat oil in large saucepan or Dutch oven. Add onion, garlic and hot pepper flakes. Cook gently until very fragrant and tender.

2. Add rice to onion mixture and combine well. Cook for 1 minute.

3. Add ½ cup/125 mL hot tomatoes and cook, stirring, until all liquid has been absorbed or evaporated (heat should be medium to medium-high). Keep adding tomatoes about ½ cup/125 mL at a time. Cook, stirring, until liquid is gone before adding next amount.

4. After all tomatoes have been added, start adding stock. After adding about 2 cups/500 mL stock, stir in beans. Heat thoroughly. Continue adding stock until rice is tender but still slightly firm.

5. Stir in salt, pepper, parsley and cheese.

PARMESAN CHEESE
Use the best Parmesan cheese that you can. I usually buy it in a chunk and grate it with a fine hand grater, but it can also be chopped in a food processor using the steel knife. Good-quality grated Parmesan cheese can be found in most supermarkets. Look for the Parmigiano Reggiano name.

PARMESAN CHEESE CRISPS
A delicious cheese "crouton" (sometimes called "frico") can be made with Parmigiano Reggiano. Simply take a few spoonfuls of grated cheese and spread it into a 3-inch/7.5 cm circle on a non-stick baking sheet. Bake at 350°F/180°C for 3 to 5 minutes, or until the cheese melts. When cool, use as a garnish for soups and salads.

PER SERVING

Calories	431
g carbohydrate	79
g fibre	7
g total fat	6
g saturated fat	2
g protein	15

Excellent: folacin
Good: thiamine; niacin; vitamin B_6; calcium; iron

mg cholesterol	7
mg sodium	401
mg potassium	657

RICE BAKED WITH SPINACH, FETA AND DILL

You can serve this with or without the feta cheese as a side dish for lamb or salmon. You can also fold the spinach mixture into cooked couscous or bulgur instead of rice.

For a main course, serve this with soup and fresh rolls.

Makes 6 servings

2 cups	brown basmati rice	500 mL
3 cups	cold water	750 mL
2 tsp	olive oil	10 mL
1	onion, sliced	1
2	cloves garlic, finely chopped	2
1 lb	fresh spinach, trimmed and chopped	500 g
2 tbsp	chopped fresh dill	25 mL
2 oz	crumbled feta cheese	60 g
	Salt and pepper to taste	

1. Rinse rice well (page 171) and place in saucepan with cold water. Bring to boil. Reduce heat to medium and cook, uncovered, until water has been absorbed but top of rice is still moist. Cover and cook on very low heat for about 35 minutes, or until rice is tender.

2. Meanwhile, heat oil in large, deep non-stick skillet. Add onion and cook until browned. Add garlic and cook for a few minutes.

3. Stir in spinach and cook just until spinach wilts.

4. Add rice and combine gently. Add dill and feta and mix in gently. Season with salt and pepper.

5. Place mixture in oiled 2-qt/2 L casserole or baking dish. Cover with foil. Bake in preheated 350°F/180°C oven for 30 minutes.

PER SERVING

Calories	291
g carbohydrate	52
g fibre	6
g total fat	6
g saturated fat	2
g protein	9

Excellent: vitamin A; vitamin B$_6$; folacin
Good: thiamine; riboflavin; niacin; calcium; iron

mg cholesterol	9
mg sodium	170
mg potassium	435

POLENTA WITH ROASTED RATATOUILLE

Polenta is an Italian specialty of cooked cornmeal; it can be served with any number of sauces. Creamy-style polenta dishes are served in wide soup bowls with a topping immediately after cooking. Or the polenta can be chilled, cut into squares and grilled or pan-fried before being served with the topping. Polenta squares can even be used as a kind of bruschetta, topped with pesto (page 60) or an appetizer spread.

To make polenta you can use regular cornmeal or precooked cornmeal (which will cook in about one-quarter of the time).

Ratatouille is usually a savoury vegetable stew that is cooked on the stove, but when the vegetables are roasted, the flavours really intensify. I learned about roasting at high heat at my cottage, where the forty-year-old oven goes to about 650°F when it's set at 350°F! But when everything started turning out great, I began to crank up my oven at home, too (not quite that high, though!).

For a main course, serve this with salad and crusty bread. As a side dish, the ratatouille can be served on its own or in phyllo cups as with the Asparagus Tarts (page 52), topped with chèvre.

Makes 6 servings

4 cups	water (use 6 cups/1.5 L for creamy polenta)	1 L
1 tsp	salt	5 mL
½ tsp	pepper	2 mL
1 cup	cornmeal	250 mL
¼ cup	pesto (page 60), optional	50 mL

Roasted Ratatouille:

1	large onion, cut in 12 wedges	1
12	cloves garlic, peeled	12
¾ lb	eggplant, cut in chunks	375 g
½ lb	zucchini, cut in ½-inch/1 cm rounds	250 g
1 lb	fresh plum tomatoes, cut in 4 wedges	500 g
1	bulb fennel, trimmed and cut in 12 wedges (1 to 1½ lb/500 to 750 g)	1

SHREDDING BASIL
Fresh basil becomes bruised and turns black when it is chopped, so if I am using it to garnish a dish, I like to shred it. Stack the leaves or roll them, then slice, using a sharp knife.

PER SERVING

Calories	189
g carbohydrate	38
g fibre	7
g total fat	3
g saturated fat	trace
g protein	5

Excellent: vitamin C
Good: vitamin A; niacin; vitamin B$_6$; folacin

mg cholesterol	0
mg sodium	619
mg potassium	818

¼ lb	shiitake (without stems) or portobello (with stems) mushrooms, cut in quarters	125 g
1	sweet red pepper, cut in strips	1
1	sweet yellow pepper, cut in strips	1
1 tbsp	chopped fresh rosemary, or ½ tsp/2 mL dried	15 mL
1 tbsp	chopped fresh thyme, or ½ tsp/2 mL dried	15 mL
½ tsp	salt	2 mL
½ tsp	pepper	2 mL
¼ cup	shredded fresh basil or chopped fresh parsley	50 mL
1 tbsp	olive oil	15 mL
1 tbsp	balsamic vinegar	15 mL

1. To make polenta, bring water to boil in large saucepan. Add salt and pepper. Very slowly whisk in cornmeal. If you are using regular cornmeal, cook, stirring often, on low heat, for about 30 minutes. If you are using instant cornmeal, cook for about 5 minutes.

2. When polenta is ready, stir in pesto. Taste and adjust seasonings if necessary. Spread polenta in non-stick or parchment paper-lined 13 x 9-inch/3.5 L baking dish. Cool and refrigerate until ready to use.

3. Meanwhile, to prepare ratatouille, spread onion, garlic, eggplant, zucchini, tomatoes, fennel, mushrooms and sweet peppers in single layer in large, lightly oiled roasting pan. Sprinkle with rosemary, thyme, salt and pepper.

4. Roast vegetables in preheated 400°F/200°C oven for 45 minutes, or until tender and browned. Stir occasionally. Toss with basil, olive oil and vinegar. Taste and adjust seasonings if necessary.

5. Cut polenta into 12 3-inch/7.5 cm squares (brush with olive oil if you wish). Grill or pan-fry in non-stick skillet until lightly browned. Serve with vegetables on top.

Fresh Herb and Vegetable Lasagna

I like to serve this easy and flavourful lasagna dish with a salad. You can also stuff the ricotta and vegetable mixture into cooked cannelloni tubes and cover them with the tomato sauce. Or you can use the filling to stuff crêpes.

You can also use oven-ready lasagna noodles in this recipe. Follow the package directions.

Serve this with a salad.

Makes 6 to 8 servings

9	lasagna noodles (10 x 2 inches/25 x 5 cm each)	9
2	28-oz/796 mL tins plum tomatoes, with juices, pureed or broken up	2
	Salt and pepper to taste	
2 tsp	olive oil	10 mL
1	onion, chopped	1
3	cloves garlic, finely chopped	3
pinch	hot red pepper flakes	pinch
2	small eggplants, diced (½ lb/250 g)	2
1	medium zucchini, diced	1
1	sweet red pepper, diced	1
½ lb	mushrooms, sliced	250 g
1 tsp	chopped fresh rosemary, or pinch dried	5 mL
1 tsp	chopped fresh thyme, or pinch dried	5 mL
2 tbsp	balsamic vinegar	25 mL
1 cup	light ricotta cheese or chèvre (goat cheese)	250 mL
½ cup	chopped fresh basil or parsley	125 mL
¼ cup	grated Parmesan cheese	50 mL

1. Bring large pot of water to boil. Add noodles and cook a few at a time just until tender. Rinse under cold water. Arrange noodles on damp tea towels in single layer until ready to use.

2. Place tomatoes in Dutch oven. Bring to boil and cook over medium-high heat, stirring frequently, until reduced by half and quite thick, about 15 to 20 minutes. You should have about 3 cups/750 mL. Season with salt and pepper.

3. To make filling, heat oil in large, deep non-stick skillet or Dutch oven. Add onion, garlic and hot pepper flakes. Cook gently for a few minutes.

4. Add eggplants and zucchini and cook for 5 minutes. Add red pepper, mushrooms, rosemary and thyme. Cook until liquid has evaporated.

5. Add vinegar and cook on high heat until vinegar evaporates. Taste and season with salt and pepper. Cool.

6. Add ricotta and basil to sauce. Taste and adjust seasonings if necessary.

7. To assemble, spread a few spoonfuls of tomato sauce in bottom of 12 x 8-inch/3 L baking dish. Arrange one layer of noodles on top of sauce. Spread with half the vegetable mixture (about 1 cup/250 mL) and drizzle with one-third sauce. Place another layer of noodles on top, remaining vegetable mixture and one-third of sauce. Top with remaining noodles and sauce. Sprinkle with Parmesan.

8. Bake, uncovered, in preheated 350°F/180°C oven for 30 to 35 minutes, or until bubbling. Allow to rest for 10 minutes before serving.

BAKED BEANS IN BREWMASTER'S BARBECUE SAUCE

I used to think that if you cooked beans in barbecue sauce, the beans would absorb even more of the flavour. But in fact, beans toughen if they are cooked for a long time in a very acidic or salty mixture. They should be cooked to a tender state before adding them to the sauce.

This barbecue sauce is also good with chicken, ribs, polenta or veggie burgers. Serve the beans with a green salad and Grilled Corn Salad (page 78) for a satisfying meatless meal.

Makes 8 servings

1 lb	dried navy beans (2 cups/500 mL)	500 g

Brewmaster's Barbecue Sauce:

2 tsp	vegetable oil	10 mL
2	onions, diced	2
1	clove garlic, finely chopped	1
¼ cup	red wine vinegar	50 mL
2 tbsp	maple syrup or brown sugar	25 mL
⅓ cup	molasses	75 mL
1½ cups	pureed plum tomatoes or tomato sauce	375 mL
1	28-oz/796 mL tin plum tomatoes, with juices, broken up	1
1	12-oz/341 mL bottle beer	1
1 tbsp	chopped fresh sage, or ½ tsp/2 mL dried	15 mL
1 tbsp	Dijon mustard	15 mL
2 tsp	minced chipotles or jalapeños	10 mL
½ tsp	salt	2 mL
½ tsp	pepper	2 mL

PER SERVING

Calories	303
g carbohydrate	60
g fibre	12
g total fat	2
g saturated fat	trace
g protein	14

Excellent: thiamine; folacin; iron
Good: niacin; vitamin B$_6$; calcium

mg cholesterol	0
mg sodium	631
mg potassium	1083

1. Soak beans overnight in plenty of cold water in refrigerator. Drain. Place beans in large pot and cover with cold water. Bring to boil, reduce heat and simmer gently, uncovered, for 1 hour, or until just tender. Rinse and drain well.

2. Meanwhile, heat oil in large, deep non-stick skillet. Add onions and garlic. Cook gently until tender and fragrant.

3. Add vinegar, maple syrup, molasses, pureed tomatoes, plum tomatoes, beer, sage, mustard, chipotles, salt and pepper. Bring to boil, reduce heat and simmer for 5 minutes.

4. Stir in beans. Transfer mixture to casserole dish. Cover. Bake in preheated 350°F/180°C oven for 2 hours, stirring occasionally. Remove cover for last 20 minutes of cooking time. Allow to rest for 10 minutes before serving.

COOKING WITH DRIED BEANS

Beans are becoming more and more popular, partly for health reasons but also because people are realizing how delicious they are. However, some people find them hard to digest. Here are some tips:

• Beano is available in many drugstores and supermarkets, in pills or drops; it is an enzyme like Lactaid that helps most people digest beans. Follow the package instructions — some people need more than others.

• Cook beans thoroughly; beans cooked al dente are harder to digest.

• If you are not used to eating beans, start with small amounts.

• Although dried beans do not really need to be soaked anymore, soaking them in cold water overnight in the refrigerator, or a few hours at room temperature, and discarding the soaking liquid before cooking seems to reduce the gas.

CANNED VS. DRIED BEANS

To save time, you can substitute canned beans for dried beans, although the texture of the dish may suffer. I tend to use canned beans in bean purees and pureed soups, but in salads, side dishes and chilis, I prefer to cook my own dried beans. Canned beans are also higher in sodium, so rinse them to remove as much salt as possible before using.

COUSCOUS SOUP WITH VEGETABLES AND CHARMOULA

This is a very interesting and delicious soup. I like to use Israeli couscous (sometimes called pearl pasta), but you can also use rice or tiny pasta (e.g., orzo). Charmoula is a Middle Eastern-flavoured pesto-like mixture that carries an amazing flavour punch. It can be used as a dressing, sandwich spread or sauce.

Serve this soup in large bowls as a main course with salad and crusty bread or pita.

Makes 8 servings

2 tsp	olive oil	10 mL
1	onion, diced	1
3	cloves garlic, finely chopped	3
1 tbsp	paprika	15 mL
1 tsp	ground cumin	5 mL
¼ tsp	hot red pepper flakes	1 mL
1 cup	Israeli couscous	250 mL
1	leek, trimmed and diced	1
1	carrot, diced	1
1	zucchini, diced	1
1	sweet red pepper, peeled and diced	1
1 cup	diced butternut squash	250 mL
8 cups	homemade vegetable stock (page 57)	2 L
1	19-oz/540 mL tin chickpeas, drained and rinsed	1
1 cup	fresh or frozen peas	250 mL
1 cup	fresh or frozen corn niblets	250 mL
	Salt and pepper to taste	

SPICES

Spices are the seeds, bark and roots of certain plants. Ground spices lose their flavour quickly (within a year of being ground), so buy them in small quantities, or buy them whole and grind them as you need them (page 216).

Store spices in a cool, dry place and use them sparingly at first, until you decide whether you like them in a particular recipe. There are some traditional matches such as nutmeg with spinach or cinnamon with apples, but don't be afraid to experiment. Spices can also replace some of the flavour that is lost by limiting fat and salt in a recipe.

PER SERVING

Calories	271
g carbohydrate	45
g fibre	6
g total fat	7
g saturated fat	1
g protein	9

Excellent: vitamin A; vitamin C; folacin
Good: vitamin B$_6$; iron

mg cholesterol	0
mg sodium	301
mg potassium	476

Charmoula:

3	cloves garlic	3
1 tsp	paprika	5 mL
1 tsp	ground cumin	5 mL
½ tsp	salt	2 mL
¼ tsp	cayenne	1 mL
¼ tsp	pepper	1 mL
½ cup	chopped fresh parsley	125 mL
½ cup	chopped fresh cilantro or parsley	125 mL
3 tbsp	lemon juice	45 mL
2 tbsp	olive oil	25 mL

1. To make soup, heat oil in Dutch oven. Add onion and garlic and cook gently until tender. Add paprika, cumin and hot pepper flakes. Cook for about 30 seconds, or until fragrant.

2. Add couscous and stir to coat well.

3. Add leek, carrot, zucchini, red pepper, squash and stock. Bring to boil. Cook for about 10 minutes, or until couscous is almost tender.

4. Add chickpeas, peas and corn. Heat thoroughly. Taste and season with salt and pepper.

5. Meanwhile, to make charmoula, puree garlic in food processor. Add paprika, cumin, salt, cayenne and pepper and combine. Add parsley and cilantro and blend in. Add lemon juice and olive oil and puree (you should have about ⅓ cup/75 mL).

6. Ladle soup into bowls. Swirl spoonful of charmoula into each serving.

PIZZA WITH BLACK BEAN SALSA

Pizza crusts can be made in many different ways, but my favourite quick version is baked flour tortillas. Any of the salsas or pestos in this book can be used as a base, and crumbled chèvre, grated Parmesan or Gorgonzola all make delicious toppings.

This recipe can also be made as quesadillas (page 51).

Makes 6 servings

6	**10-inch/25 cm flour tortillas**	6
1 cup	**cooked black beans**	250 mL
2	**sweet red peppers, roasted (page 241), peeled and diced**	2
2	**tomatoes, seeded and diced**	2
1 cup	**fresh or frozen corn niblets**	250 mL
1	**chipotle (page 78) or jalapeño, finely chopped**	1
½ cup	**chopped fresh cilantro or parsley**	125 mL
1½ cups	**grated Monterey Jack or smoked mozzarella cheese (5 oz/150 g)**	375 mL

1. Prick tortillas all over with fork. Place directly on oven rack in preheated 400°F/200°C oven for 5 minutes, or until lightly browned and crisp. Arrange tortillas in single layer on three baking sheets.

2. In bowl, combine beans, red peppers, tomatoes, corn, chipotle and cilantro.

3. Spoon about ¾ cup/175 mL black bean mixture on each tortilla. Sprinkle each with ¼ cup/50 mL cheese.

4. Return to oven and bake for 7 minutes, or until cheese has melted. Serve whole or cut into wedges.

COOKING BLACK BEANS

Black turtle beans are often used in Southwestern and Mexican dishes, soups and salads. You can use canned beans or cook dry ones (they freeze well).

To cook, soak 1 lb/500 g (2 cups/500 mL) dried beans in cold water overnight in the refrigerator. Drain, rinse and place in a large saucepan. Cover generously with cold water. Add 1 peeled and quartered onion. Bring to boil, skim off scum and cook gently, covered, for 1 to 1½ hours, or until tender. Remove onion. Rinse beans and drain well.

Makes about 4 cups/1 L

PER SERVING

Calories	368
g carbohydrate	50
g fibre	5
g total fat	13
g saturated fat	6
g protein	16

Excellent: vitamin A; vitamin C; niacin; folacin; calcium; iron
Good: thiamine; riboflavin

mg cholesterol	25
mg sodium	447
mg potassium	397

Penne with Tomatoes and Arugula
(page 100)

Broken Spaghetti with Fresh Salsa and Scallops
(page 107)

LENTIL AND WILD RICE SALAD WITH FETA

This makes a great meatless main course — serve it with grilled vegetables (page 40) — but it can also be served as a side salad for a barbecue. I like to use the small green French lentils for salads, but if you cannot find them, simply use the larger green ones. Instead of the wild rice you can use brown rice (cook it for 30 to 40 minutes) or basmati rice (cook for about 12 to 15 minutes).

WILD RICE

Wild rice is actually a grass, not a grain. But when it cooks, it has a very similar texture and taste to brown rice. Wild rice takes about 50 minutes to prepare, but you can cook lots and freeze what you are not using for another time. Not only does it taste great in salads and as a side dish, it is delicious in rice pudding (page 266) and in pancakes (page 227). Be sure to cook until it puffs and looks like long grains of rice.

Makes 8 to 10 servings

1 cup	small green lentils	250 mL
1 cup	wild rice	250 mL
2 cups	fresh or frozen corn niblets	500 mL
1	sweet red pepper, diced	1
1	jalapeño, diced	1
½ cup	chopped fresh parsley	125 mL
¼ cup	chopped fresh chives or green onions	50 mL
½ cup	crumbled feta cheese (2½ oz/75 g)	125 mL

Dressing:

3 tbsp	rice vinegar or cider vinegar	45 mL
2	cloves garlic, minced	2
1 tsp	salt	5 mL
½ tsp	pepper	2 mL
3 tbsp	olive oil	45 mL

1. Rinse lentils and place in large pot. Cover generously with water and bring to boil. Cook for 25 to 30 minutes, or until tender. Drain well. Cool.

2. Bring a second large pot of water to boil. Add rice and cook until tender, about 45 to 50 minutes or until rice has puffed up. Drain well. Cool. Combine with lentils in large bowl.

3. Add corn, red pepper, jalapeño, parsley, chives and feta to rice mixture.

4. To make dressing, in small bowl, combine vinegar, garlic, salt and pepper. Whisk in oil. Toss salad gently with dressing. Taste and adjust seasonings if necessary.

PER SERVING

Calories	261
g carbohydrate	40
g fibre	6
g total fat	8
g saturated fat	2
g protein	12

Excellent: vitamin C; folacin
Good: thiamine; niacin; vitamin B$_6$; iron

mg cholesterol	7
mg sodium	380
mg potassium	479

Pizza Salad with Roasted Garlic Hummos

This is fun to serve and delicious to eat. You may want to serve it with a knife and fork, however, as the spinach tends to fall off.

The garlic hummos also makes a wonderful spread on its own. The pizza can also be topped with roasted ratatouille (page 120).

Makes 8 servings

1	10-inch/25 cm focaccia	1
2 tbsp	olive oil	25 mL
1	clove garlic, minced	1
¼ tsp	salt	1 mL
¼ tsp	pepper	1 mL

Roasted Garlic Hummos:

1	19-oz/540 mL tin chickpeas, drained and rinsed	1
1	head roasted garlic (page 131), or 2 cloves minced raw garlic	1
2 tbsp	lemon juice	25 mL
1 tsp	ground cumin	5 mL
1 tsp	sesame oil	5 mL
	Salt and pepper to taste	

Salad:

1 lb	fresh spinach, coarsely chopped	500 g
1 lb	fresh tomatoes, seeded and diced	500 g
½ cup	shredded fresh basil, optional	125 mL
3 tbsp	balsamic vinegar	45 mL
½ tsp	salt	2 mL
½ tsp	pepper	2 mL
1	clove garlic, minced	1
2 tbsp	olive oil	25 mL

GARLIC

When I use garlic in an uncooked dish like a salad dressing, spread or dip, I like to mince it or put it through a garlic press, so there are not actual pieces of raw garlic in the mixture. But minced garlic is likely to burn and stick when it is sauteed, so if I am cooking garlic I chop it finely with a knife.

When you are sauteing chopped garlic with ingredients like onions, add the other ingredients to the hot skillet first to soften the heat and help prevent the garlic from burning.

Be cautious with quantity when using raw garlic as it is very strong. But if garlic is to be cooked, you can be more generous as it becomes sweeter and more mild when cooked.

PER SERVING

Calories	291
g carbohydrate	41
g fibre	5
g total fat	11
g saturated fat	2
g protein	10

Excellent: vitamin A; folacin; iron
Good: vitamin C; thiamine; riboflavin; niacin; vitamin B₆

mg cholesterol	2
mg sodium	755
mg potassium	607

1. Slice focaccia in half horizontally.

2. In small bowl, combine olive oil with garlic. Brush over cut surfaces of bread. Sprinkle with salt and pepper. Bake in preheated 400°F/200°C oven for 10 minutes, or until warm and crusty.

3. Meanwhile, to prepare hummos, place chickpeas in food processor or blender. Squeeze garlic out of skins and add. Blend. Add lemon juice, cumin and sesame oil and blend in. Taste and season with salt and pepper. Spread hummos over cut surfaces of toasted bread (add a little water if mixture is too thick to spread).

4. Meanwhile, in large bowl, combine spinach, tomatoes and basil.

5. In small bowl, combine vinegar, salt, pepper and garlic. Whisk in oil. Toss well with salad.

6. Spoon salad over top of bread. Cut each round into quarters to serve.

ROASTED GARLIC

Roasted garlic adds a wonderful flavour to dishes, and it thickens sauces, dips, salad dressings and soups without adding fat. You can add roasted garlic to soups, salads, salad dressings, pasta sauces, potatoes, rice and vegetable dishes. It can be spread on grilled bread with some goat cheese. It lasts for a few weeks in the refrigerator, so make lots.

There are a number of ways to roast garlic. If you want a very gentle garlic flavour, trim about $1/4$ inch/5 mm off the top of garlic heads. Remove any of the parchment-like skin that comes away easily. Place the garlic in a baking dish, cut sides up. Brush lightly with olive oil if you wish and cover with foil. Bake in a preheated 300°F/150°C oven for $1 1/2$ hours. Remove foil and bake for 20 minutes longer. The garlic should be tender when you squeeze it gently.

If you prefer a stronger roasted flavour, place the garlic, cut side down, on parchment or foil-lined baking sheet and roast the garlic at 400°F/200°C, uncovered, for 40 to 45 minutes, or until tender.

To remove the garlic, turn the heads upside down and gently squeeze the garlic out of the skins.

SPICY SINGAPORE NOODLES

This is a spicy vegetarian dish containing tofu, but shrimp or strips of chicken can be used instead. If you do not like your food too spicy, omit the hot chili paste and use only half the amount of curry powder.

Makes 4 to 6 servings

½ lb	thin rice vermicelli or angelhair or spaghettini pasta	250 g

Sauce:

⅓ cup	homemade vegetable stock (page 57) or water	75 mL
2 tbsp	soy sauce	25 mL
1 tbsp	granulated sugar	15 mL
1 tbsp	sesame oil	15 mL
1 tbsp	rice wine	15 mL

To Cook:

1 tbsp	vegetable oil	15 mL
¼ lb	tofu, cut in sticks	125 g
2	cloves garlic, finely chopped	2
1 tbsp	chopped fresh ginger root	15 mL
3	green onions, finely chopped	3
1 tbsp	curry powder	15 mL
½ tsp	hot chili paste	2 mL
2	leeks, trimmed and thinly sliced	2
1	carrot, grated	1
1	sweet red pepper, thinly sliced	1
¼ lb	bean sprouts	125 g

LEEKS

I use the white and light-green portions of leeks (unless the leeks are very young, in which case the whole thing is tender). Peel off the outside layers until you reach the light-green part. Trim and dice the leek and place it in a bowl of cold water. Swish the pieces around until the grit sinks to the bottom of the bowl and the leeks float to the top. Lift out the leeks and dry them.

PER SERVING

Calories	364
g carbohydrate	62
g fibre	4
g total fat	9
g saturated fat	1
g protein	9

Excellent: vitamin A; vitamin C; vitamin B_6; iron
Good: niacin; folacin

mg cholesterol	0
mg sodium	451
mg potassium	377

1. Place rice noodles in large bowl, cover with very hot tap water and soak for 10 minutes. Drain well. (If you are using regular pasta, cook in pot of boiling water until tender.)

2. In small bowl, combine stock, soy sauce, sugar, sesame oil and rice wine.

3. Heat vegetable oil in large non-stick wok or deep skillet on medium-high heat. Rinse tofu and pat dry. Stir-fry for a few minutes until slightly browned. Remove and reserve.

4. Add garlic, ginger and green onions to wok. Cook for 30 seconds. Add curry powder and chili paste and cook for 10 to 20 seconds longer.

5. Add leeks, carrot and red pepper. Cook until barely wilted. Add bean sprouts and reserved sauce and bring to boil. Add tofu and noodles and cook together until hot and well combined. Taste and adjust seasonings if necessary.

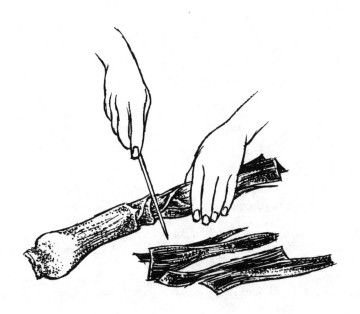

CHICKPEA AND COUSCOUS SALAD

This delicious salad can be served on its own or with other salads as a meatless main course, or as a side salad with grilled chicken, lamb or fish.

Makes 6 servings

1 cup	couscous	250 mL
1	19-oz/540 mL tin chickpeas, drained and rinsed	1
1	sweet red pepper, raw or roasted (page 241), diced	1
1 cup	fresh or frozen corn niblets	250 mL
4	chopped green onions	4
2 cups	chopped fresh cilantro or parsley	500 mL

Dressing:

1 tsp	minced chipotle (page 78), jalapeño or sweet and hot Thai sauce (page 94)	5 mL
1 tsp	ground cumin	5 mL
1 tbsp	molasses or honey	15 mL
2 tbsp	rice vinegar or cider vinegar	25 mL
¼ cup	lime juice or lemon juice	50 mL
¼ cup	orange juice	50 mL
2 tbsp	olive oil	25 mL
	Salt and pepper to taste	

1. Place couscous in 8-inch/1.5 L square glass baking dish. Pour 1 cup/250 mL boiling water over top and cover tightly. Allow to rest for 15 minutes. Fluff with fork.

2. In large bowl, combine couscous, chickpeas, red pepper, corn, green onions and cilantro.

3. For dressing, puree chipotle with cumin, molasses, vinegar, lime juice, orange juice and olive oil. Toss lightly with couscous and chickpea mixture. Taste and season with salt and pepper if necessary.

PER SERVING

Calories	289
g carbohydrate	51
g fibre	5
g total fat	6
g saturated fat	1
g protein	10

Excellent: vitamin C; folacin
Good: niacin; vitamin B$_6$

mg cholesterol	0
mg sodium	149
mg potassium	354

TOFU AND ONIONS BRAISED IN ASIAN BARBECUE SAUCE WITH NOODLES

This can be served with rice instead of noodles. Grilled Corn Salad (page 78) makes a wonderful accompaniment.

Makes 4 servings

4	onions, thinly sliced (1 lb/500 g)	4
1 lb	extra-firm tofu	500 g
½ tsp	five-spice powder (see sidebar), optional	2 mL
2	cloves garlic, minced	2
1 tbsp	minced fresh ginger root	15 mL
1½ tbsp	hoisin sauce	20 mL
1½ tbsp	oyster sauce	20 mL
⅓ cup	ketchup	75 mL
1½ tbsp	soy sauce	20 mL
2 tbsp	rice wine	25 mL
1 tsp	sesame oil	5 mL
½ tsp	hot chili paste	2 mL
½ lb	spaghetti or Chinese egg noodles	250 g
3	green onions, chopped	3

1. Arrange sliced onions in bottom of 13 x 9-inch/3.5 L baking dish. Rinse tofu and pat dry. Cut tofu into 4 pieces and arrange on top of onions.

2. In small bowl, combine five-spice powder, garlic, ginger, hoisin, oyster sauce, ketchup, soy sauce, rice wine, sesame oil and hot chili paste. Pour over tofu and onions.

3. Cover dish with foil and bake in preheated 375°F/190°C oven for 30 to 45 minutes, or until onions are very tender. Uncover and bake for 10 minutes longer. Remove tofu and slice. Keep warm.

4. Meanwhile, bring large pot of water to boil. Add noodles and cook until tender but firm. Drain well and toss with onions and sauce. Serve with tofu slices. Sprinkle with green onions.

FIVE-SPICE POWDER

Five-spice powder is an aromatic spice mixture that is used in Asian cooking. To make it, grind together equal amounts of star anise, fennel seeds, cinnamon, cloves and Sichuan peppercorns.

PER SERVING

Calories	429
g carbohydrate	70
g fibre	9
g total fat	5
g saturated fat	1
g protein	27

Excellent: calcium
Good: vitamin B$_6$; folacin

mg cholesterol	0
mg sodium	828
mg potassium	602

SPICY TOFU
WITH EGGPLANT
AND MUSHROOMS

I love tofu cooked with Asian flavours. This version is similar to the classic Ma Po bean curd that is usually made with ground meat, but I find the eggplant and mushrooms just as delicious. Serve it with Stir-fried Broccoli with Ginger (page 210).

If you do not have fresh shiitake mushrooms, use four dried mushrooms. Soak in ½ cup/125 mL warm water for 30 minutes. Discard stems, and rinse and dice caps. Strain liquid through cheesecloth and use as part of the vegetable stock. Red and yellow peppers also taste great in this.

Makes 4 to 6 servings

2 cups	homemade vegetable stock (page 57) or water	500 mL
2 tbsp	soy sauce	25 mL
2 tbsp	rice wine	25 mL
1 tbsp	hoisin sauce	15 mL
1 tbsp	cornstarch	15 mL
1 tbsp	water	15 mL
½ tsp	sesame oil	2 mL

To Cook:

2 tsp	vegetable oil	10 mL
3	cloves garlic, finely chopped	3
1 tbsp	chopped fresh ginger root	15 mL
4	green onions, chopped	4
1 tsp	hot chili paste	5 mL
1 lb	eggplant (4 small), diced	500 g
¼ lb	fresh shiitake mushrooms, stems removed, chopped	125 g
½ lb	tofu, diced	250 g
2 tbsp	chopped fresh cilantro or parsley	25 mL
4 cups	steamed rice (page 171)	1 L

PER SERVING

Calories	411
g carbohydrate	74
g fibre	5
g total fat	7
g saturated fat	1
g protein	13

Excellent: iron
Good: thiamine; niacin; vitamin B_6; folacin

mg cholesterol	0
mg sodium	540
mg potassium	573

1. Combine stock, soy sauce, rice wine and hoisin sauce.

2. In small bowl, prepare thickening mixture by combining cornstarch, water and sesame oil. Stir until smooth.

3. Heat vegetable oil in non-stick wok or large, deep skillet on medium-high heat. Add garlic, ginger, green onions and chili paste. Cook for about 30 seconds, or until fragrant.

4. Add eggplant and mushrooms to wok. Cook for a few minutes.

5. Rinse tofu and pat dry. Add tofu and sauce mixture to wok. Bring to boil and simmer, uncovered, for 20 minutes.

6. Stir up thickening mixture and add to wok. Bring to boil to thicken. Sprinkle with cilantro and serve over rice.

TOFU

Tofu, or bean curd, is a cheese-like mixture made from soy milk. You can buy soft, regular, firm and extra-firm tofu.

When you are buying tofu, look for whole pieces covered with water and check the expiry date before buying. Keep it in the refrigerator, and change the water once a day.

FRIED RICE
WITH GRILLED TOFU

Both the tofu and rice are delicious on their own, but together they make a perfect meatless main course.

Makes 4 to 6 servings

½ lb	tofu	250 g
1 tbsp	hoisin sauce	15 mL
1 tsp	sesame oil	5 mL
¼ tsp	hot chili paste	1 mL
1 tbsp	vegetable oil	15 mL
1	onion, chopped	1
1	sweet red pepper, chopped	1
4 cups	cooked rice	1 L
3 tbsp	rice vinegar or cider vinegar	45 mL
2 tbsp	orange juice concentrate	25 mL
1 tbsp	soy sauce	15 mL
¼ cup	chopped fresh cilantro or parsley	50 mL
4	green onions, chopped	4

1. Rinse tofu and pat dry. Cut into 3 or 4 pieces about 1 inch/2.5 cm thick.

2. In small bowl, combine hoisin sauce, sesame oil and chili paste. Spread all over tofu. Marinate for 10 to 60 minutes.

3. Cook tofu on lightly oiled hot grill or skillet until brown, a few minutes per side. Dice.

4. Meanwhile, heat oil in large non-stick wok or skillet. Add onion and red pepper and cook gently for a few minutes, until tender. Add rice and break up. Cook, stirring, until hot. Stir in vinegar, orange juice concentrate and soy sauce.

5. Gently fold in tofu, cilantro and green onions.

PER SERVING

Calories	398
g carbohydrate	70
g fibre	3
g total fat	8
g saturated fat	1
g protein	12

Excellent: vitamin C; iron
Good: niacin; vitamin B_6; folacin

mg cholesterol	0
mg sodium	306
mg potassium	350

FISH AND SEAFOOD

Salmon Baked in Parchment with Parsley Pesto

Salmon Fillets in Rice Paper Wrappers

Salmon Patties with Fresh Dill

Glazed Swordfish

Teriyaki Swordfish Burgers with Sweet Pickled Ginger Salsa

Halibut with Rice Wine

Oven-roasted Sea Bass

Sea Bass with Couscous Crust and Tomato Olive Vinaigrette

Cod Baked in Tomato Sauce with Onions

Baked Red Snapper with Hot Chiles

Baked Fish with Mushroom Crust

Lightly Breaded Shrimp with Hot Garlic Sauce

Stir-fried Scallops

Steamed Fish with Spinach and Black Bean Sauce

SALMON BAKED IN PARCHMENT WITH PARSLEY PESTO

Cooking fish in a sealed package is a wonderful way to keep it tender and moist. I like to use both foil and parchment paper, but you could use just one or the other. (The parchment paper doesn't affect the taste of the fish, and the foil provides a good seal.)

Serve this with Basmati Rice Pilaf with Garam Masala (page 221).

Makes 6 servings

1 cup	packed fresh parsley leaves	250 mL
½ cup	packed fresh basil leaves	125 mL
1 tbsp	capers, well drained	15 mL
1 tsp	salt	5 mL
½ tsp	pepper	2 mL
1 tbsp	olive oil	15 mL
6	salmon fillets, skin removed (4 oz/125 g each and 1 inch/2.5 cm thick)	6
2	sweet red peppers, roasted (page 241) and peeled	2

1. Place parsley and basil in food processor or blender and chop. Blend in capers, salt and pepper. Add olive oil and blend until mixture forms rough paste.

2. Pat fish dry. Spread pesto mixture on top of each piece of salmon.

3. Cut peppers into ¾-inch/2 cm strips and arrange on top of pesto.

4. Line baking sheet with foil. Place same-sized sheet of parchment paper on top. Arrange salmon pieces on one half of baking sheet. Fold parchment and foil over salmon and seal edges to enclose fish.

5. Bake in preheated 425°F/220°C oven for 15 minutes, or until salmon is just cooked through.

PER SERVING

Calories	182
g carbohydrate	4
g fibre	1
g total fat	9
g saturated fat	1
g protein	21

Excellent: vitamin C; riboflavin; niacin; vitamin B_6; vitamin B_{12}
Good: vitamin A; thiamine; folacin

mg cholesterol	57
mg sodium	457
mg potassium	643

SALMON FILLETS IN RICE PAPER WRAPPERS

This is a rather fancy dish, but it is not difficult to prepare. Serve it with Carrot Salad with Moroccan Dressing (page 80) and Rice Salsa Salad (page 84). For a dipping sauce use sweet and hot Thai chili sauce or peanut sauce (page 54).

You can also steam this dish. Brush a piece of parchment paper with oil and pierce holes in the paper. Place fish packages on top and steam (page 158) for 5 to 7 minutes.

Makes 6 servings

12	6-inch/15 cm rice paper wrappers	12
1	clove garlic, minced	1
2 tbsp	chopped fresh ginger root	25 mL
pinch	hot red chili flakes	pinch
½ tsp	sesame oil	2 mL
½ cup	chopped fresh cilantro or parsley	125 mL
¼ cup	chopped fresh chives or green onions	50 mL
¼ tsp	salt	1 mL
½ tsp	pepper	2 mL
6	salmon fillets, skin removed (4 oz/125 g each)	6
1 tsp	vegetable oil	5 mL

1. Soak rice paper wrappers, one at a time, in warm water for about 20 seconds. Arrange in single layer on clean damp tea towel.

2. Meanwhile, to make herb mixture, in small bowl, combine garlic, ginger, chili flakes, sesame oil, cilantro, chives, salt and pepper

3. Pat salmon dry. Cut each fillet in half. Place 2 tsp/10 mL herb mixture in centre of each rice paper wrapper and spread to size of salmon pieces. Place piece of salmon on top of mixture. Fold in ends of wrapper and roll up salmon, enclosing it completely in rice paper.

4. Just before serving, brush oil over bottom of non-stick skillet and heat on high. Place salmon packages in pan folded side down. Reduce heat to medium and cook for 4 minutes per side, or until salmon is just cooked through and wrappers are lightly browned. Serve 2 packages per person.

RICE PAPER WRAPPERS

Rice paper wrappers come in different shapes and sizes. They are used in Asian dishes and can be used raw, steamed, baked or fried. Soak two or three at a time in a large bowl of warm water until they are pliable — about 30 seconds. Arrange the wrappers in a single layer on a damp tea towel. Place the filling down the middle of the wrapper, fold in the ends and roll up. The moist wrappers should stick together well.

Rice paper wrappers can be found in Asian food stores. In some recipes you can use lettuce leaves (if the recipe calls for the wrappers to be used raw or steamed) or spring roll wrappers (if the wrappers are to be fried or baked).

PER SERVING

Calories	194
g carbohydrate	8
g fibre	trace
g total fat	8
g saturated fat	1
g protein	21

Excellent: riboflavin; niacin; vitamin B$_6$; vitamin B$_{12}$
Good: thiamine

mg cholesterol	57
mg sodium	142
mg potassium	545

SALMON PATTIES WITH FRESH DILL

Salmon patties are an old-fashioned favourite. Although all types of canned salmon have similar nutritional values, I think sockeye has the best taste, colour and texture.

If you are making mashed potatoes just for this dish, peel ½ lb/250 g baking potatoes and cut into chunks. Cook in boiling water until tender and mash with ¼ cup/50 mL hot milk or potato-boiling water.

Serve these patties with Spicy Rice Pilaf (page 220) and Glazed Winter Vegetables with Maple and Ginger (page 219).

Makes 4 servings

1	6½-oz/184 g tin sockeye salmon	1
1 cup	mashed potatoes, or fresh whole wheat or white breadcrumbs	250 mL
2	egg whites, or 1 whole egg	2
2 tbsp	low-fat yogurt	25 mL
1 tbsp	Dijon mustard	15 mL
1 tsp	Worcestershire sauce	5 mL
2 tbsp	chopped green onions	25 mL
2 tbsp	chopped fresh dill or parsley	25 mL
¼ tsp	pepper	1 mL

1. Drain salmon and remove skin. Leave in bones (for added calcium) or remove.

2. In bowl, mash salmon with potatoes. Beat in egg whites, yogurt, mustard, Worcestershire, green onions, dill and pepper.

3. Shape mixture into 8 small patties or 4 large ones, about ½ inch/1 cm thick.

4. Place salmon on parchment paper-lined baking sheet and bake in preheated 375°F/190°C oven for 15 to 20 minutes, turning once, until brown and crusty. Or, cook in a non-stick pan brushed with 1 tbsp/15 mL unflavoured oil for about 5 minutes per side.

PER SERVING

Calories	117
g carbohydrate	11
g fibre	1
g total fat	4
g saturated fat	1
g protein	10

Excellent: vitamin B$_{12}$
Good: niacin

mg cholesterol	10
mg sodium	225
mg potassium	322

GLAZED SWORDFISH

Although most people love thick pieces of swordfish, I prefer them quite thin. If you cook slices that are ½ inch/1 cm thick for about 5 minutes in total, they won't be overcooked. If your fish store won't cut the fish that thinly for you, buy thicker pieces and cut them yourself. Or you can cook pieces that are 1 inch/2.5 cm thick for 10 minutes in total.

Try serving this with Tabbouleh Salad with Fresh Herbs (page 83) and steamed spinach tossed with ½ tsp/2 mL sesame oil.

Makes 6 servings

¼ cup	homemade (page 144) or commercial teriyaki sauce	50 mL
1 tbsp	honey	15 mL
1 tbsp	orange juice concentrate	15 mL
1 tbsp	sweet and hot Thai chili sauce (page 94), or ½ tsp/2 mL hot chili paste	15 mL
½ tsp	five-spice powder (page 135)	2 mL
6	pieces boneless swordfish, ½ inch/1 cm thick, skin removed (4 oz/125 g each)	6

1. In medium saucepan, combine teriyaki sauce, honey, orange juice concentrate, chili sauce and five-spice powder. Bring to boil and cook for about 3 minutes, or until slightly thickened. Cool.

2. Pat fish dry and brush both sides with glaze. Grill for 1 minute. Turn, brush top with glaze and cook for 1 minute longer. Keep brushing and turning fish until it has cooked for 5 to 6 minutes in total.

SWORDFISH KEBABS

Cut 1 lb/500 g swordfish steaks into 1-inch/2.5 cm cubes. In large bowl, combine 3 tbsp/45 mL balsamic vinegar or lemon juice, 1 tbsp/15 mL olive oil, ½ tsp/2 mL pepper, 1 tbsp/15 mL each chopped fresh rosemary and thyme (½ tsp/2 mL dried), 1 minced clove garlic and ½ tsp/2 mL salt. Marinate fish for 10 minutes. Thread onto skewers and grill for 6 to 8 minutes, turning occasionally, until just cooked through.

Makes 4 servings

TERIYAKI SWORDFISH BURGERS WITH SWEET PICKLED GINGER SALSA

Swordfish burgers are a delicious change from traditional hamburgers. When you order the fish, be sure to say that you are grinding it and that you will take irregular pieces at a cheaper price (or have the fish store grind it for you).

Fresh tuna and salmon make great burgers, too. Serve these on their own or with Roasted "French-fried" Potatoes (page 217).

Makes 6 servings

Teriyaki Sauce:

3 tbsp	soy sauce	45 mL
3 tbsp	water	45 mL
3 tbsp	rice wine	45 mL
¼ cup	granulated sugar	50 mL
1	clove garlic, peeled and smashed	1
1	1-inch/2.5 cm piece fresh ginger root, smashed	1
1	1-inch/2.5 cm piece lemon peel	1

Sweet Pickled Ginger Salsa:

½ cup	chopped pink pickled ginger (sushi ginger)	125 mL
¼ cup	chopped fresh cilantro or parsley	50 mL
¼ cup	chopped fresh chives or green onions	50 mL
1	5-inch/12 cm sheet nori, toasted and broken into small pieces, optional	1
1	ripe mango	1

PICKLED GINGER
Pickled ginger (sometimes called pink ginger or sushi ginger) is sliced ultra-thin and made from young spring ginger roots. It is available at Japanese and Asian food stores or fish markets. In a pinch, try buying some from your local Japanese restaurant.

Burgers:

1 lb	boneless fresh swordfish, skin removed	500 g
2	egg whites, or 1 whole egg	2
½ cup	fresh whole wheat or white breadcrumbs	125 mL
1 tsp	salt	5 mL
½ tsp	pepper	2 mL
2 tbsp	chopped fresh cilantro or parsley	25 mL
1 tbsp	sesame oil	15 mL
6	Kaiser rolls or sesame buns	6

1. For teriyaki sauce, in small saucepan, combine soy sauce, water, rice wine, sugar, garlic, ginger and lemon peel. Bring to boil and cook until mixture is reduced by half and is quite thick. Cool.

2. To make salsa, in large bowl, combine pickled ginger, cilantro, chives and nori. Peel and dice mango (page 279). Mix into salsa.

3. To make burgers, pat fish dry and cut into 1-inch/2.5 cm chunks. Chop in food processor until pieces are very small and then blend in egg whites, breadcrumbs, salt, pepper and cilantro. Shape into patties about ½ inch/1 cm thick. Brush with sesame oil.

4. Grill burgers for about 2 minutes per side. Brush with teriyaki sauce. Cook for 1 minute, then turn and brush again. Repeat once. Burgers should be just cooked through. Serve burgers in buns with salsa on top.

HALIBUT WITH RICE WINE

This is a great way to prepare halibut, cod, sea bass or salmon. Serve it with couscous (see sidebar) or rice and Sauteed Greens (page 209).

Makes 6 servings

1 tsp	vegetable oil	5 mL
2	shallots, or 1 small onion, finely chopped	2
2	cloves garlic, finely chopped	2
1 tbsp	black bean sauce	15 mL
½ cup	rice wine	125 mL
1 tbsp	soy sauce	15 mL
1 tbsp	rice vinegar or cider vinegar	15 mL
6	halibut fillets, 1 inch/2.5 cm thick, skin removed (4 oz/125 g each)	6
1 tsp	sesame oil	5 mL
¼ tsp	pepper	1 mL
2 tbsp	chopped fresh cilantro or parsley	25 mL

1. To make sauce, heat oil in non-stick saucepan. Add shallots and garlic and cook gently until fragrant but not brown.

2. Add black bean sauce, rice wine and soy sauce. Bring to boil and cook until reduced by half. Add vinegar. Reserve.

3. Pat fish dry. Rub with sesame oil and sprinkle with pepper.

4. Grill fish for about 5 minutes per side, or just until cooked through. Sprinkle with cilantro. Serve with sauce poured over top.

COUSCOUS

Almost all the couscous sold in our stores is instant or quick-cooking. To prepare it, spread 1½ cups/375 mL instant couscous over bottom of 12 x 8-inch/3 L baking dish. Pour in 1½ cups/375 mL boiling water mixed with 1 tbsp/15 mL honey and ½ tsp/2 mL salt. Cover tightly and allow to rest for 10 to 15 minutes. Fluff with fork and serve.

Makes about 3 cups/750 mL

PER SERVING

Calories	126
g carbohydrate	3
g fibre	trace
g total fat	3
g saturated fat	trace
g protein	16

Excellent: niacin; vitamin B$_{12}$
Good: vitamin B$_6$

mg cholesterol	24
mg sodium	223
mg potassium	404

OVEN-ROASTED SEA BASS

This is one of my favourite ways to cook fish. Brown the fish for a minute in a hot skillet on top of the stove and then finish the cooking in the oven to keep the fish very moist and tender. This method works well for salmon, halibut and any other thick fillet.

If you do not have a skillet that will go into the oven, simply transfer the fish to a baking sheet lined with parchment paper (it will probably take a few extra minutes to cook). If you are cooking for a large number of people, you can even brown the fish ahead of time and finish it in the oven just before serving.

Serve this with roasted asparagus (page 210) and Sweet Potato Mash (page 214).

Makes 6 servings

1 tbsp	honey	15 mL
1 tbsp	lemon juice	15 mL
1	clove garlic, minced	1
½ tsp	ground cumin	2 mL
½ tsp	paprika	2 mL
pinch	cayenne	pinch
¼ tsp	salt	1 mL
6	sea bass fillets, 1 inch/2.5 cm thick, skin removed (4 oz/125 g each)	6
1 tsp	vegetable oil	5 mL

1. In small bowl, combine honey, lemon juice, garlic, cumin, paprika, cayenne and salt.

2. Pat fish dry. Rub marinade into fish and marinate in refrigerator for 1 to 2 hours.

3. Brush non-stick ovenproof skillet with oil. Pat fish dry and cook for 1 minute on each side on high heat. Place skillet in preheated 425°F/220°C oven. Cook for 8 to 10 minutes, or until fish is just cooked through.

PER SERVING

Calories	123
g carbohydrate	3
g fibre	0
g total fat	3
g saturated fat	1
g protein	20

Good: niacin; vitamin B$_6$

mg cholesterol	44
mg sodium	169
mg potassium	288

SEA BASS WITH COUSCOUS CRUST AND TOMATO OLIVE VINAIGRETTE

See front cover photo.

The couscous adds a great texture, and the vinaigrette keeps the fish moist. Halibut and salmon are also delicious cooked this way. The vinaigrette is also delicious on salads.

Serve this with Glazed Beets with Balsamic Vinegar (page 208) and Mashed Baked Squash (page 216).

Makes 6 servings

¾ cup	couscous	175 mL
¾ cup	boiling water or homemade chicken stock (page 57)	175 mL
1 tsp	ground cumin	5 mL
½ tsp	salt	2 mL
½ cup	all-purpose flour	125 mL
1	egg or 2 egg whites, beaten	1
6	sea bass fillets, 1 inch/2.5 cm thick, skin removed (4 oz/125 g each)	6
1 tbsp	olive oil	15 mL
10 cups	mixed salad greens	2.5 L

Tomato Olive Vinaigrette:

2 tbsp	red wine vinegar	25 mL
2 tbsp	lemon juice	25 mL
1	clove garlic, minced	1
½ tsp	pepper	2 mL
¼ cup	tomato juice	50 mL
2 tbsp	olive oil	25 mL
2 tbsp	chopped sun-dried tomatoes	25 mL
2 tbsp	shredded fresh basil or chopped parsley	25 mL
	Salt to taste	

PER SERVING

Calories	298
g carbohydrate	26
g fibre	3
g total fat	10
g saturated fat	2
g protein	26

Excellent: vitamin A; niacin; vitamin B$_6$; folacin
Good: vitamin C; thiamine; riboflavin; vitamin B$_{12}$; iron

mg cholesterol	71
mg sodium	365
mg potassium	706

1. Place couscous in shallow baking dish. Combine boiling water with cumin and salt and pour over couscous. Cover tightly with foil and allow to rest for 15 minutes. Fluff with fork and reserve.

2. Place flour in shallow dish. Place beaten egg in second shallow dish.

3. Pat fish dry. Dip fish into flour and shake off excess. Dip into egg and allow excess to drip off. Pat couscous into fish to coat all over. Refrigerate until ready to cook.

4. For vinaigrette, in bowl, combine vinegar, lemon juice, garlic and pepper. Whisk in tomato juice and oil. Stir in tomatoes, basil and salt.

5. Heat 1 tbsp/15 mL olive oil in non-stick ovenproof skillet on high heat. Add fish and cook for 1 minute. Turn gently and cook for 1 minute longer. Transfer to preheated 425°F/220°C oven and bake for 10 minutes or until cooked through.

6. Serve fish on salad greens and drizzle with vinaigrette.

FRESH FISH

- Fresh fish should smell clean and fresh, never "fishy."
- If the fish is whole, the eyes should be clear and protruding. The gills should be red, and the skin should feel moist and smooth.
- The flesh should feel firm when you press it.
- Fresh fish can have a heady odour if it has been packed in plastic. Remove it from its plastic wrapping as soon as you get it home. Place it in a glass container, cover loosely and refrigerate. If the fish still smells after one hour, return it to the fish store.
- Use fresh fish as soon as possible.

FROZEN FISH

- If ice has formed at one side, it usually means the fish has been defrosted and refrozen.
- Use defrosted fish quickly.
- Defrost frozen fish in the refrigerator, or in a microwave according to the manufacturer's instructions.
- Do not refreeze fish.

COD BAKED IN TOMATO SAUCE WITH ONIONS

This is a wonderfully easy and quick way to prepare fish, but if you prefer to assemble the dish ahead, you can bake it in a casserole. Pour the cooked tomato sauce over top and bake at 400°F/200°C for 15 minutes before serving.

Use any thick white-fleshed fillet in this dish. Serve it with Mashed Root Vegetables (page 218) and Spicy Rice Pilaf (page 220).

Makes 6 servings

1 tbsp	olive oil	15 mL
2	onions, sliced	2
4	cloves garlic, finely chopped	4
pinch	hot red pepper flakes	pinch
1	28-oz/796 mL tin plum tomatoes with juices	1
1 tbsp	chopped fresh thyme, or ½ tsp/2 mL dried	15 mL
2 tbsp	pitted black olives, optional	25 mL
	Salt and pepper to taste	
6	pieces fresh cod, skin removed, 1 inch/2.5 cm thick (4 oz/125 g each)	6
¼ cup	chopped fresh parsley	50 mL

1. Heat oil in large, deep non-stick skillet. Add onions, garlic and hot pepper flakes. Cook gently until onions wilt.

2. Add tomatoes, thyme, salt and pepper. Break tomatoes up with spoon. Bring to boil and cook until thick, about 5 to 7 minutes. Stir often. Stir in olives, salt and pepper.

3. Pat fish dry. Add cod to skillet and spoon sauce over top. Cover and cook for 5 minutes, or until cod is just cooked through. Sprinkle with parsley before serving.

PER SERVING

Calories	152
g carbohydrate	10
g fibre	2
g total fat	3
g saturated fat	1
g protein	21

Excellent: niacin; vitamin B_{12}
Good: vitamin C; vitamin B_6

mg cholesterol	46
mg sodium	285
mg potassium	572

BAKED RED SNAPPER WITH HOT CHILES

It is always impressive to serve a whole fish, and this version is spicy and sensational. I prefer to serve the fish with the head and tail intact as I think it looks more important that way, but if your baking dish isn't big enough, cut off the head and/or tail.

You can use any small hot chile in this dish. Trim the chile and remove the seeds and ribs if you prefer less heat, and wear gloves if you have sensitive skin.

I like to serve this with couscous or brown rice and Green Beans with Garlic (page 206).

Makes 6 to 8 servings

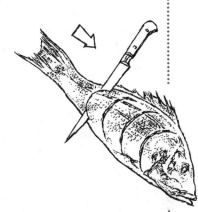

1	4-lb/2 kg red snapper, cleaned	1
3 tbsp	chopped fresh ginger root	45 mL
1	jalapeño (or any other small hot chile), chopped	1
2	cloves garlic, chopped	2
¼ cup	packed fresh cilantro or parsley leaves	50 mL
1 tsp	sesame oil	5 mL
3	green onions, cut in thirds	3
½ tsp	salt	2 mL
1 tbsp	olive oil	15 mL
1	lemon, sliced	1
	Sprigs cilantro	

1. Pat fish dry inside and out. Cut 4 diagonal slits in each side of fish.

2. In food processor or blender, combine ginger, jalapeño and garlic. Blend together into rough paste. Add cilantro, sesame oil, green onions and salt. Puree.

3. Reserve about 1 tbsp/15 mL chile mixture. Stuff remaining into slits in fish. Rub fish with olive oil mixed with reserved chile mixture and place on large baking sheet lined with foil.

4. Bake fish in preheated 425°F/220°C oven for 10 minutes per inch of thickness (a fish that is 3 inches/7.5 cm thick will take about 30 to 40 minutes). Garnish with lemon slices and cilantro sprigs.

BAKED FISH WITH MUSHROOM CRUST

The mushroom mixture can be used as a stuffing for vegetables, as a filling for dumplings, as a base for soups and sauces and as a coating for meats. If you like, you can double the mushroom mixture and freeze the extra for another time.

This recipe works well with lean fish like sole or turbot, or with thick fillets like halibut or sea bass (just cook thicker fillets for a longer time). The topping keeps the fish very moist as it bakes.

I like to serve this with boiled new potatoes and Roasted Fennel with Tomatoes (page 211).

Makes 4 servings

1 tbsp	olive oil	15 mL
1	onion, finely chopped	1
2	cloves garlic, finely chopped	2
1 lb	fresh mushrooms, finely chopped	500 g
2 tbsp	brandy, homemade chicken stock (page 57) or water	25 mL
1 tbsp	chopped fresh parsley	15 mL
1 tbsp	chopped fresh tarragon, or ½ tsp/2 mL dried	15 mL
½ tsp	salt	2 mL
¼ tsp	pepper	1 mL
½ cup	fresh whole wheat or white breadcrumbs	125 mL
4	sole fillets, about ½ inch/1 cm thick, skin removed (4 oz/125 g each)	4

COOKING FISH

The rule for cooking fish devised by the Canadian Fisheries Institute is still the norm, no matter what the cooking method. Cook fish at medium-high heat for 10 minutes per inch of thickness. If you are cooking frozen fish, double the cooking time.

PER SERVING

Calories	190
g carbohydrate	10
g fibre	3
g total fat	5
g saturated fat	1
g protein	24

Excellent: niacin; vitamin B_{12}
Good: riboflavin; vitamin B_6; iron

mg cholesterol	60
mg sodium	413
mg potassium	652

1. Heat oil in large non-stick skillet. Add onion and garlic and cook gently until tender but not brown.

2. Add mushrooms and cook until all liquid has evaporated and mixture is almost dry.

3. Add brandy, parsley, tarragon, salt, pepper and breadcrumbs. (Add a little water if mixture is so dry that it won't hold together.)

4. Pat fish dry and arrange on baking sheet lined with parchment paper. Top fish with mushroom mixture and pat down to cover each piece of fish.

5. Bake in preheated 425°F/220°C oven for 10 minutes. Topping should be slightly crusty. If not, grill under hot broiler for about 3 minutes, or until brown.

BREADCRUMBS

If you have extra stale bread, make your own fresh breadcrumbs. Grind the bread (with or without the crusts) in the food processor and freeze the breadcrumbs. For dry breadcrumbs, spread the crumbs on a baking sheet and bake in a 250°F/120°C oven for about an hour. Then grind again if you want really fine crumbs. If you do not have a food processor, simply freeze the chunk of bread and grate it on a grater. Store the crumbs in the freezer.

The latest word in breadcrumbs is the terrific Panko breadcrumbs now available in Japanese markets. They are large crumbs made from the whites of the bread only; because they are extra dry and crisp, they make a wonderful coating for breaded foods.

LIGHTLY BREADED SHRIMP WITH HOT GARLIC SAUCE

See photo opposite page 160.

If you make fresh breadcrumbs for this recipe, use the crusts, too — they brown nicely in this dish. I like to prepare more breadcrumbs than I actually need so they are easier to work with, but be sure to discard any excess breadcrumbs because of the raw shrimp juices that are in them.

The sauce can be drizzled over the shrimp or served as a dip if you want to serve this as an appetizer. For a main course serve over rice or Israeli couscous and Sauteed Greens (page 209).

Makes 6 to 8 servings

1½ lb	large shrimp, cleaned (page 73)	750 g
2 tsp	olive oil	10 mL
2	cloves garlic, minced	2
1 tsp	chopped fresh rosemary, or pinch dried	5 mL
¼ tsp	salt	1 mL
½ tsp	pepper	2 mL
2 cups	fresh whole wheat or white breadcrumbs	500 mL
4 cups	arugula or other greens	1 L

Hot Garlic Sauce:

1 tbsp	olive oil	15 mL
2	cloves garlic, finely chopped	2
¼ tsp	hot red pepper flakes	1 mL
2 tbsp	lemon juice	25 mL
2 tbsp	balsamic vinegar	25 mL
¼ tsp	salt	1 mL
¼ tsp	pepper	1 mL
¼ cup	chopped fresh parsley	50 mL

HOISIN MARINADE
This sauce/marinade is great with salmon, sea bass and shrimp. It can also be used as a sauce in stir-fried dishes.

Combine ¼ cup/50 mL hoisin sauce, 1 tbsp/15 mL orange juice concentrate, 1 tbsp/15 mL oyster sauce, 1 tsp/5 mL sesame oil, ¼ tsp/1 mL hot chili paste, 1 minced clove garlic and 1 tsp/5 mL chopped fresh ginger root. Marinade seafood for up to 4 hours in refrigerator. Grill or broil seafood, turning once, for 3 to 5 minutes, or until cooked through. Sprinkle with cilantro before serving.

Makes 4 servings

PER SERVING

Calories	167
g carbohydrate	9
g fibre	2
g total fat	6
g saturated fat	1
g protein	19

Excellent: niacin; vitamin B$_{12}$
Good: folacin; iron

mg cholesterol	130
mg sodium	390
mg potassium	303

1. Cut shrimp along top to open, but do not cut through (see diagram). Pat shrimp very dry.

2. In bowl, combine 2 tsp/10 mL olive oil, minced garlic, rosemary, salt and pepper. Toss with shrimp.

3. Place breadcrumbs in large, flat dish. Dip shrimp in crumbs and pat crumbs in gently on both sides. Arrange shrimp in single layer on baking sheets lined with parchment paper.

4. To prepare sauce, in small saucepan, warm 1 tbsp/15 mL olive oil with chopped garlic and hot pepper flakes. Add lemon juice, vinegar, salt and pepper. Remove from heat.

5. Just before serving, cook shrimp in preheated 425°F/220°C oven for 6 to 10 minutes, until just cooked through.

6. Place shrimp on bed of arugula and drizzle sauce over top. Sprinkle with parsley.

STIR-FRIED SCALLOPS

Letty Lastima, our chief produce buyer at the school, loves preparing quick stir-fries for our lunch with any meat, fish or vegetables we have left in the fridge.

This quick stir-fry is also great made with shrimp or chicken breasts. Serve it over steamed rice or noodles.

Makes 4 to 6 servings

2 tbsp	rice wine	25 mL
2 tbsp	soy sauce	25 mL
1 tsp	sesame oil	5 mL
1 lb	scallops, cut in half if large	500 g

Sauce:

2 tbsp	black bean sauce	25 mL
¾ cup	homemade chicken stock (page 57) or water	175 mL
2 tbsp	rice wine	25 mL
2 tbsp	orange juice concentrate	25 mL
1 tbsp	honey	15 mL
1 tbsp	soy sauce	15 mL
1 tbsp	cornstarch	15 mL

To Cook:

2 tbsp	vegetable oil	25 mL
3	cloves garlic, finely chopped	3
1 tbsp	chopped fresh ginger root	15 mL
½ tsp	hot chili paste	2 mL
2	large carrots, sliced on diagonal	2
1	sweet red pepper, cut in 1½-inch/4 cm chunks	1
6	green onions, cut in 1½-inch/4 cm lengths or in "brushes" (see diagram)	6

BLACK BEAN SAUCE
There are many kinds of black bean sauce on the market, but I prefer Lee Kum Kee, and it is widely available. To make your own sauce, heat 1 tsp/5 mL sesame oil in skillet. Add 2 cloves finely chopped garlic, 1 tsp/5 mL finely chopped fresh ginger root and 2 tbsp/25 mL minced fermented black beans (soak in boiling water for a few minutes if they are very dry). Cook until fragrant, about 1 minute. Add 1 to 2 tbsp/15 to 25 mL water. Be sure to use the Asian fermented black beans and not the dried black turtle beans that are used in chilis and soups. The Asian ones are usually sold in very small quantities.

1. In large bowl, combine rice wine, soy sauce and sesame oil. Add scallops and marinate for 10 minutes or up to a few hours in refrigerator.

2. In small bowl, combine black bean sauce, chicken stock, rice wine, orange juice concentrate, honey, soy sauce and cornstarch. Stir until smooth. Reserve.

3. Just before serving, heat 1 tbsp/15 mL oil in large, deep non-stick skillet or wok on high heat. Drain scallops and add to wok. Stir-fry for 1 minute, or until scallops are just beginning to turn opaque. Remove from pan and reserve.

4. Return pan to heat and add remaining oil. Add garlic, ginger and chili paste. Cook, stirring, for 30 to 60 seconds, until very fragrant.

5. Add carrots and red pepper. Stir-fry for 2 to 3 minutes (add about 1/4 cup/50 mL water if vegetables begin to stick).

6. Stir up reserved sauce and add to pan. Bring to boil. Add scallops and green onions. Cook until thoroughly heated.

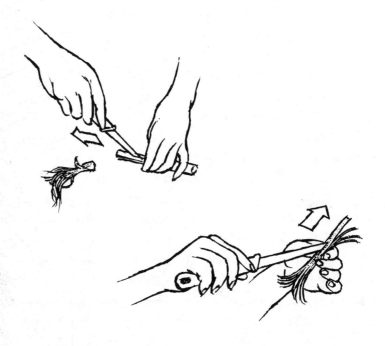

STEAMED FISH WITH SPINACH AND BLACK BEAN SAUCE

This is quick, easy, low in fat and perfectly delicious. I like it best made with halibut, salmon or sea bass, but any thick fish fillet will be good. Serve it with steamed rice and stir-fried vegetables.

Instead of being steamed, the fish can be covered with foil and baked at 425°F/220°C for 10 to 12 minutes, until just cooked through.

Makes 4 servings

1 lb	fresh spinach, trimmed and chopped	500 g
4	halibut fillets, 1 inch/2.5 cm thick, skin removed (4 oz/125 g each)	4
2 tbsp	black bean sauce	25 mL
1 tbsp	sesame oil	15 mL
1 tbsp	chopped fresh ginger root	15 mL
½ tsp	pepper	2 mL
1 tbsp	lemon juice	15 mL
¼ cup	water	50 mL
2	green onions, chopped	2
2 tbsp	chopped fresh cilantro or parsley	25 mL

1. Press spinach into bottom of 8-inch/1.5 L square or round baking dish (it will wilt when cooked). Pat fish dry and place on top in single layer.

2. In small bowl, combine black bean sauce, sesame oil, ginger, pepper, lemon juice and water. Pour over fish.

3. Set up steaming unit by placing small rack or crisscrossed set of chopsticks in bottom of wok or large deep skillet. Fill with boiling water up to bottom of rack. Set dish with fish on top. Cover wok tightly (use foil if wok does not have lid).

4. Steam fish over high heat for 10 minutes or until just cooked through. Remove to serving dish and sprinkle with green onions and cilantro.

PER SERVING

Calories	160
g carbohydrate	9
g fibre	3
g total fat	6
g saturated fat	1
g protein	19

Excellent: vitamin A; niacin; vitamin B$_6$; folacin; vitamin B$_{12}$; iron
Good: riboflavin; calcium

mg cholesterol	24
mg sodium	237
mg potassium	923

POULTRY

Barbecued Chicken Steaks

Flattened Cumin-grilled Chicken Breasts with Garlic Couscous

Twist and Shout Chicken Drumsticks

Chicken Burgers with Herbed Yogurt Sauce

Sweet and Sour Chicken Balls

Chicken "Meatloaf"

Baked Chicken with Vegetables and Balsamic Vinegar

Asian Chicken Thighs

Hunter-style Chicken with Wild Mushrooms

Chicken Jambalaya

Breaded Chicken Cutlets with Roasted Tomato Sauce

Chicken Adobo

Thai Chicken and Noodle Stir-fry

Turkey Burgers with Old-fashioned Coleslaw

Turkey Paillards

Roast Turkey Breast with Spinach Stuffing

Barbecued Butterflied Turkey Breast

Barbecued Chicken Steaks

To flatten the chicken, simply remove the "filets" or tender strips on the underside of the breasts (freeze the filets for stir-fries or chicken fingers). Place the remaining large piece of chicken between two pieces of waxed paper or parchment paper and pound until the chicken is about ½ inch/1 cm thick. The chicken will have a wonderful barbecued taste, but it will also cook very quickly without drying out or burning.

This is an especially kid-friendly recipe. Serve it with Wheat Berry Salad (page 82) or Spicy Rice Pilaf (page 220) and a Caesar salad (page 79). You can also use the marinade for grilled chicken fingers.

Makes 4 servings

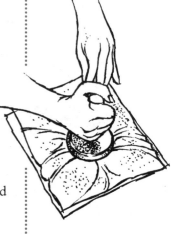

¼ cup	ketchup	50 mL
2 tbsp	cider vinegar or rice vinegar	25 mL
2 tbsp	brown sugar	25 mL
1 tbsp	Dijon mustard	15 mL
1 tbsp	Worcestershire sauce	15 mL
½ tsp	ground cumin or chili powder	2 mL
4	boneless, skinless single chicken breasts, flattened (4 oz/125 g each)	4

1. In large bowl, combine ketchup, vinegar, brown sugar, mustard, Worcestershire and cumin.

2. Add chicken, stir to coat with sauce and marinate for 30 minutes or up to overnight in refrigerator.

3. Grill chicken for 3 to 5 minutes per side, or just until cooked through (chicken can also be cooked in non-stick or lightly oiled skillet).

PER SERVING

Calories	148
g carbohydrate	6
g fibre	trace
g total fat	2
g saturated fat	trace
g protein	26

Excellent: niacin; vitamin B_6

mg cholesterol	70
mg sodium	211
mg potassium	280

Lightly Breaded Shrimp with Hot Garlic Sauce (page 154)
Couscous *(page 146)* with Sauteed Greens *(page 209)*

Flattened Cumin-grilled Chicken Breasts
with Garlic Couscous *(page 161)*

See photo opposite this page.

FLATTENED CUMIN-GRILLED CHICKEN BREASTS WITH GARLIC COUSCOUS

If you don't have roasted garlic, try stirring 2 tbsp/25 mL pesto (page 60) into the couscous, instead of the garlic paste.

ISRAELI COUSCOUS

Israeli couscous, sometimes called pearl pasta, is completely different from regular couscous. It looks like little beads and has a similar texture to barley. It should be cooked like pasta. It can be used in soups, or served with stews or stir-fried dishes instead of rice. Kids especially seem to love it. Buy it in Jewish and Italian markets or specialty stores. If you can't find it, substitute a very small pasta such as orzo.

Makes 6 servings

6	boneless, skinless single chicken breasts (4 oz/125 g each)	6
1 tbsp	olive oil	15 mL
2 tbsp	orange juice concentrate	25 mL
1 tsp	ground cumin	5 mL
2	cloves garlic, minced	2
½ tsp	salt	2 mL
½ tsp	pepper	2 mL

Garlic Couscous:

4 cups	homemade chicken stock (page 57), or 1 10-oz/284 mL tin chicken broth plus water	1 L
8 oz	Israeli couscous or orzo (2 cups/500 mL)	250 g
1	head roasted garlic (page 131), pureed (2 tbsp/25 mL)	1
	Salt and pepper to taste	

1. Remove filets from chicken breasts (page 160). Pound remaining pieces of chicken until about ½ inch/1 cm thick.

2. In small bowl, combine olive oil, orange juice concentrate, cumin, minced garlic, salt and pepper. Rub mixture into chicken breasts. Marinate for 10 minutes or up to overnight in refrigerator.

3. Grill chicken breasts on lightly oiled barbecue or grill for a few minutes per side — 3 to 5 minutes, or just until cooked through.

4. Meanwhile, to prepare couscous, bring chicken stock to boil. Add couscous and cook for 10 minutes, or until tender.

5. Stir garlic paste into couscous. Taste and season with salt and pepper. Place couscous in serving dish and arrange chicken on top.

PER SERVING

Calories	392
g carbohydrate	46
g fibre	3
g total fat	5
g saturated fat	1
g protein	37

Excellent: niacin; vitamin B$_6$
Good: vitamin B$_{12}$; iron

mg cholesterol	71
mg sodium	238
mg potassium	447

TWIST AND SHOUT CHICKEN DRUMSTICKS

My kids were enthralled when they first had Shake 'n Bake chicken at a potluck dinner. Because we don't use commercial mixes at home, they weren't familiar with the name; they said it sounded something like twist and shout chicken, and that's what we've been calling this dish ever since.

You can use drumsticks in any recipe that calls for chicken wings. Remove the skin from the drumsticks before cooking to reduce the fat. You can also make this with chicken breasts.

Serve this chicken with Buttermilk Mashed Potatoes (page 215) and Green Beans with Garlic (page 206).

Makes 6 servings

½ cup	orange juice or buttermilk	125 mL
2	cloves garlic, minced	2
12	chicken drumsticks, skin removed (3 oz/90 g each)	12
1 cup	dry breadcrumbs	250 mL
2 tbsp	cornmeal	25 mL
1 tbsp	paprika	15 mL
1 tbsp	granulated sugar	15 mL
1 tsp	chili powder	5 mL
1 tsp	salt	5 mL
1 tsp	dry mustard	5 mL
½ tsp	cayenne, optional	2 mL
½ tsp	ground cumin	2 mL

1. In large bowl, combine orange juice and garlic. Toss drumsticks in mixture and marinate for 10 minutes. Shake off excess liquid.

2. Meanwhile, in clean plastic bag, combine breadcrumbs, cornmeal, paprika, sugar, chili powder, salt, mustard, cayenne and cumin.

3. Add drumsticks to plastic bag and shake in seasoned breadcrumbs until coated. Place on non-stick or parchment paper-lined baking sheet.

4. Bake in preheated 350°F/180°C oven for 40 to 45 minutes, or until cooked through, brown and crisp.

PER SERVING

Calories	225
g carbohydrate	15
g fibre	1
g total fat	5
g saturated fat	1
g protein	28

Excellent: niacin
Good: riboflavin; vitamin B_6; vitamin B_{12}; iron

mg cholesterol	96
mg sodium	519
mg potassium	355

CHICKEN BURGERS WITH HERBED YOGURT SAUCE

This is a great casual dinner dish that is quick to prepare. Serve it with Tabbouleh Salad with Fresh Herbs (page 83).

Makes 6 servings

1 lb	lean ground chicken breast	500 g
2	egg whites, or 1 whole egg	2
1 cup	fresh whole wheat or white breadcrumbs	250 mL
1 tsp	salt	5 mL
½ tsp	pepper	2 mL
½ tsp	dried oregano	2 mL
½ tsp	paprika	2 mL
½ tsp	grated lemon peel	2 mL
2	cloves garlic, minced	2

Herbed Yogurt Sauce:

1 cup	yogurt cheese (page 229) or extra-thick yogurt	250 mL
2 tbsp	chopped fresh parsley, mint, dill or cilantro, or a combination	25 mL
½ tsp	hot red pepper sauce	2 mL
1	clove garlic, minced	1
	Salt and pepper to taste	
6	pita breads	6
2 cups	shredded lettuce	500 mL

1. In large bowl, combine chicken, egg whites, breadcrumbs, salt, pepper, oregano, paprika, lemon peel and garlic. Knead together well. Shape into 6 burgers about ½ inch/1 cm thick.

2. To make sauce, in small bowl, combine yogurt cheese, herbs, hot pepper sauce, garlic, salt and pepper.

3. Grill burgers for 5 to 7 minutes per side, or until cooked through.

4. To assemble, cut open one end of each pita to form pocket. Fit a burger and some lettuce into each pita and drizzle with sauce.

MANGO AND RED PEPPER SALSA

Serve this with grilled chicken or fish.

Combine ½ cup/125 mL finely diced ripe mango and ½ cup/125 mL finely diced roasted red pepper (page 241). Add 2 tbsp/25 mL chopped fresh cilantro or parsley and 1 tbsp/15 mL chopped fresh mint. Stir in 1 tbsp/15 mL mango vinegar or rice vinegar.

Makes about 1 cup/250 mL

PER SERVING

Calories	318
g carbohydrate	42
g fibre	1
g total fat	3
g saturated fat	1
g protein	29

Excellent: riboflavin; niacin; vitamin B$_6$; folacin; vitamin B$_{12}$
Good: thiamine; calcium; iron

mg cholesterol	48
mg sodium	734
mg potassium	474

SWEET AND SOUR CHICKEN BALLS

Everyone loves sweet and sour meatballs. These are made using lean ground chicken or turkey, and I think they are just as delicious. Serve them over rice, couscous or orzo and steamed broccoli.

Makes 6 servings

1 lb	lean ground chicken or turkey breast	500 g
1	clove garlic, minced	1
2	egg whites, or 1 whole egg	2
1 cup	fresh whole wheat or white breadcrumbs	250 mL
¼ cup	ketchup	50 mL
1 tsp	salt	5 mL
¼ tsp	pepper	1 mL
2 tbsp	chopped fresh parsley	25 mL

Sweet and Sour Sauce:

1 tbsp	vegetable oil	15 mL
1	clove garlic, finely chopped	1
1	onion, chopped	1
½ cup	ketchup	125 mL
1	28-oz/796 mL tin plum tomatoes, drained and pureed or broken up	1
½ cup	ginger ale or cranberry juice	125 mL

1. In large bowl, combine ground chicken, minced garlic, egg whites, breadcrumbs, ¼ cup/50 mL ketchup, salt, pepper and parsley. Shape into 1-inch/2.5 cm balls. Reserve.

2. To prepare sauce, heat oil in large non-stick saucepan. Add garlic and onion. Cook on low heat until fragrant but do not brown. Add ½ cup/125 mL ketchup, tomatoes and ginger ale. Bring to boil (if sauce is too thick, add about ½ cup/125 mL water or additional ginger ale). Taste and adjust seasonings if necessary.

3. Add chicken balls to boiling sauce. Reduce heat and cook gently, uncovered, for 20 to 30 minutes, or until meatballs are tender and sauce is thick.

GROUND CHICKEN
Ground chicken is very perishable, so use it the same day or freeze it. Most store-bought ground chicken is made from both light and dark meat, and sometimes it even contains skin or fat. If you have a food processor, grind boneless, skinless chicken breasts yourself so you know that the chicken is fresh and lean, or ask your butcher to do this for you.

PER SERVING

Calories	196
g carbohydrate	21
g fibre	3
g total fat	4
g saturated fat	1
g protein	21

Excellent: niacin; vitamin B₆

mg cholesterol	44
mg sodium	1040
mg potassium	625

Chicken "Meatloaf"

I love this served hot with mashed potatoes, peas and tomato sauce or ketchup. But it is also delicious cold. Try it in sandwiches with grilled onions, peppers and roasted garlic pesto (page 45). You can also make chicken burgers with this mixture.

Makes 8 servings

2 tsp	olive oil	10 mL
1	onion, chopped	1
2	cloves garlic, finely chopped	2
2 lb	lean ground chicken breast	1 kg
1	egg	1
2	egg whites, or 1 whole egg	2
1 tsp	salt	5 mL
½ tsp	pepper	2 mL
1 tbsp	Worcestershire sauce	15 mL
1 tsp	hot chili paste	5 mL
1 tbsp	Dijon mustard	15 mL
½ cup	ketchup	125 mL
1 cup	fresh whole wheat or white breadcrumbs	250 mL
2 tbsp	chopped fresh basil or parsley	25 mL
2 tbsp	chopped fresh chives or green onion	25 mL

1. Heat oil in large non-stick skillet. Add onion and garlic and cook on low heat until fragrant but not brown. Cool.

2. In large bowl, combine chicken, egg, egg whites, salt, pepper, Worcestershire, chili paste, mustard, ketchup, breadcrumbs and onion mixture. Knead together with a spoon or your hands. Add basil and chives.

3. Spoon mixture into non-stick, lightly oiled or parchment paper-lined 9 x 5-inch/2 L loaf pan. Cover with parchment paper or foil.

4. Bake for 1 hour in preheated 350°F/180°C oven. Uncover and bake for 20 minutes longer. Cool for a few minutes. Drain off any liquid accumulated in pan. Unmould and serve hot, or cool in pan and unmould before serving.

Per Serving

Calories	189
g carbohydrate	9
g fibre	1
g total fat	4
g saturated fat	1
g protein	29

Excellent: niacin; vitamin B$_6$
Good: vitamin B$_{12}$

mg cholesterol	93
mg sodium	665
mg potassium	443

BAKED CHICKEN WITH VEGETABLES AND BALSAMIC VINEGAR

Add chunks of eggplant, red peppers, zucchini and portobello mushrooms to this if you like. Serve with a salad.

Makes 6 servings

½ cup	balsamic vinegar	125 mL
2 tbsp	olive oil	25 mL
2	cloves garlic, minced	2
½ tsp	salt	2 mL
½ tsp	pepper	2 mL
2 tbsp	chopped fresh rosemary, or ½ tsp/2 mL dried	25 mL
6	single skinless chicken breasts, bone in	6
2 lb	potatoes, cut in 1½-inch/4 cm chunks	1 kg
3	onions, cut in quarters	3
1	large bulb fennel, or 2 stalks celery, trimmed and cut in chunks or wedges	1
12	whole cloves garlic, peeled	12
2 tbsp	chopped fresh parsley	25 mL

1. In small bowl, combine vinegar, oil, minced garlic, salt, pepper and rosemary.

2. Rub about ¼ cup/50 mL marinade into chicken breasts on all sides.

3. In large bowl, toss remaining marinade with potatoes, onions, fennel and whole garlic cloves.

4. Spread vegetables in large non-stick roasting pan or baking sheet lined with parchment paper or foil. Roast in preheated 400°F/200°C oven for 30 minutes, or until vegetables are beginning to brown. Stir once during cooking.

5. Reduce heat to 350°F/180°C. Place chicken on top of vegetables and continue baking until chicken is cooked through and vegetables are tender — about 30 to 40 minutes longer. Sprinkle with parsley before serving.

PER SERVING

Calories	328
g carbohydrate	38
g fibre	5
g total fat	6
g saturated fat	1
g protein	31

Excellent: niacin; vitamin B$_6$
Good: vitamin C; thiamine; folacin; vitamin B$_{12}$; iron

mg cholesterol	73
mg sodium	294
mg potassium	998

ASIAN CHICKEN THIGHS

You can now buy boneless, skinless chicken thighs in many supermarkets, but you could also use skinless thighs with the bone still in — simply cook them for an extra 15 minutes. The chicken can be grilled instead of baked — I usually start them on the barbecue for about 2 minutes per side and then finish them in the oven for about 20 minutes at 375°F/190°C.

This marinade can also be used on chicken breasts, or with lamb or pork.

Serve with rice and Grilled Corn Salad (page 78).

Makes 6 servings

2	cloves garlic, peeled	2
1	1-inch/2.5 cm piece fresh ginger root, peeled	1
¼ cup	hoisin sauce	50 mL
2 tbsp	soy sauce	25 mL
2 tbsp	lemon juice	25 mL
6	large boneless, skinless chicken thighs (or 12 small ones)	6
¼ cup	chopped fresh cilantro or parsley	50 mL

1. In food processor or blender, puree garlic, ginger, hoisin, soy sauce and lemon juice.

2. Coat chicken with marinade and marinate for 30 minutes or up to 8 hours in refrigerator.

3. Arrange chicken in single layer on non-stick or parchment paper-lined baking sheet. Bake in preheated 400°F/200°C oven for 15 minutes per side or until cooked through. Sprinkle with cilantro before serving.

PER SERVING

Calories	97
g carbohydrate	3
g fibre	0
g total fat	3
g saturated fat	2
g protein	14

Excellent: niacin

mg cholesterol	49
mg sodium	298
mg potassium	139

HUNTER-STYLE CHICKEN WITH WILD MUSHROOMS

Chicken stew is a perfect entertaining dish because it tastes even better when it has been cooked ahead and reheated. You can make this recipe with only chicken breasts, but be sure to cook them on the bone to keep the meat moist and tender and add extra flavour.

Serve this with boiled new potatoes or rice and green beans. If you can't find wild mushrooms (such as portobello, oyster, shiitake, morels, porcini or chanterelles), just use regular mushrooms.

Makes 6 servings

1	½-oz/15 g package dried wild mushrooms	1
1 cup	warm water	250 mL
1	3-lb/1.5 kg chicken, cut in pieces, skin removed	1
pinch	salt	pinch
pinch	pepper	pinch
1 tbsp	olive oil	15 mL
2	large onions, thickly sliced	2
4	cloves garlic, finely chopped	4
pinch	hot red pepper flakes	pinch
½ lb	fresh wild mushrooms, trimmed and quartered	250 g
½ cup	dry white wine or chicken stock	125 mL
1	28-oz/796 mL tin plum tomatoes with juices, chopped	1
1 tbsp	chopped fresh oregano, or ½ tsp/2 mL dried	15 mL
2 tbsp	shredded fresh basil or chopped parsley	25 mL
2 tbsp	chopped fresh parsley	25 mL

HANDLING CHICKEN

Keep chicken in the refrigerator and use it quickly, or freeze it. Chicken can be easily contaminated with salmonella and other bacteria, so it must be handled carefully. Salmonella is killed when the chicken is cooked, but the danger lies in cross-contamination to foods that will be eaten raw. Defrost it in the refrigerator or in the microwave to help prevent bacteria from growing. Be sure to prepare it on a sanitized surface, and wash the counter, utensils and your hands carefully afterwards.

PER SERVING

Calories	219
g carbohydrate	14
g fibre	3
g total fat	6
g saturated fat	1
g protein	26

Excellent: niacin; vitamin B$_6$
Good: riboflavin; iron

mg cholesterol	77
mg sodium	308
mg potassium	780

1. Soak dried mushrooms in warm water for 20 minutes. Strain liquid through sieve lined with paper towel and reserve liquid. Rinse mushrooms and chop. Reserve.

2. Pat chicken dry and season with salt and pepper.

3. Heat olive oil in large, deep non-stick skillet. Brown chicken pieces lightly. Remove from pan and reserve.

4. Return pan to heat. Add onions, garlic and hot pepper flakes. Cook gently for about 5 minutes, or until onions are wilted. If they begin to burn, add a few tablespoons of water or stock.

5. Add fresh mushrooms to pan and cook for 5 minutes longer.

6. Add wine, reserved mushroom liquid and dried mushrooms. Cook until liquid has reduced to a few tablespoons. Add chicken and combine well.

7. Add tomatoes. Cover and simmer gently for 30 minutes.

8. If sauce is too runny, remove chicken and mushrooms and cook sauce, uncovered, until thicker. Add oregano, basil and parsley to sauce. Taste and adjust seasonings if necessary. Pour sauce over chicken to serve.

Chicken Jambalaya

This is a kid-friendly one-dish meal. You can add other vegetables if you like. Serve it with Smoky Cornbread with Corn and Peppers (page 260) and a salad.

If you are using brown rice, add an extra ½ cup/125 mL chicken stock and bake the casserole for 40 minutes, or until the rice is tender.

Makes 6 servings

2 tbsp	vegetable oil, divided	25 mL
1	onion, chopped	1
2	cloves garlic, finely chopped	2
1	sweet red pepper, diced	1
1	sweet green pepper, diced	1
2	stalks celery, sliced	2
1 lb	boneless, skinless chicken breast, cut in 1½-inch/4 cm cubes	500 g
2	tomatoes, peeled, seeded and diced	2
1½ cups	long-grain rice	375 mL
½ cup	tomato juice	125 mL
2 cups	homemade chicken stock (page 57), or 1 10-oz/284 mL tin chicken broth plus water	500 mL
½ tsp	hot red pepper sauce	2 mL
1 tsp	salt	5 mL
¼ tsp	pepper	1 mL
¼ tsp	dried thyme	1 mL
¼ tsp	dried oregano	1 mL
pinch	cayenne	pinch
¼ lb	medium shrimp, cleaned and butterflied, optional	125 g
2	green onions, chopped	2

PEELING TOMATOES

To peel tomatoes, cut across on one end and then simply submerge them in boiling water for 15 to 30 seconds. When the tomatoes are cool enough to handle, the skins will slip off easily. Or, hold them over an open gas flame or grill on a fork to char them. Cool and then peel.

To seed tomatoes, slice them in half crosswise (not through the core and top) and gently squeeze out the seeds.

PER SERVING

Calories	337
g carbohydrate	44
g fibre	2
g total fat	7
g saturated fat	1
g protein	24

Excellent: vitamin C; niacin; vitamin B$_6$

mg cholesterol	44
mg sodium	534
mg potassium	570

1. Heat 1 tbsp/15 mL oil in large, flat casserole dish that can be used on stovetop. Add onion and garlic and cook over low heat for 3 to 5 minutes, until tender and fragrant. Add sweet peppers and celery. Cook for 5 minutes. Transfer mixture to bowl and reserve.

2. Heat remaining oil in pan. Add chicken and cook on medium-high heat for a few minutes. Stir so pieces brown a little on all sides.

3. Return vegetables to pan. Stir in tomatoes and rice. Cook, stirring, for 3 minutes.

4. Meanwhile, combine tomato juice, chicken stock, hot pepper sauce, salt, pepper, thyme, oregano and cayenne. Stir well.

5. Add liquid to casserole and bring to boil. Reduce heat, cover and bake in preheated 350°F/180°C oven for 20 to 25 minutes, or until liquid is absorbed and rice is tender.

6. Add shrimp to casserole. Cover and bake for another 5 minutes, or until shrimp are cooked. Sprinkle with green onions.

RICE
··········

Although there are many lengths of rice, long-grain and short-grain are the most common. Use long-grain rice in pilafs and in recipes where you want each grain to stay separate. If you want the rice to be sticky, as in risottos, sushi, paella and rice puddings, use short-grain rice.

If you make steamed rice more than twice a week, you might want to invest in an electric rice cooker. I like the 10-cup/2.5 L size (Japanese cups are smaller than North American cups, so it is not as big as it sounds).

Steamed Rice
Rinse 1½ cups/375 mL long-grain rice in a strainer until water runs clear. Drain well. Place in a saucepan with 2¼ cups/550 mL cold water. Bring to a boil, reduce heat to medium-high and cook until surface water disappears and crater-like holes appear on the surface of the rice, about 5 minutes. Cover tightly, reduce heat to very low and cook for 15 minutes. Remove from heat and allow to rest, without lifting lid, for at least 10 minutes. (For brown rice, increase the water by 1/4 cup/50 mL and cook for 30 minutes instead of 15 minutes.)

Makes about 3 cups/750 mL

Boiled Rice
For easy cooked rice, just boil it like pasta. Bring a pot of water to the boil, add the rice, and cook until tender, about 10 to 13 minutes, depending on the kind of rice. Drain it in a sieve, not a colander, and rinse with cold water if you are not using it immediately. The rice will never be sticky (this is a good method when you want rice to use in salads, soups or meatballs, or when you want to cook rice ahead and freeze it), and you won't have to worry about using exact amounts of liquid.

Sticky Rice
Buy sticky or glutinous rice at Asian markets. Rinse it only once or twice. Place 1½ cups/375 mL rice in a saucepan and cover with 2½ cups/625 mL cold water. Bring to a boil and cook for 3 or 4 minutes. Cover, reduce heat and cook for 10 minutes longer, or until the water has been absorbed. For a special treat, replace ½ cup/125 mL water with coconut milk.

Makes about 3 cups/750 mL

BREADED CHICKEN CUTLETS WITH ROASTED TOMATO SAUCE

This is great served as a main course, but it can also be made into wonderful sandwiches with the tomato sauce spooned on top. Or the cutlets can be prepared without the tomato sauce. Slice them and serve on top of a salad, or like chicken fingers with a dip.

Makes 4 servings

4	small boneless, skinless chicken breasts (4 oz/125 g each)	4
1 tsp	paprika	5 mL
½ tsp	ground cumin	2 mL
¼ tsp	salt	1 mL
¼ tsp	pepper	1 mL
pinch	cayenne	pinch
½ cup	all-purpose flour	125 mL
1	egg	1
2 cups	fresh whole wheat or white breadcrumbs	500 mL
2 tbsp	chopped fresh parsley	25 mL
1 tsp	chopped fresh thyme, or pinch dried	5 mL
1 tbsp	vegetable oil	15 mL
1	lemon	1
1	recipe Roasted Tomato Sauce (page 96) or chili sauce (page 190)	1

PER SERVING

Calories	280
g carbohydrate	31
g fibre	5
g total fat	7
g saturated fat	1
g protein	26

Excellent: vitamin A; vitamin C; niacin; vitamin B$_6$
Good: thiamine; riboflavin; folacin; vitamin B$_{12}$; iron

mg cholesterol	90
mg sodium	251
mg potassium	880

1. Remove "filets" from chicken breasts (page 160) and save for chicken fingers or stir-fries. Pat larger pieces of chicken dry. Place between two pieces of waxed paper or parchment paper and pound until ½ inch/1 cm thick.

2. In shallow dish, blend together paprika, cumin, salt, pepper, cayenne and flour.

3. Beat egg lightly and place in another shallow dish. Place breadcrumbs, parsley and thyme in third dish.

4. Dip chicken into flour mixture and dust off excess. Dip chicken into egg and allow excess to run off. Pat breadcrumb mixture into chicken. If not cooking right away, place chicken on rack, set over a baking sheet, and refrigerate.

5. To cook, heat oil in large non-stick skillet. Add chicken pieces and cook until lightly browned — 3 to 4 minutes per side, or until cooked through. (You could also place chicken on non-stick or lightly oiled baking sheet and bake at 400°F/200°C for 20 to 30 minutes, turning once, until brown and cooked through.)

6. Place chicken on platter and squeeze lemon juice over top. Serve with Roasted Tomato Sauce.

CHICKEN ADOBO

This version of the famous Filipino dish is from family friend Dely Balagtas. Children like it, too. Serve it with steamed rice (page 171) and any plain vegetable.

You can also use one small whole chicken in this recipe; cut it into serving pieces and remove the skin.

Makes 4 servings

1 tbsp	vegetable oil	15 mL
1	large onion, cut in ¼-inch/5 mm rings	1
4	skinless single chicken breasts, bone in, cut in 8 pieces	4
3	cloves garlic, minced	3
3 tbsp	lemon juice	45 mL
2 tbsp	soy sauce	25 mL
¼ cup	water	50 mL
½ tsp	pepper	2 mL
1	bay leaf	1

1. Heat oil in large, deep non-stick skillet. Add onion and cook on medium-high heat until browned. Remove from pan and reserve.

2. Add chicken, garlic, lemon juice, soy sauce, water and pepper to skillet. Stir everything together well. Add bay leaf. Cook gently, covered, for 30 minutes.

3. Return onion to skillet. Continue to cook, uncovered, until chicken is cooked through and tender, about 5 to 10 minutes. Taste and adjust seasonings if necessary.

PER SERVING

Calories	198
g carbohydrate	5
g fibre	1
g total fat	5
g saturated fat	1
g protein	31

Excellent: niacin; vitamin B$_6$
Good: vitamin B$_{12}$

mg cholesterol	76
mg sodium	504
mg potassium	422

THAI CHICKEN AND NOODLE STIR-FRY

Although coconut milk is high in fat, it adds a wonderful texture and taste to sauces, even if only a small amount is added. If you do not want to use it, simply add extra tomato juice. Be sure to remove the whole chiles after cooking (or warn guests not to eat them — unless they have iron stomachs!). Or omit the chiles and add 1 tsp/5 mL hot chili paste with the onions.

Makes 4 to 6 servings

¾ lb	linguine	375 g
1 tbsp	vegetable oil	15 mL
1 lb	boneless, skinless chicken breast, cut in 1½-inch/4 cm chunks	500 g
1	onion, thinly sliced	1
2	cloves garlic, finely chopped	2
1 tbsp	chopped fresh ginger root	15 mL
1 tsp	curry powder	5 mL
1 tbsp	Thai fish sauce or soy sauce	15 mL
⅓ cup	homemade chicken stock (page 57) or water	75 mL
⅓ cup	coconut milk	75 mL
½ cup	tomato juice	125 mL
12	small hot green chiles	12
	Handful Thai basil or regular basil, unchopped	
	Salt and pepper to taste	

1. Bring large pot of water to boil. Add linguine and cook until tender. Drain. If not using right away, rinse with cold water.

2. Heat oil on high heat in non-stick wok or large, deep skillet. Add chicken and stir-fry until it loses its raw appearance.

3. Add onion, garlic and ginger. Stir-fry for 30 to 60 seconds.

4. Stir in curry powder, fish sauce, chicken stock, coconut milk and tomato juice. Bring to boil.

5. Add chiles and basil and cook for 3 to 4 minutes.

6. Add noodles and combine well until noodles are thoroughly heated. Taste and add salt and pepper if necessary.

THAI BASIL
Thai basil, also known as holy basil, has more of an anise taste than other kinds of basil and its stems are purply green. It can usually be found in Thai and Asian markets; if you can't find it, just use regular basil.

PER SERVING

Calories	536
g carbohydrate	69
g fibre	4
g total fat	11
g saturated fat	4
g protein	39

Excellent: niacin; vitamin B_6
Good: folacin; vitamin B_{12}; iron

mg cholesterol	66
mg sodium	576
mg potassium	572

TURKEY BURGERS WITH OLD-FASHIONED COLESLAW

These burgers are favourites with most kids, but for really fussy eaters, omit the oyster sauce and grill the burgers plain.

You can omit the coleslaw entirely or serve it on the side (it should keep for about one week in the refrigerator). For a change, a grated fennel bulb would be a delicious addition.

Makes 6 burgers

1 lb	lean ground turkey breast	500 g
1	small onion, finely chopped	1
1	clove garlic, minced	1
2	egg whites, or 1 whole egg	2
1 cup	fresh whole wheat or white breadcrumbs	250 mL
1 tsp	salt	5 mL
½ tsp	pepper	2 mL
½ tsp	ground cumin	2 mL
2 tbsp	ketchup	25 mL
2 tbsp	oyster sauce	25 mL
1 cup	coleslaw (see sidebar)	250 mL
6	Kaiser rolls or sesame buns	6

1. In large bowl, combine turkey, onion, garlic, egg whites, breadcrumbs, salt, pepper, cumin and ketchup. Mix well and shape into 6 patties about ½ inch/1 cm thick.

2. Brush burgers all over with oyster sauce. Barbecue or broil until cooked through, about 5 minutes per side. Top each burger with large spoonful of coleslaw and serve in buns.

OLD-FASHIONED COLESLAW
Combine 1 grated small cabbage, 1 grated carrot and 3 finely chopped green onions. In small saucepan, bring ⅓ cup/75 mL cider vinegar, 2 tbsp/25 mL granulated sugar and 2 tbsp/25 mL vegetable oil (optional) to boil. Toss hot dressing with cabbage mixture and season with salt and pepper to taste.

Makes about 4 cups/1 L

PER SERVING

Calories	347
g carbohydrate	48
g fibre	2
g total fat	5
g saturated fat	1
g protein	27

Excellent: niacin
Good: thiamine; riboflavin; vitamin B$_6$; folacin; iron

mg cholesterol	47
mg sodium	1048
mg potassium	453

TURKEY PAILLARDS

A paillard is a "steak" of turkey, chicken, beef or lamb. It is always boneless and usually thin and lean, so it cooks quickly. Serve these with Buttermilk Mashed Potatoes (page 215) and Carrot Salad with Moroccan Dressing (page 80).

Makes 4 servings

1 lb	turkey breast scallops or cutlets	500 g
3 tsp	olive oil, divided	15 mL
1 tbsp	Worcestershire sauce	15 mL
1 tbsp	Dijon mustard	15 mL
1 tbsp	lemon juice	15 mL
1 tbsp	chopped fresh rosemary, or ½ tsp/2 mL dried	15 mL
1	clove garlic, minced	1
1 tsp	granulated sugar	5 mL
½ tsp	pepper	2 mL
¼ cup	chopped fresh cilantro or parsley	50 mL

1. Pat turkey dry. Pound until ¼ inch/5 mm to ½ inch/1 cm thick.

2. In small bowl, combine 1 tsp/5 mL olive oil, Worcestershire, mustard, lemon juice, rosemary, garlic, sugar and pepper. Rub into turkey pieces. Marinate for up to 30 minutes in refrigerator.

3. Heat remaining 2 tsp/10 mL oil in large non-stick skillet. Cook turkey for a few minutes per side, or just until cooked through. Very thin scallops will take 2 to 3 minutes per side; ½-inch/1 cm cutlets will take 4 to 5 minutes per side. Sprinkle with cilantro before serving.

ASIAN COLESLAW

Combine 1 grated small cabbage, 1 grated carrot, 3 finely chopped green onions and ½ cup/125 mL chopped cilantro. In small saucepan, combine ⅓ cup/75 mL rice vinegar, 2 tbsp/25 mL honey, 1 minced clove garlic, 1 tbsp/15 mL minced fresh ginger root and 1 tsp/5 mL sesame oil. Bring to boil. Toss with cabbage mixture and season with salt and pepper to taste.

Makes about 4 cups/1 L

PER SERVING

Calories	173
g carbohydrate	2
g fibre	0
g total fat	5
g saturated fat	1
g protein	27

Excellent: niacin; vitamin B_6
Good: vitamin B_{12}

mg cholesterol	68
mg sodium	169
mg potassium	381

ROAST TURKEY BREAST WITH SPINACH STUFFING

I first made this in a Passover Lite cooking class and used three pieces of matzo instead of the bread, but it is great either way. It sounds like a lot of spinach, but it does cook down in volume greatly.

Makes 6 to 8 servings

Stuffing:

3	slices whole wheat or white bread, broken up	3
⅓ cup	homemade chicken stock (page 57), hot	75 mL
2 tsp	vegetable oil	10 mL
1	small onion, finely chopped	1
2	cloves garlic, finely chopped	2
1½ lb	fresh spinach, cooked and chopped	750 g
1	egg white	1
½ tsp	salt	2 mL
½ tsp	pepper	2 mL
¼ tsp	grated nutmeg	1 mL
1	boneless, skinless turkey breast, opened and flattened (2 lb/1 kg)	1
1 tbsp	vegetable oil	15 mL
2	onions, thickly sliced	2
1	head garlic, cloves peeled but left whole	1
2 tbsp	chopped fresh rosemary, or ½ tsp/2 mL dried	25 mL
pinch	salt	pinch
pinch	pepper	pinch
1 cup	dry white wine or chicken stock	250 mL

GRAVY

Heat 1 tbsp/15 mL vegetable oil in saucepan. Add 3 tbsp/45 mL all-purpose flour and cook, whisking, until flour browns lightly. Whisk in 2 cups/500 mL chicken stock (if you have them, use the cooking juices from the turkey as part of this amount) and bring to boil. Add a pinch of dried thyme and sage and salt, pepper and Worcestershire sauce to taste. Cook for 10 minutes. Add 1 tbsp/15 mL brandy, sherry or lemon juice. Thin gravy with ½ cup/125 mL milk or additional stock if necessary. Taste and adjust seasonings.

Makes about 2 cups/500 mL

1. To prepare stuffing, place bread in large bowl and cover with ⅓ cup/75 mL hot chicken stock. Allow to rest for 10 minutes.

2. Heat oil in large non-stick skillet. Add onion and garlic. Cook gently until tender. Add to bread.

3. Squeeze excess water from spinach and add to bread.

4. In small bowl, combine egg white, salt, pepper and nutmeg. Add to bread and combine well.

5. Flatten turkey breast and spread with spinach stuffing. Roll up and tie with string.

6. Heat 1 tbsp/15 mL oil in roasting pan. Add turkey and brown all over. Add sliced onions, whole garlic cloves and rosemary. Sprinkle with salt and pepper. Add wine.

7. Roast turkey in preheated 400°F/200°C oven for 1½ hours, or until meat thermometer reaches 165°F/75°C. Allow roast to rest for 10 minutes before carving.

CRANBERRY SAUCE

Place 3/4 lb/375 g fresh or frozen cranberries in saucepan along with ½ cup/125 mL dried cranberries if you have them. Add 1 cup/250 mL granulated sugar and 1 cup/250 mL cranberry juice (orange, apple or grape juice can also be used). Add grated peel from 1 orange. Bring to boil, reduce heat and simmer for about 15 minutes. Sauce will thicken more when cold.

Makes about 2 cups/500 mL

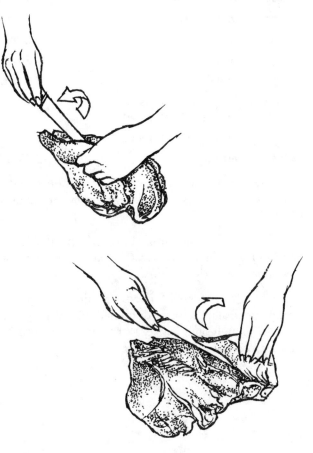

BARBECUED BUTTERFLIED TURKEY BREAST

*This recipe is quick, lower-fat, easy and reasonable in price —
what could be better? Be sure not to overcook the turkey. I like
to start it on the grill and finish it in the oven to keep it moist.
Ask your butcher to butterfly the turkey, or flatten it yourself
by cutting open the thicker sections and pounding it so it is
more even in thickness. Serve it with coleslaw (page 176) and
potato salad.*

*Any sauce used for a butterflied leg of lamb can also be used
with turkey.*

Makes 6 servings

2 lb	boneless, skinless turkey breast	1 kg
1 tbsp	olive oil	15 mL
1 tbsp	Dijon mustard	15 mL
½ tsp	salt	2 mL
½ tsp	pepper	2 mL
1 tsp	paprika	5 mL
1 tbsp	chopped fresh rosemary, or ½ tsp/2 mL dried	15 mL
2	cloves garlic, minced	2
2 tbsp	lemon juice	25 mL

1. Trim any fat from turkey breast. Cut breast open and pound if necessary so meat is even thickness (turkey should be less than 1 inch/2.5 cm thick).

2. Combine olive oil, mustard, salt, pepper, paprika, rosemary, garlic and lemon juice. Marinate turkey in mixture for up to a few hours in refrigerator.

3. Barbecue or broil turkey for about 5 minutes per side. Transfer to non-stick baking dish or dish lined with parchment paper and bake in preheated 350°F/180°C oven for 18 to 20 minutes, or until cooked through but not dry.

PER SERVING

Calories	201
g carbohydrate	1
g fibre	trace
g total fat	5
g saturated fat	1
g protein	36

Excellent: niacin; vitamin B_6
Good: vitamin B_{12}

mg cholesterol	91
mg sodium	321
mg potassium	485

MEAT

Beef and Broccoli with Baked Noodle Cake

Grilled Steak Sandwiches with Barbecued Onion Sauce

Shepherd's Pie with Garlic Mashed Potatoes

Polenta with Wild Mushroom and Meat Ragout

Giant Hamburger with Homemade Chili Sauce

Shishkebab-flavoured Butterflied Leg of Lamb

Lamb Chops with Cashew Nut Couscous

Osso Bucco (Braised Veal Shanks)

Sweet and Sour Cabbage Casserole

Braised Lamb Shanks with White Bean Puree

Barbecued Lamb Chili

Baked Pork Chops with Barbecue Sauce

Pork Tenderloin with Hoisin

Cajun Glazed Ham

BEEF AND BROCCOLI WITH BAKED NOODLE CAKE

See photo opposite page 192.

Beef with broccoli is one of the most popular Chinese dishes. You can use lamb, pork or chicken in place of the beef, and you can use peppers, beans, celery or Chinese greens in place of the broccoli.

   Serve this over steamed rice (page 171), or try this noodle cake for a change. It's fun and different (you can also serve the noodle cake as a base for an Italian dish, with the sauce spooned on top).

Makes 4 servings

½ lb	angelhair pasta or thin Chinese egg noodles or spaghetti	250 g
1 tsp	sesame oil	5 mL
¾ lb	flank steak	375 g

Marinade:

1 tbsp	soy sauce	15 mL
1 tbsp	rice wine	15 mL
2 tbsp	water	25 mL
1 tbsp	cornstarch	15 mL

To Cook:

1 tbsp	vegetable oil	15 mL
3	cloves garlic, finely chopped	3
1 tbsp	chopped fresh ginger root	15 mL
6	green onions, chopped	6
1	bunch broccoli, trimmed and cut in 1-inch/2.5 cm pieces (1 lb/500 g)	1
½ cup	water	125 mL

Sauce:

1 cup	homemade chicken stock (page 57) or water	250 mL
2 tbsp	oyster sauce	25 mL
1 tbsp	soy sauce	15 mL
1 tbsp	rice wine	15 mL
2 tbsp	cornstarch	25 mL

PER SERVING

Calories	481
g carbohydrate	59
g fibre	6
g total fat	13
g saturated fat	3
g protein	31

Excellent: vitamin C; niacin; vitamin B$_6$; folacin; vitamin B$_{12}$; iron
Good: vitamin A; thiamine; riboflavin

mg cholesterol	35
mg sodium	659
mg potassium	906

1. Bring large pot of water to boil. Add noodles and cook until tender. Drain well and toss with sesame oil. Place noodles in lightly oiled 9-inch/23 cm cake pan or pie pan.

2. Meanwhile, cut flank steak on diagonal, against grain, into thin slices (for easier slicing, freeze the meat for 20 minutes first).

3. To prepare marinade, in large bowl, combine soy sauce, rice wine, water and cornstarch. Add beef and marinate for 20 minutes at room temperature.

4. Bake noodle cake in preheated 400°F/200°C oven for 10 minutes. Broil for 3 to 5 minutes until slightly browned and crisp.

5. Meanwhile, to cook beef and broccoli, heat oil in wok or non-stick skillet on medium-high heat. Add beef and cook just until coloured but not cooked through. Remove from pan and reserve.

6. Return pan to heat. Add garlic, ginger and green onions. Cook for about 30 seconds until fragrant. Add broccoli and water. Bring to boil, cover and cook for 3 minutes, or until broccoli is tender-crisp.

7. Meanwhile, to make sauce, combine stock, oyster sauce, soy sauce, rice wine and cornstarch. Add to broccoli and bring to boil. Add meat and combine well.

8. Slide baked noodle cake out onto large platter. Spoon beef, broccoli and sauce over top.

GRILLED STEAK SANDWICHES WITH BARBECUED ONION SAUCE

This is a real treat during barbecue season, but the steak can also be broiled or pan-grilled. It is a reasonably economical dish for entertaining. Prepare the onions in advance, and either reheat or serve at room temperature. Serve the sandwiches with Grilled Corn Salad (page 78).

The steak and onions can be served in Kaiser buns instead of on a French stick. They can also be served over mashed potatoes.

Makes 8 servings

1½ lb	sirloin or flank steak, 1 inch/2.5 cm thick, trimmed of all fat	750 g
2 tbsp	balsamic vinegar	25 mL
1 tbsp	Dijon mustard	15 mL
½ tsp	pepper	2 mL
2	cloves garlic, minced	2

Barbecued Onion Sauce:

2 tsp	olive oil	10 mL
3	large onions, sliced	3
3	cloves garlic, chopped	3
½ cup	pureed canned plum tomatoes	125 mL
½ cup	brown sugar	125 mL
½ cup	rice vinegar or cider vinegar	125 mL
½ cup	strong coffee	125 mL
1 tbsp	Worcestershire sauce	15 mL
2	thin French sticks (24 inches/60 cm each)	2
¼ cup	chopped fresh parsley	50 mL

RICE VINEGAR

Rice vinegar is very mild. If you don't have it, substitute cider vinegar, although the taste will be a little more acidic. Seasoned rice vinegar (sushi su) contains salt and sugar; it is used to flavour sushi rice, but is also delicious sprinkled on salads.

PER SERVING

Calories	437
g carbohydrate	66
g fibre	3
g total fat	8
g saturated fat	2
g protein	25

Excellent: thiamine; niacin; vitamin B_{12}; iron
Good: riboflavin; vitamin B_6; folacin

mg cholesterol	40
mg sodium	552
mg potassium	555

1. Pat steak dry. In small bowl, combine balsamic vinegar, mustard, pepper and minced garlic. Rub into meat. If you are using flank steak, marinate it in refrigerator for a few hours or overnight.

2. Heat oil in large, deep non-stick skillet. Add onions and chopped garlic and cook gently until tender.

3. Add tomatoes, sugar, rice vinegar, coffee and Worcestershire sauce. Bring to boil. Simmer gently for 15 minutes.

4. Just before serving, grill steak on each side. Grill flank steak for about 3 to 6 minutes per side for rare; 4 to 6 minutes for sirloin steak depending on the thickness. Use touch test (see box). Allow to rest for 5 minutes. Slice thinly. (Steak can also be broiled or pan-grilled.)

5. Slice French stick and make sandwiches with steak and onions. Sprinkle with parsley.

GRILLING

Whether you are barbecuing outdoors or using an indoor gas or electric grill, grilling is a popular cooking method. It's easy and adds flavour to food without adding fat.

Grills can be sprayed with non-stick coating or brushed or wiped with vegetable oil before heating. (Brushes will burn if they are used on a hot grill.) Or you can follow the advice of cooking-show host Caprial Pence, who sprays the chicken, fish or meat itself to prevent it from sticking to the grill!

Testing Steak for Doneness

Grill chefs can tell when a steak or chop is ready just by touching the top of the meat. You can use the same method.

Rest your forearm on a surface in front of you. Relax and feel your bicep muscle. That's what rare steak feels like. Now hold your arm up off the table but do not tense it. Feel your bicep. That's what a medium steak feels like. Now tense your bicep muscle as hard as you can. That's well done.

SHEPHERD'S PIE WITH GARLIC MASHED POTATOES

Maureen Lollar, who manages the cookware shop at my school, is our shepherd's pie expert. Her mother had fourteen children, and she really knew how to cook ground beef! Maureen loved this version — even she didn't detect the chickpeas, which lower the fat and increase the fibre in the recipe.

Serve this with a salad.

Makes 8 to 10 servings

2 lb	baking potatoes, peeled and cut in 2-inch/5 cm pieces	1 kg
12	cloves garlic, peeled	12
¾ cup	hot potato cooking liquid or milk	175 mL
	Salt and pepper to taste	
1 lb	extra-lean ground beef	500 g
2	onions, chopped	2
2	cloves garlic, finely chopped	2
2 cups	cooked chickpeas, chopped	500 mL
1½ cups	chili sauce, tomato sauce, ketchup or pureed canned tomatoes	375 mL
1 tbsp	Worcestershire sauce	15 mL
¼ tsp	hot red pepper sauce	1 mL
1 cup	fresh whole wheat or white breadcrumbs	250 mL
½ cup	fresh or frozen peas	125 mL
½ cup	fresh or frozen corn niblets	125 mL
1 tbsp	paprika	15 mL

SHEPHERD'S PIE VARIATIONS

Shepherd's pie can be varied in many different ways. In place of ground beef, you can use ground chicken or turkey (page 164). You can use lentils or beans instead of chickpeas; add lots of fresh herbs to the meat or potato mixture; add hot chiles, cumin and cilantro to the meat to give it a Southwestern twist; or add ginger, hoisin sauce, soy sauce and sesame oil for an Asian version. Instead of the mashed potatoes you can top the meat with any pureed root vegetable mixture (page 218) or with pureed white kidney beans (page 199) or polenta (page 120). And that's just the beginning of the possibilities!

PER SERVING

Calories	323
g carbohydrate	51
g fibre	8
g total fat	6
g saturated fat	2
g protein	20

Excellent: niacin; vitamin B_6; folacin; vitamin B_{12}; iron
Good: vitamin C; thiamine; riboflavin

mg cholesterol	30
mg sodium	784
mg potassium	842

1. Place potatoes and whole garlic cloves in pot and cover with water. Bring to boil and cook for 20 minutes, or until tender. Drain well, reserving about 1 cup/250 mL cooking liquid. With potato masher or food mill, mash potatoes with ½ cup/125 mL hot cooking liquid. Add salt and pepper to taste. Add additional liquid if necessary.

2. Meanwhile, heat large, deep non-stick skillet. Add beef and brown. Add onions and chopped garlic and cook until tender. Drain off any fat if necessary.

3. Add chickpeas and chili sauce. Bring to boil. Reduce heat and cook gently for about 10 minutes.

4. Add Worcestershire, hot pepper sauce, breadcrumbs, peas and corn and combine well. Season to taste with salt and pepper.

5. Transfer mixture to lightly oiled 10 x 8-inch/2.5 L casserole. Spread or pipe mashed potatoes on top. Dust with paprika. Bake in preheated 400°F/200°C oven for 30 minutes.

UTENSILS FOR A LOW-FAT KITCHEN

- heavy non-stick skillets (pots, Dutch ovens and saucepans do not need to be non-stick)
- woks are useful in a low-fat kitchen, as you can cook a lot of food in very little oil; buy a large one so there is plenty of room to stir things around, and choose a wok with handles on both sides as well as a lid, so you can use it for steaming
- pasta pot with built-in strainer for pasta and for making homemade chicken stock (the meat, bones and vegetables can just be lifted out)
- measuring cups and spoons
- grill pan for indoor barbecues; they give food a better taste than broilers, and the clean-up is easier
- pastry brush for spreading just a small amount of oil in the bottom of pans before sauteing; a spray bottle also works well
- parchment paper for lining baking pans so no oil is needed to prevent sticking
- kitchen scale
- yogurt strainer (you can easily use a strainer and cheesecloth to make yogurt cheese, but the new yogurt strainers are fast, non-spill and efficient)

POLENTA WITH WILD MUSHROOM AND MEAT RAGOUT

This is a delicious all-purpose meat sauce. It is also wonderful served over pasta (cook about 1 lb/500 g dry pasta), mashed potatoes or rice. Just a little bit of sausage adds a lot of flavour, but you can omit it if you prefer.

Makes 4 servings

Wild Mushroom and Meat Ragout:

½ oz	dried wild mushrooms	15 g
1 cup	warm water	250 mL
2 tsp	olive oil	10 mL
1	onion, chopped	1
3	cloves garlic, finely chopped	3
¼ tsp	hot red pepper flakes, optional	1 mL
1	sweet red pepper, diced	1
½ lb	extra-lean ground beef	250 g
1	extra-lean Italian sausage, removed from casing (2 oz/60 g), optional	1
1	28-oz/796 mL tin plum tomatoes, with juices, pureed or broken up	1
	Salt and pepper to taste	

Polenta:

6 cups	water	1.5 L
1 tsp	salt	5 mL
½ tsp	pepper	2 mL
1 cup	cornmeal (regular or instant)	250 mL
2 tbsp	grated Parmesan cheese	25 mL
2 tbsp	chopped fresh parsley	25 mL

PER SERVING

Calories	314
g carbohydrate	43
g fibre	5
g total fat	8
g saturated fat	3
g protein	18

Excellent: vitamin A; vitamin C; niacin; vitamin B$_6$; vitamin B$_{12}$
Good: thiamine; riboflavin; folacin; iron

mg cholesterol	32
mg sodium	1006
mg potassium	764

1. Cover mushrooms with warm water and let soak for 30 minutes. Strain liquid through paper towel-lined sieve and reserve. Rinse mushrooms thoroughly and chop. Reserve.

2. Heat oil in large, deep non-stick skillet. Add onion, garlic and hot pepper flakes. Cook gently until tender but do not brown.

3. Add red pepper and cook for a few minutes. Add beef and sausage meat and brown. Drain off and discard any excess fat.

4. Add mushrooms, mushroom liquid and tomatoes. Bring to boil and cook for 30 minutes, or until sauce is quite thick. Add salt and pepper.

5. To cook polenta, add water, salt and pepper to large pot and bring to boil. Slowly whisk in cornmeal. Stirring with long-handled wooden spoon, cook over medium heat for 25 to 30 minutes for regular cornmeal or 5 to 10 minutes for instant. Polenta should be tender. Taste and adjust seasonings if necessary.

6. Serve polenta in individual bowls or pour into 9-inch/2 L square baking dish. Top with sauce and sprinkle with cheese and parsley.

- Make lower-sodium soy sauce by combining your favourite regular soy sauce with the same amount of water as you use it.
- Make lower-fat soft cheese by blending your favourite regular-fat cheese with low-fat cottage cheese or firm yogurt cheese (page 229).
- Make lower-fat mayonnaise by combining regular mayonnaise with soft yogurt cheese.

WAYS TO REDUCE SALT

- Boost the flavour of food by using very fresh, good-quality ingredients. Add lots of fresh herbs, or add dried herbs discreetly. Use hot chiles, citrus peel, vinegars, wine and juices.
- Be aware that canned and processed foods contain hidden salt. Rinse canned beans, chiles, capers, etc., before using.

- Make your own lower-sodium soy sauce by combining equal parts soy sauce and water. It is cheaper and better-tasting than the commercial product.
- Take two bites of a dish before salting (you tend to miss the salt right away, and other flavours may not register immediately).

Giant Hamburger with Homemade Chili Sauce

This gigantic burger is a lot of fun. To turn it, use a cookie sheet without sides or the flat base of a springform pan. Slip the pan under the burger, invert it onto another flat pan and then slide it gently back onto the grill.

A round Italian loaf may be too thick for this recipe. If so, cut the loaf in half and pull out some of the bread from the inside. Use it to make the breadcrumbs for the burger or freeze for another use.

The chili sauce can be pureed (leave it slightly chunky) and used whenever commercial chili sauce is called for in this book.

Makes 10 servings

1 lb	extra-lean ground beef	500 g
2 cups	cooked green lentils	500 mL
2	eggs	2
1 tbsp	Dijon mustard	15 mL
1 tbsp	Worcestershire sauce	15 mL
2 cups	fresh whole wheat or white breadcrumbs	500 mL
2	cloves garlic, minced	2
1 tsp	minced fresh ginger root	5 mL
1	onion, finely chopped	1
1	sweet red, green or yellow pepper, finely chopped	1
3 tbsp	chopped fresh cilantro or parsley	45 mL
3	green onions, finely chopped	3
1 tsp	salt	5 mL
¼ tsp	pepper	1 mL

CILANTRO

Cilantro is also known as Chinese parsley or fresh coriander. Some people love its citrus, fresh, clean taste; others think it tastes like soap. But if it is given a fair chance and eaten in small quantities at first, most people come to love it. Usually only the leaves are added to a dish, but in many Thai, Indian and Asian recipes the stems and roots are also used.

PER SERVING

Calories	373
g carbohydrate	58
g fibre	5
g total fat	6
g saturated fat	2
g protein	22

Excellent: vitamin C; thiamine; niacin; folacin; vitamin B_{12}; iron
Good: vitamin A; riboflavin; vitamin B_6

mg cholesterol	67
mg sodium	961
mg potassium	638

Chili Sauce:

2 tsp	olive oil	10 mL
1	onion, chopped	1
3	cloves garlic, finely chopped	3
1	hot banana pepper, chopped, optional	1
2	stalks celery, chopped	2
1	sweet green pepper, chopped	1
1	sweet red pepper, chopped	1
½ cup	ketchup	125 mL
1	28-oz/796 mL tin plum tomatoes, drained and pureed or broken up, or 2 cups/500 mL tomato sauce	1
	Salt and pepper to taste	
1	10-inch/25 cm round loaf bread	1

1. In large bowl, combine ground beef, lentils, eggs, mustard, Worcestershire, breadcrumbs, minced garlic, ginger, onion, pepper, cilantro, green onions, salt and pepper. Shape mixture into one large hamburger, about 9 inches/23 cm in diameter and 1 inch/2.5 cm thick. Refrigerate until ready to cook.

2. To make sauce, heat oil in large non-stick saucepan. Add onion, chopped garlic, banana pepper and celery. Cook gently until vegetables are wilted. Add sweet peppers and cook for 5 minutes.

3. Add ketchup and tomatoes. Bring to boil and simmer gently for 15 to 20 minutes, until thick. Season with salt and pepper.

4. Meanwhile, grill hamburger for about 10 minutes per side, or until cooked through.

5. Cut bread in half horizontally. Place burger on bottom half and spread sauce (hot or cold) on top. Top with other half of bun. Cut into 10 wedges.

SHISHKEBAB-FLAVOURED BUTTERFLIED LEG OF LAMB

This marinade is also great on shishkebabs. Just cut the lamb into 1½ inch/4 cm cubes and thread on metal skewers, alternating with onion wedges. Serve with Basmati Rice Pilaf with Garam Masala (page 221) and Carrot Salad with Moroccan Dressing (page 80).

Makes 8 servings

3 lb	butterflied leg of lamb	1.5 kg
1	onion, cut in quarters	1
4	cloves garlic	4
1 tbsp	ground cumin	15 mL
1 tbsp	paprika	15 mL
½ tsp	ground ginger	2 mL
2 tbsp	honey	25 mL
2 tbsp	lemon juice	25 mL
¼ cup	chopped fresh cilantro or parsley	50 mL
½ cup	low-fat yogurt	125 mL

1. Trim lamb of all fat.

2. In food processor, puree onion, garlic, cumin, paprika and ginger. Stir in honey, lemon juice, cilantro and yogurt. Pour over lamb and marinate in refrigerator for at least 30 minutes or up to overnight.

3. Just before cooking, scrape marinade from lamb. Grill lamb for about 10 minutes per side. (You could also brown lamb in skillet and finish cooking in preheated 400°F/200°C oven for 25 to 30 minutes.) Lamb should reach 130 to 140°F/55 to 60°C for medium-rare.

4. Allow lamb to rest for 5 minutes before carving on diagonal.

PER SERVING

Calories	211
g carbohydrate	4
g fibre	trace
g total fat	8
g saturated fat	3
g protein	30

Excellent: riboflavin; niacin; vitamin B$_{12}$
Good: iron

mg cholesterol	106
mg sodium	55
mg potassium	246

Beef and Broccoli with Baked Noodle Cake
(page 182)

Grilled Chicken Sandwich
(page 240)

LAMB CHOPS WITH CASHEW NUT COUSCOUS

If you think lamb is too strong-tasting, try buying fresh lamb, trimming it of all fat and cooking it just until pink — it should be mild-tasting and tender!

Mould the couscous into shapes for a neat, tidy presentation. You can scoop it with an ice-cream scoop or pack it firmly into ramekins before unmoulding onto serving plates.

Makes 4 servings

8	rib lamb chops, trimmed of all fat (2 oz/60 g each)	8
1 tsp	ground cumin	5 mL
½ tsp	paprika	2 mL
¼ tsp	pepper	1 mL
1 tbsp	lemon juice	15 mL

Cashew Nut Couscous:

1½ cups	couscous	375 mL
1½ cups	boiling water	375 mL
½ tsp	curry powder	2 mL
½ tsp	salt	2 mL
2 tbsp	orange juice concentrate	25 mL
1	carrot, grated (¾ cup/175 mL)	1
2 tbsp	chopped cashews, toasted (see sidebar)	25 mL
2 tbsp	chopped fresh cilantro or parsley	25 mL

1. Pat lamb dry. In small bowl, combine cumin, paprika and pepper. Stir in lemon juice to make a paste. Rub paste into lamb chops and marinate in refrigerator until ready to cook.

2. Meanwhile, place couscous in 9-inch/2 L square baking dish. In bowl or measuring cup, combine boiling water, curry powder, salt and orange juice concentrate. Stir into couscous along with grated carrot. Cover tightly with foil and allow to rest for 10 minutes. Fluff lightly and stir in cashews and cilantro.

3. Grill, broil or pan-fry (in a non-stick skillet or grill pan) chops for 5 minutes per side, or until cooked. Serve with couscous.

TOASTING NUTS

Nuts are delicious, but they are also expensive and high in fat. You can double their flavour by toasting them before using — you won't need to use so many. Spread nuts in a single layer on a baking sheet and toast at 350°F/180°C until lightly coloured, about 10 minutes.

PER SERVING

Calories	386
g carbohydrate	61
g fibre	4
g total fat	7
g saturated fat	2
g protein	19

Excellent: vitamin A; niacin; vitamin B₁₂
Good: thiamine; folacin; iron

mg cholesterol	36
mg sodium	329
mg potassium	357

OSSO BUCCO
(BRAISED VEAL SHANKS)

Osso bucco, meaning "bone with a hole," is one of the most delicious braised dishes. The longer it cooks, the better it tastes, so this is a perfect dish to make ahead and reheat! I like the veal shanks cut about 1½ inches/4 cm thick (thicker shanks take longer to cook). If you want to serve the meat on the bone, this recipe will serve six, but you can easily serve eight if you take the meat off the bone. Although osso bucco is often served with risotto, I also like to serve it with simply cooked short-grain rice and peas.

Makes 8 servings

¼ cup	all-purpose flour	50 mL
¼ tsp	salt	1 mL
½ tsp	pepper	2 mL
6	pieces veal shank (8 oz/250 g each), trimmed of any fat	6
2 tsp	vegetable oil	10 mL
2	onions, chopped	2
4	cloves garlic, finely chopped	4
2	stalks celery, chopped	2
2	carrots, chopped	2
2 cups	dry white wine or chicken stock	500 mL
1	28-oz/796 mL tin plum tomatoes, with juices	1
2 tbsp	lemon juice	25 mL
1 tbsp	chopped fresh rosemary, or ½ tsp/2 mL dried	15 mL
½ tsp	pepper	2 mL
2 cups	short-grain Italian rice	500 mL
1 cup	fresh or frozen peas	250 mL
	Salt to taste	

PER SERVING

Calories	437
g carbohydrate	55
g fibre	4
g total fat	9
g saturated fat	3
g protein	32

Excellent: vitamin A; niacin; vitamin B$_6$; vitamin B$_{12}$
Good: vitamin C; thiamine; riboflavin; folacin; iron

mg cholesterol	110
mg sodium	365
mg potassium	908

Herb Topping:

¼ cup	chopped fresh parsley	50 mL
1 tbsp	grated lemon peel	15 mL
2	cloves garlic, finely chopped	2

1. Combine flour, salt and pepper. Pat veal dry and dust with seasoned flour.

2. Heat oil in large, deep ovenproof skillet. Brown veal on medium-high heat on all sides. Remove meat and reserve. Remove all but 2 tsp/10 mL fat from pan.

3. Add onions, garlic, celery and carrots. Reduce heat and cook gently for about 10 minutes, until fragrant and tender.

4. Add wine and increase heat. Bring to boil and let half the wine evaporate. Add tomatoes, breaking them up with spoon. Add lemon juice, rosemary and pepper.

5. Return veal to pan. Cover and simmer gently in preheated 350°F/180°C oven for 2 to 4 hours, or until veal is very tender (you can also transfer everything to a casserole dish and cover it tightly with a lid or foil). If sauce is not thick enough, remove veal to platter and keep warm. Bring sauce to boil and cook until desired thickness.

6. Before serving, bring large pot of water to boil (use at least 5 qt/5 L water). Add rice. Return to boil and cook for 10 to 12 minutes until tender. Add peas and allow to rest for 2 minutes. Drain rice and peas in sieve. Taste and season with salt.

7. To make topping, in small bowl, combine parsley, lemon peel and garlic. Serve veal over rice with sauce. Sprinkle with herb topping.

SWEET AND SOUR CABBAGE CASSEROLE

Cabbage rolls are very popular, but it takes time to roll up all those cabbage leaves. Try just layering the leaves with the stuffing and sauce — you'll have the same traditional flavours without the fuss.

The meat and rice mixture can also be made into meatballs. Poach them in the sauce without even browning them first.

Makes 6 to 8 servings

1 lb	extra-lean ground beef	500 g
2 cups	cooked rice (page 171)	500 mL
1	clove garlic, minced	1
1	egg	1
¼ cup	dry breadcrumbs	50 mL
¼ cup	ketchup	50 mL
1 tsp	salt	5 mL
¼ tsp	pepper	1 mL
6 tbsp	chopped fresh parsley, divided	75 mL
1 tsp	vegetable oil	5 mL
1	clove garlic, finely chopped	1
1	onion, chopped	1
¼ cup	brown sugar	50 mL
2 tbsp	lemon juice	25 mL
1	28-oz/796 mL tin plum tomatoes, with juices	1
½ cup	cranberry juice or pineapple juice	125 mL
	Salt and pepper to taste	
1	large cabbage	1

1. In large bowl, combine ground beef, rice, minced garlic, egg, breadcrumbs, ketchup, salt, pepper and 2 tbsp/25 mL parsley. Reserve.

2. To make sauce, heat oil in large non-stick saucepan. Add chopped garlic and onion. Cook gently for a couple of minutes until fragrant but do not brown.

3. Add sugar, lemon juice, tomatoes and cranberry juice. Bring to boil. Add 2 tbsp/25 mL parsley. Cook for 15 to 20 minutes, breaking up tomatoes with spoon. If sauce is too thick, add about ½ cup/125 mL water or additional juice. Taste and season with salt and pepper.

4. Meanwhile, separate cabbage leaves and place in large bowl. Cover with boiling water. Cover bowl and allow to rest for 5 minutes. Drain well and pat leaves dry.

5. Line bottom of 11 x 7-inch/2 L baking dish with one-third of cabbage leaves. Spread with half of meat mixture and one-third of sauce. Repeat with cabbage, meat and sauce. Top with remaining cabbage and sauce.

6. Bake in preheated 350°F/180°C oven for 45 minutes. Sprinkle with remaining parsley and allow to rest for 10 minutes before serving. Cut into squares, being careful to cut right through all cabbage leaves.

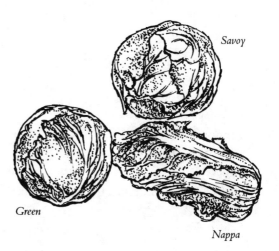

Savoy

Green

Nappa

Braised Lamb Shanks with White Bean Puree

Lamb shanks are sometimes served on the bone, but they can take over the entire plate and look somewhat intimidating! I like to take the cooked meat off the bone, reheat it in the sauce and then serve it over bean puree, mashed potatoes or soft polenta (page 120), with beets on side.

The bean puree also makes a great dip or spread.

Makes 8 servings

6	lamb shanks (8 oz/250 g each)	6
1	onion, chopped	1
2	cloves garlic, minced	2
2 cups	dry red wine or chicken stock	500 mL
½ tsp	pepper	2 mL
1 tbsp	chopped fresh rosemary, or ½ tsp/2 mL dried	15 mL
1 tbsp	chopped fresh thyme, or ½ tsp/2 mL dried	15 mL

Sauce:

1 tsp	olive oil	5 mL
6	onions, sliced	6
6	cloves garlic, finely chopped	6
¼ tsp	hot red pepper flakes	1 mL
1 tbsp	chopped fresh rosemary, or ½ tsp/2 mL dried	15 mL
1 tbsp	chopped fresh thyme, or ½ tsp/2 mL dried	15 mL
½ tsp	pepper	2 mL
1	28-oz/796 mL tin plum tomatoes, with juices	1
	Salt to taste	

OLIVE OIL

I like to cook with olive oil, partly because it is a monounsaturated fat, but also because it adds the delicious taste of olives to recipes. Extra-virgin olive oil has less acidity than regular olive oil; it is made with ripe olives without the use of heat or chemicals.

Buy olive oil in small quantities and, once it has been opened use it up within a month or two. Otherwise, keep it in the refrigerator (the oil may firm up and become cloudy, but it will be fine when it returns to room temperature).

If I don't want the taste of olives in a dish, I usually use safflower, corn or canola oil.

White Bean Puree:

2	19-oz/540 mL tins white kidney beans, drained and rinsed	2
3	cloves garlic, finely chopped	3
1 tsp	ground cumin	5 mL
½ tsp	pepper	2 mL
1 tbsp	lemon juice	15 mL
½ tsp	hot red pepper sauce	2 mL
½ cup	chopped fresh parsley	125 mL

1. Trim lamb shanks of all fat. In large bowl, combine chopped onion, minced garlic, wine, pepper, rosemary and thyme. Add lamb and marinate in refrigerator for 2 hours or overnight.

2. Drain shanks well and pat dry. Strain juices and reserve.

3. Heat olive oil in large Dutch oven on medium-high heat. Add shanks and brown well, a few at a time if necessary. Remove and reserve. Discard all but 1 tbsp/15 mL fat from pan.

4. Add sliced onions, chopped garlic and hot pepper flakes. Reduce heat and cook gently until tender and fragrant, about 10 minutes.

5. Add rosemary, thyme, pepper, strained marinade juices and tomatoes. Bring to boil. Return lamb to pan, cover and cook in preheated 350°F/180°C oven for 2 to 3 hours, until lamb is very tender. Skim fat from sauce. If sauce is too liquidy, remove shanks and cook sauce over medium-high heat until it reduces to the consistency you wish. Add salt to taste.

6. Cool lamb shanks slightly and remove meat from bones. Return meat to sauce.

7. Meanwhile, place beans, garlic, cumin and pepper in large saucepan and cover with 6 cups/1.5 L water. Bring to boil, reduce heat and cook gently for 20 minutes. Drain, reserving cooking liquid.

8. In food processor, puree beans with lemon juice and hot pepper sauce. Add enough cooking liquid to achieve consistency you wish.

9. Spread bean puree on each serving plate and top with lamb, onions and juices. Sprinkle with parsley.

BARBECUED LAMB CHILI

Barbecuing or broiling the lamb first gives this chili an appealing smoky taste, but you can also use leftover cooked lamb or beef (you will need about 3 cups/750 mL cubed cooked meat). You can also use two 19-oz/540 mL tins of kidney beans; just add them to the chili during the last half hour of cooking.

Serve this chili on steamed rice (page 171) or, for a more casual meal, in flour tortillas with all the toppings.

Makes 8 to 10 servings

2 cups	dried red kidney beans	500 mL
1	small butterflied leg of lamb, all fat removed (2 lb/1 kg)	1
2 tbsp	honey	25 mL
1 tbsp	Dijon mustard	15 mL
1 tsp	chopped fresh rosemary, or ¼ tsp/1 mL dried	5 mL
¼ tsp	pepper	1 mL
2 tsp	olive oil	10 mL
3	onions, chopped	3
6	cloves garlic, finely chopped	6
2 tbsp	paprika	25 mL
1½ tbsp	ground cumin	20 mL
1 tbsp	chili powder	15 mL
1 tsp	dried oregano	5 mL
½ tsp	cayenne	2 mL
1	chipotle (page 78), minced, or 1 jalapeño, finely chopped	1
2	28-oz/796 mL tins plum tomatoes, with juices, pureed or broken up	2
1 cup	water	250 mL
	Salt and pepper to taste	
8 cups	steamed basmati or other fragrant rice (page 171)	2 L

WRAPS

A great way to serve chilis and other thick and saucy mixtures is to make wraps. Take a big flour tortilla. Spread cooked rice down the centre and top with chili, followed by a sauce or salsa. Fold in the ends and roll up securely. You can also try combining rice, stir-fried chicken (page 175) and peanut sauce (page 54), or rice, ratatouille (page 120) and pesto (page 60) mixed with tomato sauce.

PER SERVING

Calories	672
g carbohydrate	108
g fibre	16
g total fat	9
g saturated fat	3
g protein	41

Excellent: vitamin A; vitamin C; thiamine; riboflavin; niacin; vitamin B$_6$; folacin; vitamin B$_{12}$; iron
Good: calcium

mg cholesterol	72
mg sodium	429
mg potassium	1430

Toppings:

1 cup	low-fat yogurt	250 mL
¼ cup	chopped fresh cilantro or parsley	50 mL
1 cup	chopped fresh tomatoes	250 mL

1. Rinse beans and soak in plenty of cold water overnight in refrigerator. Rinse and drain beans well and reserve.

2. Pat lamb dry. Combine honey, mustard, rosemary and pepper and spread over lamb.

3. Grill lamb on hot grill for 5 to 8 minutes per side, until lamb is well seared, or broil for 4 to 5 minutes per side. Dice into ½-inch/1 cm pieces (do not worry if lamb is still very rare).

4. Heat oil in large Dutch oven. Add onions and garlic. Cook gently for 10 minutes, or until onions have wilted.

5. Add paprika, cumin, chili powder, oregano and cayenne and cook for 30 seconds.

6. Add lamb and beans and coat well with onions. Stir in chipotle, tomato puree and water. Cook, covered, for 2 hours, or until beans and lamb are almost tender. Remove lid and continue to cook until chili is as thick as you like, about 20 to 30 minutes. Season with salt and pepper. Serve chili over rice, along with toppings.

BAKED PORK CHOPS WITH BARBECUE SAUCE

Baking pork chops in barbecue sauce makes them tender and juicy and gives them an outdoor flavour all year round. The sauce can be doubled and frozen for future use as an all-purpose barbecue sauce.

If you prefer, you can grill the chops for 2 minutes per side and then baste with the sauce. Continue to cook for about 5 minutes per side, basting often.

Serve these with roasted potatoes, green beans and coleslaw (page 176).

Makes 6 servings

1 cup	chili sauce, homemade (page 191) or commercial	250 mL
½ cup	ketchup	125 mL
1 tbsp	Worcestershire sauce	15 mL
2 tbsp	rice vinegar or cider vinegar	25 mL
1 tsp	ground cumin	5 mL
¼ cup	brown sugar	50 mL
2 tbsp	Dijon mustard	25 mL
1	chipotle (page 78), minced, or 1 jalapeño, finely chopped, optional	1
1	onion, finely chopped	1
2	cloves garlic, minced	2
2 lb	baking potatoes, peeled and cut in ¼-inch/5 mm slices	1 kg
6	pork chops, ¾ inch/2 cm thick, trimmed of all fat (6 oz/175 g each)	6

1. In saucepan, combine chili sauce, ketchup, Worcestershire, vinegar, cumin, sugar, mustard, chipotle, onion and garlic. Bring to boil. Simmer gently, uncovered, for 10 to 15 minutes, or until thickened. Stir often during cooking. (Sauce can be used immediately or refrigerated for up to 5 days.)

2. Spread a little sauce in bottom of 13 x 9-inch/3.5 L baking dish. Arrange sliced potatoes on top. Arrange chops on top of potatoes in single layer. Spoon remaining sauce over chops.

3. Bake, covered, in preheated 375°F/190°C oven for 1 hour. Uncover and baste. Bake for another 45 minutes.

PER SERVING

Calories	392
g carbohydrate	47
g fibre	4
g total fat	9
g saturated fat	3
g protein	31

Excellent: vitamin C; thiamine; riboflavin; niacin; vitamin B$_6$; vitamin B$_{12}$
Good: iron

mg cholesterol	72
mg sodium	667
mg potassium	1317

PORK TENDERLOIN WITH HOISIN

This idea comes from Anne Apps, who works with me in the school and cookware shop and is a great cook and cooking teacher in her own right. The pork is sauteed in a marinade with no extra fat. Serve over rice with Sauteed Greens (page 209).

Makes 4 to 5 servings

1¼ lb	pork tenderloin	625 g
3 tbsp	soy sauce	45 mL
2 tbsp	hoisin sauce	25 mL
1½ tbsp	rice wine	20 mL
½ tsp	hot chili paste	2 mL
2	cloves garlic, minced	2
1 tbsp	minced fresh ginger root	15 mL
1	green onion, chopped	1
1 tbsp	chopped fresh cilantro or parsley	15 mL

1. Cut pork into ¼-inch/5 mm slices.

2. In large bowl, combine soy sauce, hoisin, rice wine, chili paste, garlic, ginger, green onion and cilantro. Add pork and toss in marinade. Refrigerate for a few hours.

3. Heat large non-stick skillet over medium heat. Cook pork with marinade for 7 to 10 minutes, turning occasionally. Be careful not to let pork burn.

PER SERVING

Calories	192
g carbohydrate	5
g fibre	trace
g total fat	4
g saturated fat	1
g protein	31

Excellent: thiamine; riboflavin; niacin; vitamin B_6; vitamin B_{12};
Good: iron

mg cholesterol	80
mg sodium	865
mg potassium	568

CAJUN GLAZED HAM

This is a different and exciting way to prepare ham. The glaze is quite spicy, so if you want to reduce the heat, omit the jalapeño and cayenne. Serve with Sweet Potato Mash (page 214) and Sauteed Greens (page 209).

This glaze is also good on turkey or lamb.

Makes 16 servings

4 lb	boneless cooked ham	2 kg

Glaze:

1 cup	brown sugar	250 mL
4	jalapeños, seeded and chopped	4
2	cloves garlic, minced	2
2 tbsp	white wine vinegar	25 mL
2 tbsp	grainy mustard or Dijon mustard	25 mL
1 tbsp	paprika	15 mL
1 tsp	pepper	5 mL
½ tsp	cayenne or hot red pepper sauce	2 mL
½ tsp	dried thyme	2 mL
½ tsp	dried oregano	2 mL

1. Trim ham of all fat. Pierce ham all over with long skewer and score surface.

2. In bowl, combine brown sugar, jalapeños, garlic, vinegar, mustard, paprika, pepper, cayenne, thyme and oregano.

3. Place ham on foil-lined baking sheet. Spread with one-third of glaze.

4. Bake in preheated 350°F/180°C oven for 20 minutes. Baste with one-third more glaze. Bake for 20 minutes longer. Repeat. Total cooking time should be 1 to 1½ hours. Baste often.

5. Allow to rest for about 15 minutes before carving.

PER SERVING

Calories	180
g carbohydrate	9
g fibre	trace
g total fat	6
g saturated fat	2
g protein	22

Excellent: thiamine; niacin; vitamin B$_{12}$
Good: vitamin B$_6$

mg cholesterol	56
mg sodium	1277
mg potassium	339

VEGETABLES AND SIDE DISHES

Green Beans with Garlic

Asparagus with Thai Dipping Sauce

Glazed Beets with Balsamic Vinegar

Sauteed Greens

Stir-fried Broccoli with Ginger

Roasted Fennel with Tomatoes

Caramelized Onions

Wild Mushrooms with Herbs

Sweet Potato Mash

Buttermilk Mashed Potatoes

Mashed Baked Squash

Roasted "French-fried" Potatoes

Mashed Root Vegetables

Glazed Winter Vegetables with Maple and Ginger

Spicy Rice Pilaf

Basmati Rice Pilaf with Garam Masala

Israeli Couscous with Squash and Peppers

Barley and Wild Mushroom Risotto

Risotto with Rapini

GREEN BEANS WITH GARLIC

This recipe works equally well with green or yellow beans. You can freeze the anchovies that you do not use. Place them in a single layer on a plate lined with plastic wrap. When they are frozen, put them in a bag — you'll be able to remove one or two fillets easily as you need them.

If your sun-dried tomatoes have been packed in oil, rinse them before using. Store the opened jar in the refrigerator; the olive oil will become cloudy, but it will turn clear again when it is brought to room temperature.

Makes 6 servings

1 lb	green or yellow beans, or a combination (4 cups/1 L)	500 g
1 tsp	olive oil	5 mL
1	clove garlic, finely chopped	1
1	anchovy, finely chopped	1
1 tbsp	diced sun-dried tomatoes	15 mL
1 cup	water	250 mL
	Salt to taste	

1. Trim beans and cut in half.

2. Heat oil in large non-stick skillet. Add garlic, anchovy and tomatoes. Cook on low heat until very fragrant, about 2 minutes.

3. Add beans and coat with garlic mixture. Add water and bring to boil. Cook, uncovered, until water evaporates and beans are glazed with garlic mixture — about 10 minutes. Stir occasionally during cooking. Taste and add salt only if necessary.

PER SERVING

Calories	33
g carbohydrate	6
g fibre	2
g total fat	1
g saturated fat	trace
g protein	2
mg cholesterol	1
mg sodium	42
mg potassium	224

ASPARAGUS WITH THAI DIPPING SAUCE

Many people feel that asparagus is so special you should serve it as a separate course. This recipe makes a great appetizer, or you can serve it as a side dish. You can also serve it cold as a salad — chill the asparagus under cold water after cooking and pat dry before combining with the sauce.

I prefer thick asparagus stalks, as they seem much meatier. But thin asparagus is usually more delicate in taste and doesn't need peeling. Both have their advantages.

Makes 4 to 6 servings

1 lb	asparagus (20 to 24 stalks)	500 g
1 tbsp	lime juice	15 mL
1 tbsp	granulated sugar	15 mL
1 tbsp	Thai fish sauce or soy sauce	15 mL
1 tbsp	water	15 mL
1 tbsp	rice vinegar or cider vinegar	15 mL
1	clove garlic, minced	1
¼ tsp	hot chili paste or sweet and hot Thai chili sauce (page 94)	1 mL

1. Cut 1 inch/2.5 cm from bottom of asparagus stalks. Peel stalks about 2 inches/5 cm up from bottom if stalks are thick.

2. Bring large skillet of water to boil. Add asparagus and cook for 3 to 4 minutes, or until asparagus is bright green and stalks bend slightly when held up. Drain well and place on serving dish.

3. Meanwhile, in small bowl, whisk together lime juice, sugar, fish sauce, water, vinegar, garlic and chili paste. Drizzle over asparagus or use as dipping sauce.

ASPARAGUS

I usually trim an inch or two from the stalks of asparagus. If the stalks are thick, I then peel an inch or two up from the bottom, so the stems cook at the same rate as the tips. I cook the asparagus in boiling water lying down in a skillet. To find out whether it is cooked, hold a spear upright; if it just begins to bend over, it is ready.

GLAZED BEETS WITH BALSAMIC VINEGAR

Beets are so delicious and so underrated. They have stunning colour, great texture and sweet taste. Baking beets brings out all the flavour!

Makes 6 servings

2 lb	beets (6 medium)	1 kg
2 tsp	olive oil	10 mL
¼ cup	balsamic vinegar	50 mL
2 tbsp	brown sugar	25 mL
1 tsp	chopped fresh rosemary, or pinch dried	5 mL
½ cup	water	125 mL
	Salt and pepper to taste	
¼ cup	chopped fresh chives or green onions	50 mL

1. Wrap beets in foil in single layer. Bake in preheated 400°F/200°C oven until very tender, about 1 hour. Pierce with tip of sharp knife to see if they are ready.

2. Cool beets slightly. Trim ends and peel while still warm (it is easier). Cut into wedges.

3. Heat oil in large non-stick skillet. Add beets and toss to coat with oil. Add vinegar and sugar. Bring to boil.

4. Add rosemary and water. Cook until liquid evaporates and beets are well glazed. Season with salt and pepper. Sprinkle with chopped chives before serving.

PER SERVING

Calories	68
g carbohydrate	13
g fibre	3
g total fat	2
g saturated fat	trace
g protein	1

Excellent: folacin

mg cholesterol	0
mg sodium	58
mg potassium	389

See photo opposite page 160.

SAUTEED GREENS

Many leafy green vegetables can be cooked in this healthful and delicious way. Use beet greens, bok choy, spinach, kale, curly endive, Swiss chard or any combination. The greens can be served as a side dish, or under grilled fish or chicken.

Don't be surprised at the large amount of raw greens; they will cook way down!

Makes 6 servings

2 tsp	olive oil	10 mL
2	cloves garlic, finely chopped	2
2	shallots, finely chopped	2
2 lb	leafy greens (12 to 16 cups/3 to 4 L)	1 kg
½ cup	dry white wine, homemade chicken stock (page 57) or water	125 mL
	Salt and pepper to taste	

1. Heat oil in large, deep non-stick skillet or Dutch oven. Add garlic and shallots and cook on low heat until soft and fragrant (add a bit of water if vegetables start to stick).

2. Add greens and toss with garlic mixture.

3. Add wine and bring to boil. When greens start to wilt, turn them. Cover and cook for a few minutes longer. Season with salt and pepper.

PER SERVING

Calories	54
g carbohydrate	6
g fibre	3
g total fat	2
g saturated fat	trace
g protein	3

Excellent: vitamin A; vitamin C; folacin
Good: iron

mg cholesterol	0
mg sodium	107
mg potassium	625

STIR-FRIED BROCCOLI WITH GINGER

You can also prepare this recipe with asparagus; use about 1 lb/500 g asparagus (20 to 24 stalks) and reduce the water to 2 tbsp/25 mL.

Makes 4 to 6 servings

1	bunch broccoli (1½ lb/750 g)	1
1 tsp	vegetable oil	5 mL
1	clove garlic, finely chopped	1
1 tbsp	finely chopped fresh ginger root	15 mL
3	green onions, chopped	3
3 tbsp	water	45 mL
1 tbsp	soy sauce	15 mL
1 tbsp	hoisin sauce	15 mL

1. Trim broccoli and cut into 1-inch/2.5 cm chunks. Keep stems and florets separate.

2. Heat oil in large non-stick wok or skillet on high heat. Add garlic, ginger and green onions. Cook for 30 seconds.

3. Add broccoli stems and stir-fry for about 2 minutes. Stir in florets.

4. Add water, soy sauce and hoisin sauce and bring to boil. Cook, stirring, for 3 to 4 minutes, until broccoli is bright green and glazed with sauce.

ROASTED ASPARAGUS

Trim 1 lb/500 g asparagus stalks (page 207). Peel the base of the stalks if they are thick. Arrange asparagus in single layer on parchment paper- or foil-lined baking sheet. Drizzle with olive oil and sprinkle with salt and pepper. Bake in a preheated 425°F/220°C oven for 15 minutes. Drizzle with a little lemon juice before serving. Serve hot or at room temperature.

Makes 4 to 6 servings

PER SERVING

Calories	60
g carbohydrate	9
g fibre	3
g total fat	2
g saturated fat	trace
g protein	4

Excellent: vitamin C; folacin
Good: vitamin A

mg cholesterol	0
mg sodium	324
mg potassium	385

ROASTED FENNEL WITH TOMATOES

Fennel is an anise-flavoured vegetable. Eaten raw in a salad, it has a strong licorice taste, but when it is cooked, the taste is much milder.

Makes 4 to 6 servings

2	large bulbs fennel (2 lb/1 kg)	2
4	fresh plum tomatoes (1 lb/500 g)	4
1 tbsp	olive oil	15 mL
¼ tsp	salt	1 mL
2 tbsp	balsamic vinegar	25 mL
1	clove garlic, minced	1
	Salt and pepper to taste	
½ cup	shredded fresh basil or chopped parsley	125 mL

1. Trim fennel (see diagram). Cut fennel bulb in half. Cut each half into 6 wedges through core. Cut tomatoes lengthwise into quarters.

2. Place fennel and tomatoes in single layer in lightly oiled or parchment paper-lined roasting pan. Toss with oil and salt. Bake in preheated 350°F/180°C oven for about 45 minutes, or until fennel is cooked and tomatoes have dried out a bit.

3. Meanwhile, in small bowl, whisk together vinegar and garlic. Whisk in salt and pepper.

4. Place vegetables in serving bowl and sprinkle with basil. Drizzle dressing over vegetables. Serve hot or at room temperature.

PER SERVING

Calories	105
g carbohydrate	18
g fibre	6
g total fat	4
g saturated fat	1
g protein	3

Excellent: vitamin C
Good: folacin

mg cholesterol	0
mg sodium	238
mg potassium	941

CARAMELIZED ONIONS

Caramelized onions can be used in so many ways — on top of steaks or chops, inside quesadillas (page 51) with a bit of smoked cheese, on top of bruschetta (pages 44 or 45), in frittatas and omelettes or beaten into mashed potatoes. You can also serve them as a side dish.

You can double the batch, but cook the onions in two large skillets, or they will not brown properly. And have patience and cook them slowly.

Makes about 1 cup/250 mL

2 tsp	olive oil	10 mL
4	medium onions, thinly sliced (1 lb/500 g)	4
2	cloves garlic, finely chopped	2
1 tbsp	granulated sugar	15 mL
1 tbsp	balsamic vinegar	15 mL
	Salt to taste	
1 tbsp	chopped fresh parsley	15 mL

1. Heat oil in large non-stick skillet on high heat. Add onions and garlic, reduce heat to medium and cook for a few minutes without stirring to allow onions to brown a little on bottom. Stir and cook for 5 minutes longer, until onions are evenly golden and wilted.

2. Sprinkle onions with sugar and vinegar. Continue to cook for 10 minutes, until onions are browned, tender and very fragrant.

3. Season with salt and stir in parsley. Serve warm or at room temperature.

PER ¼ CUP (50 mL)

Calories	76
g carbohydrate	13
g fibre	2
g total fat	2
g saturated fat	trace
g protein	1
mg cholesterol	0
mg sodium	3
mg potassium	170

WILD MUSHROOMS WITH HERBS

This dish can be served on its own as a vegetable, but it is also great on steaks or chops, in mashed potatoes or rice, as a topping for bruschetta (pages 44 or 45) or on top of greens for a warm salad. Different wild mushrooms are available at different times of the year, and prices vary, but most of the time they are fairly expensive. So if cost or availability is a problem, simply substitute plain white or brown mushrooms.

Makes 4 to 6 servings

2 tsp	olive oil	10 mL
2	shallots, finely chopped	2
4	cloves garlic, finely chopped	4
1 lb	wild mushrooms, cleaned and sliced (6 cups/1.5 L)	500 g
1 tsp	chopped fresh rosemary, or pinch dried	5 mL
1 tsp	chopped fresh thyme, or pinch dried	5 mL
2 tbsp	chopped fresh parsley	25 mL
2 tbsp	chopped fresh chives or green onions	25 mL
	Salt and pepper to taste	

1. Heat oil in large non-stick skillet. Add shallots and garlic and cook on low heat until very fragrant.

2. Add mushrooms. When mushrooms begin to ooze their juices, increase heat to medium-high. Cook, stirring often, until mushrooms are cooked and any juices have evaporated. Add rosemary and thyme after mushrooms have cooked for a few minutes.

3. Before serving, sprinkle with parsley, chives, salt and pepper.

PER SERVING

Calories	50
g carbohydrate	6
g fibre	2
g total fat	3
g saturated fat	trace
g protein	2

Good: riboflavin; niacin

mg cholesterol	0
mg sodium	4
mg potassium	321

SWEET POTATO MASH

The colour of this mashed potato mixture is like sunshine, and the potatoes taste sweetly wonderful.

    When you mash vegetables other than regular potatoes, you will probably need less liquid, as most vegetables do not contain as much starch as potatoes.

Makes 6 servings

2 lb	baking potatoes (4 large)	1 kg
1 lb	sweet potatoes (1 large or 2 small)	500 g
1 tbsp	olive oil	15 mL
⅓ cup	hot milk or cooking liquid from potatoes	75 mL
	Salt and pepper to taste	

1. Peel baking potatoes and sweet potatoes. Cut into large chunks (about 2 inches/5 cm). Place in large pot of cold water. Bring to boil and cook gently for about 30 minutes, or until potatoes are very tender.

2. Drain potatoes well. Return to pot. Mash with fork or potato masher. Beat in oil and hot milk. Season with salt and pepper.

PER SERVING

Calories	191
g carbohydrate	39
g fibre	3
g total fat	3
g saturated fat	trace
g protein	3

Excellent: vitamin A; vitamin B$_6$
Good: vitamin C

mg cholesterol	1
mg sodium	21
mg potassium	506

BUTTERMILK MASHED POTATOES

Buttermilk is low in fat but still has a marvellously creamy texture. Heat it gently to prevent it from separating. Although you can substitute unflavoured yogurt, buttermilk does have a distinctive tang and aroma.

Instead of cooking the whole garlic cloves with the potatoes, you could squeeze two whole heads of roasted garlic (page 131) into the buttermilk while you are heating it.

Makes 4 to 5 servings

2 lb	baking potatoes, peeled and cut in half	1 kg
6	whole cloves garlic, peeled	6
½ cup	buttermilk	125 mL
2 tbsp	olive oil, optional	25 mL
	Salt and pepper to taste	
1 tbsp	chopped fresh chives or green onions	15 mL

1. Place potatoes and garlic in large pot and cover with cold water. Bring to boil. Reduce heat and cook for 20 to 30 minutes, or until potatoes are tender. Drain well.

2. Meanwhile, in small saucepan, warm buttermilk gently so that it does not separate.

3. Mash potatoes and garlic with potato masher or a food mill, with buttermilk and oil. Season with salt and pepper. Stir in chives.

PER SERVING

Calories	162
g carbohydrate	36
g fibre	2
g total fat	trace
g saturated fat	trace
g protein	4

Excellent: vitamin B$_6$

mg cholesterol	1
mg sodium	41
mg potassium	609

MASHED BAKED SQUASH

Any kind of winter squash can be used in this recipe, but butternut squash is particularly rich in texture and taste.

Makes 6 servings

3 lb	butternut squash	1.5 kg
2 tbsp	brown sugar or maple sugar (page 267)	25 mL
1 tsp	cinnamon	5 mL
¼ tsp	ground nutmeg	1 mL
¼ tsp	salt	1 mL
¼ tsp	pepper	1 mL

1. Cut squash in half. Scoop out seeds and stringy pulp.

2. Place squash, cut side down, on baking sheet. Bake in preheated 350°F/180°C oven for 45 to 50 minutes, or until very tender.

3. Meanwhile, in small bowl, combine brown sugar, cinnamon, nutmeg, salt and pepper.

4. Scoop out squash into bowl and discard skin. Mash squash with brown sugar mixture. Serve immediately, or spoon into casserole dish and keep warm until ready to serve.

SPICE GRINDERS
The original spice grinder was the mortar and pestle (this is where pesto sauce got its name), and they still work well. You can also buy an electric spice mill, or use a coffee grinder that you save only for spices.

PER SERVING

Calories	103
g carbohydrate	27
g fibre	trace
g total fat	trace
g saturated fat	0
g protein	2

Excellent: vitamin A; vitamin C
Good: vitamin B$_6$; folacin

mg cholesterol	0
mg sodium	105
mg potassium	619

ROASTED "FRENCH-FRIED" POTATOES

These really are crisp and delicious. Serve them with burgers as a side dish, or with a dip for an appetizer or snack. Vary the flavours by adding chili powder or other spices to the coating mixture.

Makes 4 to 6 servings

4	baking potatoes (2 lb/1 kg)	4
¼ cup	cornstarch	50 mL
¼ cup	water	50 mL
2 tbsp	chopped fresh rosemary or thyme (or a combination), or 1 tsp/5 mL dried	25 mL
1	clove garlic, minced	1
1 tsp	salt	5 mL
½ tsp	pepper	2 mL
1 tsp	vegetable oil	5 mL

1. Clean or peel potatoes and cut into sticks as for French fries.

2. In large bowl, combine cornstarch, water, rosemary, garlic, salt and pepper. Stir until smooth.

3. Add potatoes to cornstarch mixture and toss well.

4. Arrange potatoes in single layer (potatoes should not touch) on large baking sheet lined with parchment paper (use 2 pieces if necessary) and brushed with oil.

5. Bake potatoes in preheated 425°F/220°C oven for 15 minutes. Turn potatoes and continue to bake for 10 to 15 minutes longer, until brown, crisp and cooked through.

MASHED ROOT VEGETABLES

Rutabagas and turnips can be used interchangeably, although rutabagas are actually the large yellow root vegetables, and turnips are smaller and white. The rutabagas take a little longer to cook, so dice them into smaller pieces than the other veggies.

If you cannot find fresh thyme, simply add a pinch of dried thyme to the milk or cooking liquid.

For a really great addition (in this or any other mashed vegetable dish), squeeze two heads of roasted garlic (page 131) into the vegetables when pureeing.

Makes 4 to 6 servings

1 lb	baking potatoes (2 large or 4 medium), peeled and cut in 2-inch/5 cm pieces	500 g
1 lb	rutabaga or turnip, peeled and cut in 1-inch/2.5 cm pieces	500 g
1	sweet potato, peeled and cut in 2-inch/5 cm pieces (¾ lb/375 g)	1
2	parsnips or carrots, peeled and cut in 2-inch/5 cm pieces (½ lb/250 g)	2
½ cup	hot milk, or cooking liquid from vegetables	125 mL
1 tsp	finely chopped fresh thyme, or pinch dried	5 mL
	Salt and pepper to taste	
pinch	nutmeg	pinch

1. Place potatoes, rutabaga, sweet potato and parsnips in large pot and cover with cold water. Bring to boil. Cook gently for 20 to 30 minutes, or until vegetables are very tender. Drain vegetables well. Reserve some cooking liquid if you are using it.

2. Mash vegetables with potato masher, in food mill or mixer. Beat in enough hot milk or cooking liquid to achieve texture you desire. Season with thyme, salt, pepper and nutmeg.

PER SERVING

Calories	233
g carbohydrate	53
g fibre	8
g total fat	1
g saturated fat	trace
g protein	5

Excellent: vitamin A; vitamin C; vitamin B$_6$; folacin
Good: thiamine; niacin

mg cholesterol	1
mg sodium	49
mg potassium	1041

GLAZED WINTER VEGETABLES WITH MAPLE AND GINGER

The maple and ginger make Brussels sprouts taste so good that even people who don't like sprouts like this dish. In the spring and summer when sprouts are hard to find, use cauliflower or green beans instead.

Makes 6 servings

2 tsp	vegetable oil	10 mL
1 tbsp	chopped fresh ginger root	15 mL
1 lb	carrots, sliced on diagonal	500 g
1 lb	Brussels sprouts, trimmed and halved	500 g
2 tbsp	maple syrup	25 mL
1 cup	homemade chicken stock (page 57), or water	250 mL
½ tsp	salt	2 mL
¼ tsp	pepper	1 mL

1. Heat oil in large non-stick skillet. Add ginger and cook gently for a few minutes until very fragrant.

2. Add carrots and Brussels sprouts. Drizzle with maple syrup and turn to coat well.

3. Add chicken stock, salt and pepper. Bring to boil and cook, uncovered, until liquid evaporates and vegetables are glazed.

PER SERVING

Calories	95
g carbohydrate	18
g fibre	5
g total fat	2
g saturated fat	trace
g protein	3

Excellent: vitamin A; vitamin C
Good: vitamin B$_6$; folacin

mg cholesterol	0
mg sodium	254
mg potassium	431

Spicy Rice Pilaf

If you remove the ribs and seeds from jalapeños, they will be milder. For the full hit, just chop up the whole thing! Or, if you do not like spicy food, omit the jalapeño and cayenne entirely.

Makes 6 servings

1½ cups	long-grain rice	375 mL
1 tbsp	olive oil	15 mL
1	onion, chopped	1
2	cloves garlic, finely chopped	2
1	jalapeño, chopped	1
½ tsp	ground cumin	2 mL
pinch	cayenne	pinch
2½ cups	hot homemade chicken stock (page 57), or 1 10-oz/284 mL tin chicken broth plus water	625 mL
	Salt and pepper to taste	
¼ cup	chopped fresh cilantro or parsley	50 mL
¼ cup	chopped fresh chives or green onions	50 mL

1. Place rice in sieve and rinse under running water until water runs clear. Drain well.

2. Heat oil in large non-stick saucepan. Add onion, garlic and jalapeño. Cook on low heat until tender and fragrant, about 5 minutes. Add cumin and cayenne.

3. Add rice and stir well to coat with vegetables. Add hot chicken stock and bring to boil. Reduce heat, cover and cook gently for 30 to 40 minutes for brown rice and 15 to 20 minutes for white rice, or until rice is tender.

4. Season with salt and pepper. Gently stir in cilantro and chives.

Per Serving	
Calories	213
g carbohydrate	39
g fibre	1
g total fat	3
g saturated fat	1
g protein	6
mg cholesterol	1
mg sodium	17
mg potassium	181

BASMATI RICE PILAF WITH GARAM MASALA

Our family cottage near Kinmount, Ontario, is fairly isolated. That's why it was such a surprise to learn that Mitchell Davis, director of publications for The James Beard Foundation in New York, also has a family cottage nearby. At one dinner there, his sister Carrie (a caterer who is writing a book on desserts made with natural sugars) made a rice dish similar to this, and I've been making it ever since.

Makes 8 servings

2 cups	basmati or other fragrant rice	500 mL
1 tbsp	vegetable oil	15 mL
1	onion, chopped	1
1	clove garlic, finely chopped	1
1 tbsp	garam masala	15 mL
3 cups	hot homemade chicken stock (page 57), or 1 10-oz/284 mL tin chicken broth plus water	750 mL
	Salt to taste	

1. Place rice in sieve and rinse until water runs clear. Drain well.

2. Heat oil in large non-stick saucepan. Add onion and garlic and cook gently for a few minutes until fragrant but not brown. Stir in garam masala and cook for 30 seconds until very fragrant.

3. Add rice and cook for a few minutes, stirring constantly, until rice is well coated with onion mixture.

4. Add hot chicken stock and bring to boil. Cook, uncovered, for about 5 minutes. Cover and cook gently for 30 to 35 minutes for brown rice or 10 to 15 minutes for white rice. Allow rice to rest for 10 minutes before serving. Season with salt to taste.

GARAM MASALA

Garam masala is a spice mixture that can be purchased at any Indian food store. You can also make your own by blending together 1 tbsp/15 mL each ground cardamom, cinnamon and ground coriander, and 1 tsp/5 mL each ground cloves, black pepper and nutmeg.

PER SERVING

Calories	205
g carbohydrate	38
g fibre	1
g total fat	3
g saturated fat	trace
g protein	6
mg cholesterol	0
mg sodium	15
mg potassium	153

ISRAELI COUSCOUS WITH SQUASH AND PEPPERS

Israeli couscous is more like a pearl-shaped pasta than couscous. If it is not available, use regular rice-shaped pasta (orzo), plain rice or any tiny soup pasta.

Makes 6 to 8 servings

1 tbsp	olive oil	15 mL
1	onion, chopped	1
2	cloves garlic, finely chopped	2
1 tsp	ground cumin	5 mL
1½ cups	Israeli couscous (8 oz/250 g) or orzo	375 mL
2	sweet red peppers, seeded and diced	2
2 cups	diced butternut squash	500 mL
3 cups	hot homemade chicken stock (page 57), or 1 10-oz/284 mL tin chicken broth plus water	750 mL
	Salt and pepper to taste	
⅓ cup	chopped fresh cilantro or parsley	75 mL

1. Heat oil in large, deep non-stick skillet. Add onion and garlic. Cook on low heat until golden.

2. Add cumin and couscous. Brown lightly. Add red peppers and squash and mix together well.

3. Add hot chicken stock and bring to boil. Reduce heat, cover and simmer gently for 10 to 14 minutes until couscous is tender. Taste and season with salt and pepper if necessary. Sprinkle with cilantro before serving.

TOASTING CUMIN
Madhur Jaffrey taught us to toast cumin seeds before grinding them. Your first taste and smell will convince you that she is right. Place whole cumin seeds in a dry skillet and shake over medium-high heat until the colour changes slightly — about 2 minutes. Cool and grind in a spice grinder or with a mortar and pestle.

PER SERVING

Calories	237
g carbohydrate	42
g fibre	4
g total fat	4
g saturated fat	1
g protein	9

Excellent: vitamin C
Good: vitamin A; niacin

mg cholesterol	1
mg sodium	21
mg potassium	384

BARLEY AND WILD MUSHROOM RISOTTO

The texture of cooked barley is very much like risotto, so it lends itself easily to the traditional risotto cooking method. Although it takes 30 to 40 minutes for the barley to become tender, you do not have to stir it constantly as with traditional risotto.

This dish is very high in dietary fibre. It makes a great appetizer, side dish or meatless main course (use vegetable broth instead of chicken stock).

Makes 4 servings

1 oz	dried wild mushrooms	30 g
2 cups	warm water	500 mL
1 tbsp	olive oil	15 mL
1	onion, finely chopped	1
2	cloves garlic, finely chopped	2
1 cup	pearl barley	250 mL
1 cup	dry white wine or stock	250 mL
6 cups	hot homemade chicken stock (page 57), or 1 10-oz/284 mL tin chicken broth plus water	1.5 L
	Salt and pepper to taste	
½ cup	grated Parmesan cheese, optional	125 mL
2 tbsp	chopped fresh parsley	25 mL

1. Soak mushrooms in warm water for 30 minutes. Strain liquid through a few layers of paper towels and reserve. Rinse mushrooms in cold water and chop.

2. Heat oil in large non-stick saucepan. Add onion and garlic and cook gently until tender and fragrant. Add barley and coat well with onion mixture. Add mushrooms and combine.

3. Stirring constantly, add wine. Cook on medium heat until wine has evaporated or been absorbed by barley. Add mushroom liquid and cook, stirring occasionally, until it has been absorbed.

4. Start adding hot chicken stock 1 cup/250 mL at a time, stirring often, over medium heat. Do not add the next batch of liquid until barley is almost dry again. When barley is tender, after about 30 to 40 minutes, stop adding stock, whether it has all been used or not.

5. Add salt and pepper to taste. Stir in cheese and parsley and serve immediately.

PER SERVING

Calories	209
g carbohydrate	34
g fibre	6
g total fat	4
g saturated fat	1
g protein	8

Excellent: niacin
Good: iron

mg cholesterol	1
mg sodium	41
mg potassium	430

RISOTTO WITH RAPINI

Although risotto must be cooked just before serving, it is well worth the trouble. Cook it for guests you don't mind having in the kitchen while you finish the dish. Planning is also important when you are serving risotto — make sure there isn't anything else on the menu that you have to prepare at the last minute.

When the risotto is ready it should be a creamy mass, but each grain of rice should still be separate. Serve it right away on hot plates or directly from the pot or a heated serving bowl.

If you serve this as a vegetarian main course (make it with vegetable stock), it will make 4 to 6 servings.

RAPINI

Rapini is a broccoli/turnip green combination with a slightly bitter but interesting taste. Trim off the ends of the stems and use the rest of the stems, leaves and flowers.

Makes 8 servings

1 lb	rapini or broccoli, trimmed and chopped	500 g
1 tbsp	olive oil	15 mL
2	cloves garlic, finely chopped	2
1	onion, chopped	1
pinch	hot red pepper flakes	pinch
2 cups	short-grain rice, preferably Arborio	500 mL
6 cups	hot homemade chicken stock (page 57), or 1 10-oz/284 mL tin chicken broth plus water	1.5 L
	Salt and pepper to taste	
½ cup	grated Parmesan cheese, optional	125 mL

1. Bring large pot of water to boil. Add rapini and cook for 5 minutes. Drain well and reserve.

2. Heat oil in large non-stick saucepan. Add garlic, onion and red pepper flakes. Cook gently until garlic and onion are tender.

3. Add rice. Stir to coat well with onion mixture (dish can be made ahead up to this point).

4. Stir in rapini. Add hot chicken stock one ladleful at a time and cook over medium or medium-high heat, stirring almost constantly. Do not add next batch of stock until previous batch evaporates or is absorbed. This should take about 15 minutes. Stop cooking when rice is barely tender (you may or may not have to use all the stock).

5. Add salt and pepper and stir in cheese. Serve immediately.

PER SERVING

Calories	248
g carbohydrate	44
g fibre	2
g total fat	3
g saturated fat	1
g protein	9

Good: vitamin A; niacin

mg cholesterol	1
mg sodium	34
mg potassium	475

Lemon Polenta Waffles
(page 234)

Blueberry Bran Muffins *(page 246)*
Rhubarb Cinnamon Muffins *(page 247)*
Lemon Poppy Seed Muffins *(page 249)*
Mini Berry Cornmeal Muffins *(page 251)*

BREAKFASTS AND BRUNCHES

Breakfast Brûlée

Wild Rice Blueberry Pancakes

Buckwheat Crêpes with Caramelized Apples

Yogurt Cheese

Summer Crêpes with Berry Berry Salad

Breakfast Honey Bread

Lemon Polenta Waffles

Baked Potatoes with Tuna Salad and Lemon Mayonnaise

Pasta Frittata

Feta and Spinach Frittata Sandwiches

Chicken Burritos with Cooked Tomato Salsa

Grilled Chicken Sandwiches with Charmoula

Chilly Cappuccino

Fara's European Fruit Salad "Drink"

Tropical Smoothie

Yogurt Fruit Shake

BREAKFAST BRÛLÉE

If you love crème brûlée but know you should not be eating anything quite that rich anymore, try Baked Wild Rice Pudding Brûlée (page 266) or this breakfast version, which is sensational. You can serve it as a breakfast or brunch dish, but it also makes a great dessert.

You can place the custard dishes under the broiler, or use a blowtorch as professional chefs do.

Makes 6 servings

1½ cups	fresh raspberries or blueberries	375 mL
3 cups	yogurt cheese (page 229)	750 mL
⅔ cup	brown sugar	150 mL

1. Divide berries among 6 custard cups. Spread yogurt cheese evenly over berries.

2. Press brown sugar through sieve to get rid of any lumps. Sprinkle top of each custard cup with about 2 tbsp/25 mL sugar.

3. Place custard cups on baking sheet and broil for 1 to 2 minutes, watching carefully, until sugar melts and begins to brown (it burns very easily). Allow to rest for a few minutes until topping is firm, then serve immediately.

WILD RICE BLUEBERRY PANCAKES

These pancakes make an interesting brunch dish served as is or topped with thin slices of smoked salmon. (They can also be served as a side dish with lamb.) Make small or large pancakes, or use the batter in waffles (this recipe will make about 12 waffles; use about ⅓ cup/75 mL or ½ cup/125 mL batter per waffle, depending on your machine).

The wild rice should be well cooked for these pancakes. Serve them with fresh fruit and/or maple syrup. Brown rice or wehani rice could be used instead of wild rice.

Makes 6 8-inch/20 cm pancakes

2	eggs	2
1½ cups	buttermilk or low-fat yogurt	375 mL
2 tbsp	maple syrup	25 mL
½ cup	whole wheat flour	125 mL
½ cup	all-purpose flour	125 mL
1 tsp	baking soda	5 mL
1 tbsp	soft margarine, melted	15 mL
1 cup	cooked wild rice	250 mL
1 cup	fresh or frozen blueberries or cranberries, or ½ cup/125 mL dried cranberries or cherries	250 mL

1. In large bowl, beat together eggs, buttermilk and maple syrup.

2. In second bowl, stir together whole wheat flour, all-purpose flour and baking soda.

3. Stir flour mixture into egg mixture. Stir in melted margarine, rice and blueberries.

4. Heat 8-inch/20 cm non-stick pan. Brush with a little oil. Add about ¾ cup/175 mL batter to pan and swirl to cover bottom. Cook until surface loses its sheen. Flip and cook second side for 1 to 2 minutes. Keep warm while making remaining pancakes.

PER PANCAKE

Calories	195
g carbohydrate	32
g fibre	3
g total fat	5
g saturated fat	1
g protein	8

Good: riboflavin

mg cholesterol	74
mg sodium	309
mg potassium	225

BUCKWHEAT CRÊPES WITH CARAMELIZED APPLES

These crêpes are also terrific filled with a little grated Swiss cheese; bake them just until the cheese has melted.

Makes 8 servings

3	eggs	3
1¼ cups	milk	300 mL
¼ tsp	salt	1 mL
2 tbsp	granulated sugar	25 mL
½ cup	all-purpose flour	125 mL
½ cup	buckwheat flour or whole wheat flour	125 mL
1 tbsp	soft margarine, melted	15 mL

Caramelized Apples:

¾ cup	granulated sugar	175 mL
2 tbsp	cold water	25 mL
6	apples, peeled, cored and sliced	6
1 cup	apple juice	250 mL
2 tbsp	icing sugar, sifted	25 mL

1. In large bowl, beat together eggs and milk. Beat in salt, sugar, all-purpose flour, buckwheat flour and melted margarine. Cover tightly and let batter rest in refrigerator for at least 1 hour. (If batter is too thick, add a little water until it is the consistency of buttermilk.)

2. Meanwhile, to make apples, combine sugar and water in large, deep skillet. Stir together and bring to boil. Cook on medium-high heat, without stirring, until sugar turns golden. Carefully, standing back (as sugar is very hot), add apples. Cook for about 20 minutes. Mixture will at first be very sticky, but apples will start to lose their juices into the caramel and smooth it out. Add a little of the apple juice during cooking if apples stick or burn.

3. To make crêpes, heat 10-inch/25 cm non-stick pan and brush with oil. Add ladleful of batter and swirl around bottom of pan. Pour back into bowl any batter that does not stick.

PER SERVING

Calories	270
g carbohydrate	55
g fibre	3
g total fat	4
g saturated fat	1
g protein	6
mg cholesterol	82
mg sodium	136
mg potassium	271

4. Cook crêpe until browned, about 2 minutes. Flip and cook second side for 30 to 60 seconds. Remove to plate and cook remaining crêpes — you should have about 8 crêpes.

5. Add remaining apple juice to apples and bring to boil. Cook until juice evaporates a bit.

6. Remove apples from pan and divide among crêpes (leaving juices in pan). Roll up crêpes. Place crêpes back in pan with juices (add a little more juice if pan is dry). Cook until crêpes are hot and juice has been absorbed. Dust with icing sugar.

YOGURT CHEESE

Cooks in the Middle East have been making yogurt cheese for a thousand years, but it is still an exciting and delicious addition to a low-fat kitchen. It can be used in place of sour cream or cream cheese in dips and spreads, as a garnish for soups or baked potatoes, in place of mayonnaise in sandwiches or salad dressings, or it can be mixed with sugar, honey or maple syrup to top desserts.

Makes 1½ cups/375 mL

3 cups	unflavoured yogurt (low-fat or regular)	750 mL

1. Line strainer with cheesecloth (or paper towel or coffee filter). Place over bowl.

2. Place yogurt in strainer. Allow to rest for 3 hours or up to overnight in refrigerator. About half the volume of yogurt will strain out into the bowl as liquid. The longer the yogurt sits, the thicker it gets.

3. Discard liquid (or use for cooking rice or making bread). Spoon thickened yogurt cheese into another container. Cover and refrigerate. Use as required.

YOGURT CHEESE DIP

Combine 1½ cups/375 mL yogurt cheese, 2 minced cloves garlic, 3 tbsp/45 mL each chopped fresh cilantro, parsley and chives. Add ½ tsp/2 mL salt, ¼ tsp/1 mL pepper and dash hot red pepper sauce. (You can use either dill or basil in place of the cilantro.)

Makes about 1½ cups/375 mL

YOGURT CHEESE DESSERT TOPPING

Combine 1½ cups/375 mL yogurt cheese, 3 tbsp/45 mL brown sugar, icing sugar, honey or maple syrup. Stir in 1 tsp/5 mL vanilla or grated orange peel or ½ tsp/2 mL cinnamon.

Makes about 1½ cups/375 mL

PER TABLESPOON

Calories	15
g carbohydrate	1
g fibre	0
g total fat	trace
g saturated fat	trace
g protein	1
mg cholesterol	2
mg sodium	13
mg potassium	46

SUMMER CRÊPES WITH BERRY BERRY SALAD

These crêpes are delicious all year round, but they are especially wonderful made with summer berries. In the winter they can be filled with sliced bananas and yogurt cheese (page 229) or light sour cream. And at any time of year I love to eat the crêpes plain — drizzled with lemon juice, sprinkled with sugar and rolled up. The berry salad is also great on its own, over angel cake or sorbet.

Crêpes freeze well, but after freezing the texture changes, so they taste best when they are reheated in a sauce before serving.

Makes 6 servings

4	eggs	4
2 tbsp	granulated sugar	25 mL
½ tsp	vanilla	2 mL
1 cup	all-purpose flour	250 mL
1 cup	milk	250 mL
2 tsp	soft margarine, melted	10 mL

Berry Berry Salad:

4 cups	sliced fresh strawberries	1 L
1 cup	fresh blueberries	250 mL
1 cup	fresh raspberries	250 mL
1	10-oz/300 g package frozen raspberries, defrosted and drained	1
2 tbsp	granulated sugar	25 mL
2 tbsp	raspberry or orange liqueur, or raspberry or orange juice concentrate	25 mL
½ cup	yogurt cheese (page 229) or thick yogurt	125 mL
2 tbsp	brown sugar	25 mL
½ tsp	vanilla	2 mL
2 tbsp	sifted icing sugar	25 mL

PER 2 CRÊPES

Calories	360
g carbohydrate	63
g fibre	7
g total fat	6
g saturated fat	2
g protein	11

Excellent: vitamin C; riboflavin; folacin
Good: niacin; vitamin B$_{12}$; calcium; iron

mg cholesterol	147
mg sodium	102
mg potassium	479

1. In large bowl, whisk together eggs, sugar and vanilla. Add flour and whisk until smooth.

2. Whisk in milk and melted margarine. Mixture should be the consistency of buttermilk. Cover bowl with plastic wrap and refrigerate for 1 hour or up to overnight. Mixture should thicken a little.

3. To prepare berries, in large bowl, gently combine strawberries, blueberries and raspberries.

4. Puree frozen raspberries with granulated sugar and liqueur in food mill or in blender or food processor (strain through sieve if you wish to remove seeds). Gently combine with fresh berries.

5. In small bowl, combine yogurt cheese with brown sugar and vanilla.

6. To cook crêpes, brush 8-inch/20 cm or 9-inch/23 cm non-stick skillet with a little oil. Ladle about ½ cup/125 mL batter into skillet. Swirl it around and pour back into bowl any batter that doesn't cling to pan. (The longer batter stays in pan, the thicker crêpes will be.) Place pan on heat and cook crêpes until browned. Flip gently and cook second side for a few seconds (the first side will always look the best and should be the "showy" side).

7. Cook remaining crêpes (you should have about 12). As crêpes are ready, they can be stacked on top of each other.

8. To assemble, spoon about ½ cup/125 mL berries on each crêpe and roll up. Top with spoonful of yogurt cheese and dust with icing sugar.

COOKING CRÊPES

• Crêpes can be made ahead and frozen, although defrosted crêpes taste best if they are reheated in a sauce. Stack them as they are cooked, placing a piece of waxed paper between each one only if you will be using them one or two at a time.

• You can buy a special crêpe pan, but omelette pans also work well. Use a non-stick pan if you can.

• Place the filling on the second side of the crêpes, so that the nice side shows.

BREAKFAST HONEY BREAD

This is similar to challah, which is usually very rich, laden with eggs and sometimes butter or oil. This is a lower-fat version. You can also use the bread in French toast and bread puddings.

Makes 1 loaf (12 slices)

1 cup	warm water	250 mL
1 tbsp	granulated sugar	15 mL
1	package dry yeast	1
1	egg	1
¼ cup	honey	50 mL
¼ cup	vegetable oil	50 mL
1 tsp	salt	5 mL
4 cups	all-purpose flour (more if necessary)	1 L
½ cup	raisins or other chopped dried fruit, optional	125 mL

Glaze:

1	egg white	1
¼ tsp	salt	1 mL
1 tbsp	sesame seeds	15 mL

1. In small bowl, combine warm water and sugar. Sprinkle yeast over water and allow to rest for 10 minutes. Mixture should bubble up and double in volume.

2. Meanwhile, in separate bowl, combine egg, honey, oil and salt.

3. Place 3 cups/750 mL flour in large bowl.

4. When yeast mixture has doubled, stir it down and combine with egg mixture. Add egg mixture to flour and combine well. Dough should be very sticky. Add extra flour until dough comes together into ball and you are able to knead it (you should need between ½ cup/125 mL and 1½ cups/375 mL more flour). Do not add so much flour that dough is dry.

PER SLICE	
Calories	231
g carbohydrate	39
g fibre	1
g total fat	6
g saturated fat	1
g protein	6

Good: folacin

mg cholesterol	18
mg sodium	251
mg potassium	75

5. Place dough in oiled bowl, cover with oiled plastic wrap and put in warm place to rise for 1 hour. Dough should double in volume.

6. Punch dough down and knead in raisins. To shape dough into crown, roll into rope about 24 inches/60 cm long. Holding one end, wind rest of dough around it so you have fairly tight spiral that is higher in centre than at edges. Or braid loaf by dividing dough into three equal pieces. Roll each piece into rope about 12 inches/30 cm long, pinch ends together and braid.

7. Place round loaf on parchment paper-lined or oiled baking sheet. Cover loosely with oiled plastic wrap and allow to rise until doubled — about 45 minutes. (Place braided loaf in parchment paper-lined loaf pan and let rise for 50 to 60 minutes or until doubled.)

8. In small bowl, combine egg white and salt. Brush gently over bread. Sprinkle with sesame seeds. Bake in preheated 350°F/180°C oven for 25 minutes. Reduce heat to 325°F/160°C and bake for 25 minutes longer. The braided loaf can also be baked in a loaf pan for easier slicing.

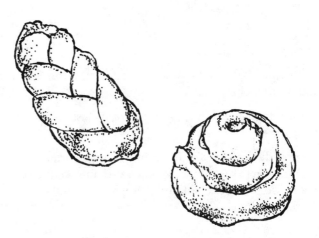

LEMON POLENTA WAFFLES

See photo opposite page 224.

Waffles are popular with adults and kids alike, and now you can buy waffle irons in many different shapes (hearts to squares) and sizes (deep or shallow).

Melissa Mertl, who works in my cookware shop, is a master of creative display and presentation. She loves the way these waffles look on a breakfast table.

If you do not have a waffle iron, simply make these as pancakes (the recipe will make about 32 3-inch/7.5 cm pancakes). Serve them with maple syrup or cinnamon sugar.

Makes 8 large waffles

3	eggs	3
1¼ cups	buttermilk or low-fat yogurt	300 mL
1 cup	all-purpose flour	250 mL
½ cup	cornmeal	125 mL
2 tbsp	granulated sugar	25 mL
1 tbsp	grated lemon peel	15 mL
1 tsp	baking soda	5 mL
1 tbsp	soft margarine, melted	15 mL

1. In bowl, whisk eggs with buttermilk.

2. In second bowl, combine flour, cornmeal, sugar, lemon peel and baking soda.

3. Stir dry ingredients into egg mixture. Whisk in melted margarine.

4. Heat waffle iron for about 5 minutes, or according to manufacturer's directions. Spoon batter into centre of hot grill and close. Cook for a couple of minutes, or until waffles are done.

PER WAFFLE	
Calories	157
g carbohydrate	24
g fibre	1
g total fat	4
g saturated fat	1
g protein	6
mg cholesterol	82
mg sodium	230
mg potassium	113

BAKED POTATOES WITH TUNA SALAD AND LEMON MAYONNAISE

This is a brunch version of the popular stuffed baked potato (see page 117 for a vegetarian version). Salmon salad could also be used.

Makes 4 servings

2	baking potatoes (½ lb/250 g each)	2
1	7-oz/198 g tin white tuna (water-packed), drained and flaked	1
1 cup	fresh or frozen corn niblets	250 mL
1	stalk celery, finely chopped	1
2	green onions, chopped	2

Lemon Mayonnaise:

2 tbsp	yogurt cheese (page 229) or thick yogurt	25 mL
1 tbsp	mayonnaise	15 mL
1 tbsp	lemon juice	15 mL
2 tbsp	chopped fresh dill, chives or parsley	25 mL

1. Prick potatoes and bake in preheated 400°F/200°C oven for 1 hour.

2. Meanwhile, in bowl, combine tuna, corn, celery and green onions.

3. In small bowl, combine yogurt cheese and mayonnaise with lemon juice. Add to tuna mixture and combine gently. Taste and adjust seasonings if necessary.

4. Cut cooked potatoes in half lengthwise. Fluff the potato and mound one-quarter of tuna mixture (about ½ cup/125 mL) on each. Sprinkle with dill.

PER SERVING

Calories	208
g carbohydrate	29
g fibre	3
g total fat	4
g saturated fat	1
g protein	14

Excellent: niacin; vitamin B_6; vitamin B_{12}
Good: folacin

mg cholesterol	19
mg sodium	196
mg potassium	589

PASTA FRITTATA

What a great dish to make with leftover pasta! This is so good, in fact, that you may cook extra pasta just to have the leftovers.

Makes 8 servings

2 tbsp	olive oil, divided	25 mL
1	small onion, finely chopped	1
1	clove garlic, finely chopped	1
½ cup	pureed plum tomatoes, or commercial or homemade tomato sauce	125 mL
2	eggs	2
6	egg whites	6
3 cups	cooked pasta (plain or with sauce)	750 mL
½ tsp	pepper	2 mL
2 tbsp	grated Parmesan cheese, optional	25 mL
2 tbsp	chopped fresh parsley	25 mL

1. Heat 1 tbsp/15 mL oil in large non-stick, ovenproof skillet. Add onion and garlic and cook gently until tender and fragrant, about 4 minutes. Add pureed tomatoes and heat.

2. In large bowl, beat together eggs and egg whites. Add onion mixture and blend in. Stir in pasta, breaking up any clumps with spoon. Stir in pepper (add ½ tsp/2 mL salt if pasta is plain).

3. Heat remaining 1 tbsp/15 mL oil in same skillet. Add egg/pasta mixture and cook on medium-high heat until bottom is brown and crusty. Occasionally lift edge so some of uncooked eggs can run under frittata.

4. Sprinkle top of frittata with cheese. Place under preheated broiler (about 10 inches/25 cm from element) and cook until eggs are set and top is brown. Serve in wedges from pan or slide frittata onto serving platter and then cut into wedges. (Flip every other wedge over for an interesting presentation.) Sprinkle with parsley before serving.

PER SERVING

Calories	143
g carbohydrate	17
g fibre	1
g total fat	5
g saturated fat	1
g protein	7
mg cholesterol	54
mg sodium	82
mg potassium	120

FETA AND SPINACH FRITTATA SANDWICHES

You can serve these individual frittatas alone with tomato sauce, or in the pita breads. You can also make the mixture into one large frittata if you wish. If your feta cheese is not very salty, you may want to add a little salt to the egg mixture before baking. The frittata can also be made with four extra egg whites instead of the two whole eggs.

Makes 6 servings

1 lb	fresh spinach, or 1 10–oz/300 g package frozen spinach, defrosted and well drained	500 g
2	eggs	2
10	egg whites	10
½ tsp	pepper	2 mL
½ tsp	nutmeg	2 mL
3 tbsp	chopped fresh dill	45 mL
2 oz	feta cheese, rinsed and crumbled	60 g
6	8-inch/20 cm pita breads	6
¾ cup	Cooked Salad (page 43), or commercial or homemade tomato sauce	175 mL

1. Trim spinach and wash well. Place in skillet just with water that is clinging to leaves. Cook, turning with tongs, until wilted. Squeeze gently. Chop coarsely. (Chop defrosted frozen spinach if you are using it.)

2. In large bowl, beat together eggs, egg whites, pepper, nutmeg and dill. Add spinach and feta and combine well.

3. Brush 8-inch/20 cm skillet with oil. Add about ½ cup/125 mL egg mixture and cook until bottom is set — about 4 or 5 minutes. Loosen eggs, slip onto plate and flip back into pan. When cooked, remove to plate and reserve. Repeat until you have 6 frittatas and all egg mixture has been used.

4. Open pita breads at top and place frittata in each one. Smear with a few spoonfuls of tomato sauce. Serve warm or at room temperature.

EGG WHITES

You can now find egg whites sold in cartons in the dairy case of some supermarkets and specialty stores. Because the whites are pasteurized, they can't be beaten until stiff (e.g., for use in meringues and angelfood cakes), but they can be used in frittatas, omelettes and many baked goods.

PER SERVING

Calories	399
g carbohydrate	65
g fibre	3
g total fat	6
g saturated fat	2
g protein	22

Excellent: vitamin A; vitamin C; thiamine; riboflavin; niacin; folacin; iron
Good: vitamin B$_6$; vitamin B$_{12}$; calcium

mg cholesterol	80
mg sodium	633
mg potassium	634

CHICKEN BURRITOS WITH COOKED TOMATO SALSA

I became friends with Linda Molitor when Paul was playing for the Blue Jays.

Linda loves good food and is very conscious about eating a healthful, low-fat diet. This is one of her favourite dishes. You can use 2 cups/500 mL commercial salsa, or make your own.

Makes 8 burritos

Cooked Tomato Salsa:

1 cup	canned plum tomatoes, drained and crushed	250 mL
2	fresh tomatoes, seeded and chopped (½ lb/250 g)	2
2	cloves garlic, minced	2
2	jalapeños, chopped	2
1	small onion, chopped (¼ cup/50 mL)	1
1	sweet red pepper, diced	1
2 tbsp	lime juice	25 mL
½ tsp	ground cumin	2 mL
⅓ cup	chopped fresh cilantro or parsley	75 mL
	Salt and pepper to taste	

Chicken Burritos:

¾ lb	boneless, skinless chicken breast, cut in 1-inch/2.5 cm strips	375 g
1 tsp	chili powder	5 mL
4	10-inch/25 cm flour tortillas	4
3 cups	shredded lettuce	750 mL
1 cup	grated light Monterey Jack cheese, optional	250 mL

TORTILLAS
Flour tortillas are now easy to find. They are used in quesadillas, fajitas and burritos. Corn tortillas are a little more difficult to find, but they are delicious for nachos, tacos, enchiladas and tortilla soup (page 68). Both types of tortillas freeze well, so keep plenty on hand.

PER BURRITO

Calories	161
g carbohydrate	22
g fibre	2
g total fat	3
g saturated fat	1
g protein	13

Excellent: vitamin C; niacin
Good: vitamin B$_6$

mg cholesterol	25
mg sodium	177
mg potassium	339

1. To prepare salsa, in bowl, combine canned tomatoes, fresh tomatoes, garlic, jalapeños, onion, sweet pepper, lime juice, cumin and cilantro. Taste and season with salt and pepper.

2. In bowl, toss chicken strips with chili powder.

3. Heat large non-stick skillet. Add chicken and cook for 1 to 2 minutes, just until chicken has lost its raw appearance. Add salsa, bring to boil and cook for a few minutes until chicken is cooked through.

4. Meanwhile, wrap tortillas in foil and heat for about 10 minutes in preheated 350°F/180°C oven. (Or heat, wrapped in napkin, in microwave for about 30 seconds on Medium-High.)

5. Divide chicken mixture among tortillas and top with lettuce and cheese. Fold up bottom and wrap up tightly. Serve 1 or 2 burritos per person.

HOT CHILES

Although chiles are often described as being mild, medium or hot, these terms are only guidelines. Some "mild" chiles can be very hot, and some hot chiles can be very mild. The heat varies according to where the chiles grow, how much sun or water they receive and where on the plant they are found. So be careful, and never fully trust a chile! In general, however, poblanos are mild, jalapeños and banana peppers are medium hot, serranos are slightly hotter, and Scotch bonnets and habañeros (sometimes called cascabels) are very, very hot.

Be careful when you handle chiles, as it is hard to tell exactly how hot they are before it is too late. If you have sensitive skin, wear plastic gloves and try not to touch your eyes, lips or any other sensitive parts of your body. There are many cures for "chile fingers," such as washing your hands in salt or soaking them in milk, but time and lots of washing will also work in the end.

Chiles will be milder if you remove the ribs and seeds, which are the hottest parts.

Grilled Chicken Sandwiches with Charmoula

See photo opposite page 193.

These days, every casual restaurant and bar offers a grilled chicken sandwich of some kind. Besides this one, another favourite is the one I concocted for the photo opposite page 193, made with cumin-grilled chicken (page 161), hummos, tomato salsa and grilled vegetables.

You can assemble the sandwiches before serving, or arrange the grilled vegetables in a shallow bowl and let guests serve themselves.

Makes 6 servings

6	boneless, skinless chicken breasts	6
2 tbsp	lemon juice	25 mL
½ tsp	ground cumin	2 mL
¼ tsp	pepper	1 mL
¼ tsp	salt	1 mL
1	clove garlic, minced	1
2	sweet red peppers, halved	2
1	large onion, sliced	1
¾ lb	eggplant, sliced	375 g
6	Kaiser rolls or sesame buns	6

Charmoula:

¼ cup	yogurt cheese (page 229) or thick yogurt	50 mL
1 tsp	ground cumin	5 mL
1 tsp	paprika	5 mL
1 tbsp	lemon juice	15 mL
pinch	cayenne	pinch
1	clove garlic, minced, or 1 head roasted garlic	1
2 tbsp	mayonnaise	25 mL
½ cup	chopped fresh cilantro or parsley	125 mL

LOWER-FAT SANDWICH SPREADS

- pesto (page 60)
- salsas
- yogurt cheese (page 229), plain or mixed with salsa or pesto
- salad dressings, such as Creamy Roasted Garlic Dressing (page 79)
- hummos (page 48)
- dips and spreads (pages 34 – 43)
- peanut sauce (page 54)
- pureed roasted red peppers (see box)
- chutney
- cranberry sauce (page 179)

PER SERVING

Calories	391
g carbohydrate	51
g fibre	4
g total fat	8
g saturated fat	1
g protein	29

Excellent: vitamin C; thiamine; niacin; vitamin B$_6$
Good: vitamin A; riboflavin; folacin; vitamin B$_{12}$; iron

mg cholesterol	60
mg sodium	574
mg potassium	583

1. Trim any fat from chicken. Remove tender filets (page 160) and reserve for chicken fingers or stir-fries. Pound chicken breasts between pieces of parchment or waxed paper until thin.

2. In small bowl, combine lemon juice, cumin, pepper, salt and garlic. Rub into chicken pieces and marinate in refrigerator until ready to cook.

3. Grill or broil peppers, skin side down, until black. Cool and remove skins. Cut peppers into strips. Grill onion and eggplant slices until cooked on both sides.

4. To prepare charmoula, in small bowl, whisk together yogurt cheese, cumin, paprika, lemon juice, cayenne, garlic and mayonnaise. Stir in cilantro.

5. Just before serving, grill chicken for 3 to 4 minutes per side, or just until cooked through.

6. To assemble sandwiches, place piece of chicken on bottom half of each bun. Top with grilled vegetables. Spread about 1 tbsp/15 mL charmoula on top half of buns.

ROASTING PEPPERS

Roasting and peeling peppers, while not necessary, gives the peppers an earthy, smoky taste. It also makes them much sweeter and easier to digest. There are many methods — you can roast the peppers whole, or cut them in half. I like to cut off the tops and bottoms of the peppers, cut through one side and remove the core, ribs and seeds, leaving the pepper in one long piece. The skin side of the pepper can then be grilled, broiled or roasted until black. When the peppers are cool enough to handle, the charred skins will slip right off, and the pepper can be cut up according to the recipe.

Red peppers can be expensive, so buy and roast lots when they are in season and then freeze them. Line a baking sheet with plastic wrap, foil or waxed paper and spread out the roasted peppers in a single layer (I leave them in large pieces). Freeze, then pack the peppers into freezer bags or containers. The pieces will stay separate, and you can defrost small amounts at a time.

CHILLY CAPPUCCINO

With fancy coffee shops opening up on every street corner, you could spend a lot of money on lattes, cappuccinos, espressos, machaccinos and frappaccinos. Here's a delicious coffee drink you can make on your own.

Makes 2 large drinks

¼ cup	hot espresso or very strong coffee	50 mL
¼ cup	corn syrup	50 mL
3 tbsp	cocoa	45 mL
¾ cup	milk	175 mL
2 cups	ice	500 mL
	Granulated sugar to taste	

1. Combine espresso, corn syrup and cocoa. Whisk together and place in blender.

2. Add milk and ice. Blend until drink is frothy and ice is well chopped. Add sugar to taste.

PER DRINK

Calories	184
g carbohydrate	39
g fibre	3
g total fat	3
g saturated fat	2
g protein	5

Good: iron

mg cholesterol	4
mg sodium	140
mg potassium	224

FARA'S EUROPEAN FRUIT SALAD "DRINK"

This is wonderful to serve as a cool summer snack, as it is a fruit salad and drink all in one. When my stepdaughter, Fara, was backpacking through Europe, she would see these drinks all lined up in the take-out shops with a spoon for eating and a straw for drinking. They looked so colourful and refreshing.

I like to serve these for brunch when guests first arrive. I serve them in wineglasses and often add a tiny bit of orange liqueur or rum.

SMOOTHIES

There are many ways to serve smoothies (page 244). If you use just a small amount of juice and serve them right away, they make great sorbets. If you add more juice, they are fabulous fruit shakes. They will have a creamy texture as long as you add bananas or mangoes.

Try these variations:
- **Jungle Madness:** half banana and half berries
- **Exotic Fantasy:** half mango, one-quarter kiwi and one-quarter raspberries
- **Purple Pleasure:** half banana and half blueberries

Makes 8 servings

¼	seedless watermelon, cut in 1-inch/2.5 cm chunks (4 cups/1 L)	¼
3	kiwi fruit, peeled and cut in chunks (1 cup/250 mL)	3
2 cups	quartered strawberries	500 mL
½	cantaloupe, cut in chunks (1½ cups/375 mL)	½
2 cups	lemon soda, lemonade or ginger ale	500 mL

1. Place watermelon, kiwi, strawberries and cantaloupe in large bowl and combine.

2. For each serving, fill a tall glass with fruit salad (about 1 cup/250 mL fruit). Add lemon soda to the top. Place a straw and fork in each glass and allow flavours to mingle for about 10 minutes in refrigerator. Serve cold.

PER SERVING

Calories	89
g carbohydrate	22
g fibre	2
g total fat	1
g saturated fat	0
g protein	1

Excellent: vitamin C

mg cholesterol	0
mg sodium	13
mg potassium	343

TROPICAL SMOOTHIE

You can serve this as a dessert or a drink. Served right out of the food processor or blender, it's a delicious dessert sorbet; served in a glass with a straw, it makes a refreshing cooler (add an extra ½ cup/125 mL juice if you are serving it as a drink right away).

Makes 2 large drinks or 4 dessert servings

1	banana	1
½ cup	sliced strawberries	125 mL
½ cup	cubed mango	125 mL
½ cup	orange juice	125 mL
1 tbsp	honey, or more to taste	15 mL
1 tbsp	lemon juice	15 mL

1. Cut up banana. Spread banana, strawberries and mango on baking sheet and place in freezer. Freeze until solid, about 2 hours.

2. Place frozen fruit in food processor or blender. Add orange juice, honey and lemon juice. Puree until smooth. Serve in dessert dishes with a spoon, or in a glass with a straw.

YOGURT FRUIT SHAKE

This makes a delicious quick breakfast if you are in a hurry. For a more leisurely breakfast or brunch, set up a fruit shake bar. Have all the ingredients in separate bowls and let guests make up their own concoction — any fruit combination can be used. Add sugar only if necessary.

Makes 2 servings

1	ripe banana	1
½ cup	halved strawberries	125 mL
½ cup	cubed mango	125 mL
½ cup	cubed pineapple	125 mL
½ cup	unflavoured yogurt, fruit juice or milk	125 mL
1 cup	ice	250 mL

1. Peel and break banana into blender. Add strawberries, mango, pineapple and yogurt and puree.

2. Add ice and blend until ice is very fine and drink is very frothy. Serve in tall glasses with straws.

BREADS

Blueberry Bran Muffins

Rhubarb Cinnamon Muffins

Apple Spice Muffins

Lemon Poppy Seed Muffins

Cappuccino Muffins

Mini Berry Cornmeal Muffins

Cheddar Sage Biscuits

Buttermilk Drop Biscuits

Prince Edward Island Dinner Rolls

Banana Bread

Beer Bread with Rosemary

Potato Sweet Rolls

Baked Boston Brown Bread

Smoky Cornbread with Corn and Peppers

Whole Wheat Focaccia

Grain and Seed Bread

BLUEBERRY BRAN MUFFINS

See photo opposite page 225.

My friend Evelyn Zabloski has the busiest coffee shop (Evelyn's Coffee Bar) in Banff. She bakes the most delicious homemade muffins, scones, cookies, pies and cakes. This recipe reminds me of the muffins she sells at her shop. They travel well for munching in the car or on the subway on the way to work.

If you are using frozen berries, add them to the batter while they are still frozen.

Makes 18 large muffins

2 cups	all-purpose flour	500 mL
1½ cups	wheat bran	375 mL
¾ cup	whole wheat flour	175 mL
¾ cup	brown sugar	175 mL
4 tsp	baking powder	20 mL
2 tsp	baking soda	10 mL
½ cup	molasses	125 mL
¼ cup	vegetable oil	50 mL
1	egg or 2 egg whites	1
2 cups	buttermilk or low-fat yogurt	500 mL
1½ cups	fresh or frozen blueberries	375 mL

1. In bowl, combine all-purpose flour, wheat bran, whole wheat flour, brown sugar, baking powder and baking soda. Mix together well.

2. In large bowl, combine molasses, oil, egg and buttermilk. Blend well.

3. Add dry ingredients to large bowl and stir into wet ingredients just until moistened. Quickly stir in berries.

4. Spoon batter into 18 large non-stick, lightly oiled or paper-lined muffin cups. Bake in preheated 375°F/190°C oven for 25 minutes.

BRAN

Wheat bran (insoluble fibre) encourages regularity, whereas oat bran (soluble fibre) helps to control blood sugar and blood cholesterol levels. You can always add a little wheat bran to bread and muffin recipes as it does not absorb much liquid; if you want to add oat bran to recipes, reduce the other dry ingredients (e.g., flour) to compensate.

I usually use natural wheat bran in muffins, but bran cereals work well, too.

PER MUFFIN

Calories	185
g carbohydrate	36
g fibre	4
g total fat	4
g saturated fat	1
g protein	4
mg cholesterol	13
mg sodium	225
mg potassium	266

See photo opposite page 225.

RHUBARB CINNAMON MUFFINS

I love the tart taste of rhubarb. For these muffins you can use frozen or fresh rhubarb (if you are using frozen, add it to the batter while it is still frozen).

Makes 12 large muffins

1½ cups	all-purpose flour	375 mL
1 cup	whole wheat flour	250 mL
1 tsp	baking powder	5 mL
1 tsp	baking soda	5 mL
pinch	salt	pinch
1	egg or 2 egg whites	1
1 cup	buttermilk or low-fat yogurt	250 mL
¾ cup	brown sugar	175 mL
¼ cup	soft margarine, melted	50 mL
1 tsp	vanilla	5 mL
2 cups	diced rhubarb	500 mL

Topping:

¼ cup	brown sugar	50 mL
½ tsp	cinnamon	2 mL
2 tbsp	finely chopped toasted pecans (page 193), optional	25 mL

1. In bowl, combine all-purpose flour, whole wheat flour, baking powder, baking soda and salt. Mix very well.

2. In large bowl, combine egg, buttermilk, brown sugar, melted margarine and vanilla. Beat together well.

3. Add dry ingredients to wet ingredients and combine just until moistened. Stir in rhubarb.

4. Scoop batter into 12 large non-stick, lightly oiled or paper-lined muffin cups.

5. In small bowl, combine brown sugar, cinnamon and nuts. Sprinkle on muffins. Bake in preheated 400°F/200°C oven for 20 to 25 minutes.

PER MUFFIN

Calories	213
g carbohydrate	39
g fibre	2
g total fat	5
g saturated fat	1
g protein	4
mg cholesterol	19
mg sodium	203
mg potassium	211

APPLE SPICE MUFFINS

These muffins contain a double hit of apples — grated fresh apples and apple juice.

Makes 12 muffins

1 cup	all-purpose flour	250 mL
1 cup	whole wheat flour	250 mL
½ cup	granulated sugar	125 mL
1 tbsp	baking powder	15 mL
1 tsp	cinnamon	5 mL
¼ tsp	nutmeg	1 mL
¼ tsp	cardamom	1 mL
¼ tsp	salt	1 mL
1	egg or 2 egg whites	1
1 cup	apple juice	250 mL
¼ cup	vegetable oil	50 mL
2	apples, unpeeled, seeded and grated (1 cup/250 mL)	2

Topping:

¼ cup	all-purpose flour	50 mL
¼ cup	brown sugar	50 mL
¼ tsp	cinnamon	1 mL
1 tbsp	soft margarine, cold, cut in bits	15 mL

1. In bowl, combine all-purpose flour, whole wheat flour, granulated sugar, baking powder, cinnamon, nutmeg, cardamom and salt. Mix well.

2. In large bowl, blend together egg, apple juice and oil.

3. Add dry ingredients to large bowl and stir just until combined. Do not overmix.

4. Stir in grated apples. Scoop batter into 12 medium non-stick, lightly oiled or paper-lined muffin cups.

5. To make topping, in small bowl, combine flour, brown sugar and cinnamon. Cut in margarine until crumbly. Sprinkle over top of muffins.

6. Bake in preheated 375°F/190°C oven for 25 to 30 minutes.

PER MUFFIN

Calories	211
g carbohydrate	36
g fibre	2
g total fat	6
g saturated fat	1
g protein	3
mg cholesterol	18
mg sodium	133
mg potassium	129

See photo opposite page 225.

LEMON POPPY SEED MUFFINS

This batter can also be baked in a 9 x 5-inch/2 L loaf pan for 45 to 50 minutes.

Makes 12 large muffins

2½ cups	all-purpose flour	625 mL
1 tbsp	baking powder	15 mL
¾ tsp	baking soda	4 mL
¼ tsp	salt	1 mL
¼ cup	vegetable oil	50 mL
½ cup	granulated sugar	125 mL
2	eggs	2
1½ cups	buttermilk or low-fat yogurt	375 mL
¼ cup	poppy seeds	50 mL
2 tbsp	grated lemon peel	25 mL

Syrup:

⅓ cup	lemon juice	75 mL
⅓ cup	granulated sugar	75 mL

1. In bowl, combine flour, baking powder, baking soda and salt. Mix well.

2. In large bowl, beat oil with sugar, eggs, buttermilk, poppy seeds and lemon peel.

3. Add dry ingredients to large bowl and combine just until moistened.

4. Spoon batter into 12 large non-stick, lightly oiled or paper-lined muffin cups. Bake in preheated 400°F/200°C oven for 20 to 25 minutes.

5. Meanwhile, in small saucepan, bring lemon juice and sugar to boil. Cool for a few minutes.

6. When muffins come out of oven, prick in a few places with toothpick. Spoon syrup over top and allow to soak into muffins. Cool and remove muffins from pan.

PER MUFFIN

Calories	232
g carbohydrate	37
g fibre	1
g total fat	7
g saturated fat	1
g protein	5
mg cholesterol	37
mg sodium	229
mg potassium	117

CAPPUCCINO MUFFINS

Here is your cup of java and your muffin rolled into one for a really quick breakfast! Use an ice-cream scoop to spoon the batter into the pans, for nicely rounded tops.

Makes 12 muffins

2 cups	all-purpose flour	500 mL
1 tbsp	baking powder	15 mL
½ tsp	baking soda	2 mL
2 tbsp	instant espresso powder	25 mL
½ tsp	cinnamon	2 mL
¼ tsp	salt	1 mL
1	egg or 2 egg whites	1
⅔ cup	granulated sugar	150 mL
¼ cup	vegetable oil	50 mL
1 cup	buttermilk or low-fat yogurt	250 mL

Topping:

⅓ cup	brown sugar	75 mL
1 tbsp	cocoa	15 mL
1 tsp	instant espresso powder	5 mL
¼ tsp	cinnamon	1 mL

1. In bowl, combine flour, baking powder, baking soda, espresso powder, cinnamon and salt. Mix well.

2. In large bowl, beat egg with granulated sugar, oil and buttermilk.

3. Add dry ingredients to large bowl and stir just until combined.

4. To make topping, in small bowl, combine brown sugar, cocoa, espresso powder and cinnamon.

5. Spoon half of batter into 12 medium non-stick, lightly oiled or paper-lined muffin cups. Sprinkle with half of topping mixture. Top with remaining batter and sprinkle with remaining topping.

6. Bake in preheated 375°F/190°C oven for 20 or 25 minutes.

PER MUFFIN	
Calories	201
g carbohydrate	35
g fibre	1
g total fat	5
g saturated fat	1
g protein	4
mg cholesterol	19
mg sodium	194
mg potassium	123

See photo opposite page 225.

MINI BERRY CORNMEAL MUFFINS

These muffins have great texture because of the slight crunch from the cornmeal, which also gives them a bright, sunny look. Instead of raspberries or blueberries (if you are using frozen berries, use them in the frozen state), you can use fresh or dried cranberries or cherries.

Makes 24 mini muffins or 12 medium muffins

1½ cups	all-purpose flour	375 mL
¾ cup	cornmeal	175 mL
½ cup	granulated sugar	125 mL
1 tbsp	grated lemon peel	15 mL
4 tsp	baking powder	20 mL
pinch	salt	pinch
1 cup	fresh or frozen raspberries or blueberries	250 mL
1 cup	milk	250 mL
2	egg whites, or 1 whole egg	2
1 tsp	vanilla	5 mL
¼ cup	vegetable oil	50 mL
2 tbsp	coarse sugar	25 mL

1. In bowl combine flour, cornmeal, granulated sugar, lemon peel, baking powder and salt. Combine 2 tbsp/25 mL of this mixture with berries in separate bowl.

2. In large bowl, combine milk, egg whites, vanilla and oil. Blend together well.

3. Add dry ingredients to large bowl and stir just until combined. Stir in berries very gently.

4. Spoon batter into non-stick, lightly oiled or paper-lined muffin cups. Sprinkle with coarse sugar. Bake in preheated 400°F/200°C oven for 15 to 25 minutes for mini muffins or 25 to 30 minutes for medium muffins, until lightly browned.

MUFFIN SHAPES

- bake muffins in tiny muffin pans; bake for half the time the recipe calls for, test, and bake longer if necessary

- bake muffin batter in a cake pan and then cut into bars; increase the cooking time slightly — bake until the top springs back when lightly pressed in the centre

- bake muffin batter in a loaf pan and cut into slices; bake for about one-third longer than the specified cooking time; test to see if it's ready

- bake muffin batter in a brioche or soufflé dish; bake for about 40 to 50 minutes or until done

PER MINI MUFFIN

Calories	94
g carbohydrate	16
g fibre	1
g total fat	3
g saturated fat	trace
g protein	2
mg cholesterol	0
mg sodium	53
mg potassium	44

CHEDDAR SAGE BISCUITS

See photo opposite page 65.

I never really liked sage until I started using it fresh; these delicate little biscuits showcase the herb perfectly!

Makes 12 biscuits

2 cups	all-purpose flour	500 mL
1 tbsp	baking powder	15 mL
1 tsp	salt	5 mL
3 tbsp	soft margarine, cold	45 mL
½ cup	grated old Cheddar cheese (2 oz/60 g)	125 mL
3 tbsp	chopped fresh sage	45 mL
1 cup	milk	250 mL

1. In large bowl, combine flour, baking powder and salt.

2. With pastry blender, cut margarine into flour until it is in tiny bits. Stir in cheese and sage.

3. Pour milk over flour mixture and stir in. Gather together with your hands to form dough. Turn out on floured board and pat to thickness of about ½ inch/1 cm. Cut into 2-inch/5 cm shapes.

4. Place biscuits on baking sheet. Bake in preheated 425°F/220°C oven for 12 to 14 minutes, or until lightly browned.

PER BISCUIT

Calories	130
g carbohydrate	17
g fibre	1
g total fat	5
g saturated fat	2
g protein	4
mg cholesterol	6
mg sodium	333
mg potassium	63

BUTTERMILK DROP BISCUITS

A rich version of these tender biscuits is served as table bread at a famous Los Angeles restaurant where many stars eat. But I am very near-sighted and even have trouble recognizing my friends, so I go for the biscuits, not the stars!

This versatile dough can also be used on cobblers (page 268), on shepherd's pie instead of mashed potatoes (page 186) or as a base for pizza.

Makes 10 biscuits

1½ cups	all-purpose flour	375 mL
¼ cup	granulated sugar	50 mL
1½ tsp	baking powder	7 mL
½ tsp	baking soda	2 mL
¼ tsp	salt	1 mL
3 tbsp	soft margarine, cold	45 mL
¼ cup	raisins or dried cherries	50 mL
¾ cup	buttermilk or low-fat yogurt	175 mL

1. In large bowl, combine flour, sugar, baking powder, baking soda and salt. Stir together very well.

2. With pastry cutter or finger tips, cut margarine into flour mixture until it is in tiny bits. Stir in raisins.

3. Pour buttermilk over flour mixture and stir until a rough batter is formed. Drop batter in 10 mounds on non-stick or parchment paper-lined baking sheet.

4. Bake in preheated 425°F/220°C oven for 12 to 18 minutes, or until lightly browned.

BUTTERMILK

Although buttermilk is thick and creamy, it is a low-fat dairy product. It tastes and smells wonderful in baked goods, pancakes and waffles. If you don't have it, use low-fat yogurt or make sour milk by placing 1 tbsp/15 mL lemon juice or vinegar in a measuring cup. Add milk until you have 1 cup/250 mL.

PER BISCUIT

Calories	138
g carbohydrate	24
g fibre	1
g total fat	4
g saturated fat	1
g protein	3
mg cholesterol	1
mg sodium	220
mg potassium	82

PRINCE EDWARD ISLAND DINNER ROLLS

These light, tender rolls seem to be served everywhere in Prince Edward Island. They are usually made with only white flour, but I like to use half whole wheat flour for a nuttier, more coarsely textured roll. In P.E.I. these are called dinner rolls, but don't stand on ceremony — they are great for breakfast and lunch, too.

Makes 12 rolls

1 tsp	granulated sugar	5 mL
¼ cup	warm water	50 mL
1	package dry yeast	1
1 cup	milk	250 mL
2 tbsp	vegetable oil	25 mL
3 tbsp	granulated sugar	45 mL
1½ tsp	salt	7 mL
1	egg	1
1½ cups	all-purpose flour (more or less as necessary)	375 mL
1½ cups	whole wheat flour	375 mL

1. In small bowl, dissolve 1 tsp/5 mL sugar in warm water. Sprinkle yeast over top. Allow mixture to rest for 10 minutes, or until yeast bubbles up and doubles in volume.

2. Meanwhile, combine milk, oil, 3 tbsp/45 mL sugar and salt in small saucepan and heat until just warm. Whisk in egg. Combine milk mixture with yeast.

3. In large bowl, combine 1 cup/250 mL all-purpose flour with whole wheat flour. Add yeast/milk mixture. Stir until sticky dough is formed. Add enough additional all-purpose flour, a little at a time, until dough is smooth and moist but not sticky.

4. Transfer dough to floured work surface. Knead for 10 minutes by hand, 5 minutes in heavy-duty mixer fitted with dough hook or 1 minute in food processor.

PER ROLL

Calories	158
g carbohydrate	28
g fibre	3
g total fat	3
g saturated fat	1
g protein	5
mg cholesterol	19
mg sodium	304
mg potassium	128

5. Place dough in lightly oiled bowl and turn to coat with oil. Cover with oiled plastic wrap. Set in warm place to rise for 1 to 2 hours, or until dough doubles in size.

6. Punch dough down and knead lightly. Divide into 12 pieces. Cut each piece in half and roll into balls.

7. Place 2 balls in each cup of non-stick or lightly oiled muffin pan. Cover loosely with oiled plastic wrap and set in warm place to rise for 30 to 45 minutes, or until double in size.

8. Bake in preheated 350°F/180°C oven for 20 minutes, or until puffed and golden brown. Remove from pan and cool on racks.

WORKING WITH YEAST

Yeast is a living organism, which is probably why many people are afraid to use it (after all, you could kill it!). But it is not difficult to work with. Just remember that yeast loves warm, cosy places — the water that it is dissolved in and the rising location should not be too hot or too cold.

The recipes in this book use dry yeast. Each package contains a scant tablespoon and should be enough for about 5 cups/1.25 L flour in a bread recipe.

I always "proof" yeast by dissolving it in a little warm sugared water to see if it is active. (The water should be between 110 and 120°F/43 to 50°C.) If the yeast does not bubble up, either the water was too hot, or the yeast is inactive. Do not use inactive yeast — if the yeast won't rise in the water, it won't rise in the bread.

BANANA BREAD

Here's a delicious lower-fat quickbread that can also be made as muffins. Spoon the batter into 12 muffin cups and bake for about 20 minutes.

You can use only whole wheat flour or only all-purpose flour in this recipe, but I prefer a mix of the two.

Makes 1 small loaf (12 slices)

1 cup	mashed very ripe bananas (2 medium)	250 mL
1 tsp	baking soda	5 mL
½ cup	low-fat yogurt	125 mL
¼ cup	vegetable oil	50 mL
¾ cup	brown sugar	175 mL
1	egg or 2 egg whites	1
1 tsp	vanilla	5 mL
1 cup	all-purpose flour	250 mL
½ cup	whole wheat flour	125 mL
1 tsp	baking powder	5 mL
pinch	salt	pinch

1. In small bowl, combine bananas, baking soda and yogurt. Allow to rest.

2. In separate bowl, combine oil, sugar, egg and vanilla. Blend together well.

3. In large bowl, combine all-purpose flour, whole wheat flour, baking powder and salt. Mix together well.

4. Combine banana mixture with oil mixture. Add to dry ingredients in large bowl and stir together just until moistened.

5. Spoon batter into non-stick, lightly oiled or parchment paper-lined 8 x 4-inch/1.5 L loaf pan. Bake in preheated 350°F/180°C oven for 50 to 60 minutes, or until loaf springs back when gently touched.

PER SLICE

Calories	178
g carbohydrate	30
g fibre	1
g total fat	5
g saturated fat	1
g protein	3
mg cholesterol	18
mg sodium	136
mg potassium	182

Dried Fruit Compote *(page 274)*
Crispy Chocolate Cookies *(page 282)*

Pavlova with Berries and Flowers
(page 275)

BEER BREAD WITH ROSEMARY

I am always amazed that quickbreads made with beer have such a yeasty aroma and taste. Use your favourite drinking beer in this recipe.

If you cannot find self-rising flour, just combine 3 cups/ 750 mL all-purpose flour with 1 tbsp/15 mL baking powder and 1½ tsp/7 mL salt.

Makes 1 small loaf (12 slices)

3 cups	self-rising flour	750 mL
3 tbsp	granulated sugar	45 mL
1 tbsp	chopped fresh rosemary or ½ tsp/2 mL dried	15 mL
1½ cups	beer (12-oz/341 mL bottle or can)	375 mL

Topping:

1 tsp	olive oil	5 mL
1 tsp	chopped fresh rosemary, or ¼ tsp/1 mL dried	5 mL
½ tsp	coarse salt	2 mL

1. In large bowl, combine flour, granulated sugar and rosemary. Stir in beer until batter is formed.

2. Transfer batter to non-stick, lightly oiled or parchment paper-lined 8 x 4-inch/1.5 L loaf pan.

3. Brush top of loaf with olive oil. Sprinkle with rosemary and salt.

4. Bake loaf in preheated 350°F/180°C oven for 75 to 90 minutes, or until firm when pressed gently in centre.

GARLIC BREAD

Cut baguette into 1-inch/ 2.5 cm slices (leave the bottoms of the slices attached). In small bowl, combine 2 tbsp/25 mL olive oil, 3 minced cloves garlic, ½ tsp/2 mL coarse salt, ¼ tsp/1 mL pepper and ½ tsp/2 mL dried rosemary. With pastry brush, brush seasoned oil on bread slices. Wrap bread in foil and bake in preheated 350°F/180°C oven for 15 minutes. Unwrap and bake for 5 minutes longer.

PER SLICE

Calories	133
g carbohydrate	27
g fibre	1
g total fat	1
g saturated fat	trace
g protein	3
mg cholesterol	0
mg sodium	495
mg potassium	47

POTATO SWEET ROLLS

Potatoes and potato water make a bread very moist and tender and the taste and aroma very yeasty. This recipe was developed by my good friend and colleague Linda Stephen, who teaches the bread-baking classes at my school. For an interesting mellow flavour, try adding 1 tsp/5 mL anise seeds, cumin seeds, caraway seeds or fennel seeds to the dry ingredients.

Makes 18 rolls

1 lb	baking potatoes (2 large)	500 g
1 tsp	granulated sugar	5 mL
2	packages dry yeast	2
2 tsp	salt	10 mL
2 tbsp	soft margarine, melted	25 mL
¼ cup	honey	50 mL
2	eggs	2
2 cups	all-purpose flour	500 mL
2 cups	whole wheat flour	500 mL

1. Peel potatoes and cut into large pieces. Place in saucepan and cover with water. Bring to boil, reduce heat and cook until tender.

2. Drain potatoes, reserving 1 cup/250 mL cooking liquid. Mash potatoes and reserve.

3. In small bowl, dissolve sugar in ½ cup/125 mL warm potato water. Sprinkle with yeast. Allow to rise for 10 minutes, or until doubled in volume.

4. In large bowl, stir salt and melted margarine into remaining ½ cup/125 mL warm potato liquid. Add honey, eggs and mashed potatoes. Blend until smooth. Add yeast mixture.

5. In separate bowl, combine flours. Add 2 cups/500 mL flour to liquid mixture and combine well. Dough should be very sticky. Add remaining flour (more if necessary) to form dough that is moist but not sticky. Knead dough for 10 minutes by hand, 5 minutes in heavy-duty mixer fitted with dough hook or 1 minute in food processor.

6. Place dough in oiled bowl. Turn until oiled on all sides. Cover bowl with oiled plastic wrap and allow to rise in warm spot for 1 hour, or until doubled in bulk.

PEAR BUTTER

Fruit butters make delicious fat-free spreads for toast, rolls or bagels.

Peel and core 8 large pears and cut into chunks (if you have a food mill you can strain out the cores and peel after cooking). Combine in large saucepan with ½ cup/125 mL pear juice and ¼ tsp/1 mL nutmeg or cinnamon. Bring to boil, reduce heat, cover and cook gently for 20 minutes. Uncover and cook until very thick (you should have 2 cups/500 mL). Puree.

Makes about 1½ cups/375 mL

PER ROLL

Calories	149
g carbohydrate	29
g fibre	3
g total fat	2
g saturated fat	trace
g protein	5

Good: folacin

mg cholesterol	24
mg sodium	282
mg potassium	159

7. Punch dough down. Divide into 18 pieces and roll each piece into ball. Arrange half the balls in lightly oiled 9-inch/23 cm springform pan or round baking pan. Repeat with remaining balls. Cover loosely with oiled plastic wrap and allow to rise for 40 to 60 minutes, or until doubled in bulk.

8. Bake in preheated 400°F/200°C oven for 25 to 30 minutes. Remove from pan and cool on racks.

BAKED BOSTON BROWN BREAD

This unusual recipe originated in Boston and is considered a traditional New England favourite. It is quite dense but very flavourful.

The bread is usually steamed for a few hours, but I bake it for more immediate gratification, and it comes out very nicely. You can also bake the batter in muffin pans for about 25 minutes.

Makes 10 to 12 slices

½ cup	whole wheat flour	125 mL
½ cup	rye flour	125 mL
½ cup	cornmeal	125 mL
1 tsp	baking soda	5 mL
½ tsp	salt, optional	2 mL
½ cup	molasses	125 mL
1 cup	milk	250 mL
½ cup	currants or raisins	125 mL

1. In large bowl, combine whole wheat flour, rye flour, cornmeal, baking soda and salt. Stir together well.

2. In small bowl, combine molasses and milk. Add wet ingredients to large bowl and stir just until combined. Stir in raisins.

3. Transfer batter to non-stick, lightly oiled or parchment paper-lined 8 x 4-inch/1.5 L loaf pan. Bake in preheated 350°F/180°C oven for 45 minutes.

PER SLICE

Calories	138
g carbohydrate	31
g fibre	2
g total fat	1
g saturated fat	trace
g protein	3
mg cholesterol	1
mg sodium	74
mg potassium	333

SMOKY CORNBREAD
WITH CORN AND PEPPERS

Grilled corn, roasted peppers and smoked cheese make this delicious bread extra-special. But it can easily be made with corn niblets, raw peppers and plain Cheddar if you prefer.

To barbecue the corn, shuck the cobs and place them directly on a hot grill. Keep turning them until they brown. To remove the niblets from the cob, break the cob in half, stand it on a cutting board (cut side down) and slice off the niblets from top to bottom (page 88).

Makes 12 servings

1½ cups	all-purpose flour	375 mL
1½ cups	cornmeal	375 mL
3 tbsp	granulated sugar	45 mL
1 tsp	salt	5 mL
1 tbsp	baking powder	15 mL
½ tsp	baking soda	2 mL
2	eggs	2
1¼ cups	buttermilk or low-fat yogurt	300 mL
3 tbsp	olive oil	45 mL
2	ears barbecued corn, niblets cut from cobs (1 cup/250 mL)	2
1	sweet red pepper, roasted (page 241), peeled and diced (½ cup/125 mL)	1
1 cup	grated smoked mozzarella or other smoked cheese	250 mL

1. In large bowl, combine flour, cornmeal, sugar, salt, baking powder and baking soda. Stir well.

2. In separate bowl, beat eggs with buttermilk and oil. Stir wet ingredients into flour mixture until just combined.

3. Gently stir in corn, peppers and cheese.

4. Spoon batter into lightly oiled 12 x 8-inch/3 L baking dish. Bake in preheated 375°F/190°C oven for 40 to 45 minutes, or until nicely browned and top springs back when pressed gently. Cool for 10 minutes before cutting into squares.

PER SERVING

Calories	233
g carbohydrate	34
g fibre	2
g total fat	7
g saturated fat	2
g protein	8
mg cholesterol	45
mg sodium	384
mg potassium	152

WHOLE WHEAT FOCACCIA

You can serve this as an appetizer or with a meal, or use it as a base for pizza.

Makes 8 servings

1 tsp	granulated sugar	5 mL
1 cup	warm water	250 mL
1	package dry yeast	1
1½ cups	all-purpose flour (more or less as necessary)	375 mL
1 cup	whole wheat flour	250 mL
½ tsp	salt	2 mL
3 tbsp	chopped black olives, well drained, optional	45 mL
1 tbsp	olive oil	15 mL
2 tbsp	chopped fresh rosemary, or 1 tsp/5 mL dried	25 mL
1 tsp	coarse salt	5 mL

1. In small bowl, dissolve sugar in ¾ cup/175 mL warm water. Sprinkle yeast over top and allow to rest for 10 minutes. Mixture should bubble up and double in volume.

2. Meanwhile, in large bowl, combine 1 cup/250 mL all-purpose flour, whole wheat flour and salt.

3. When yeast has bubbled up, stir it down and add remaining ¼ cup/50 mL warm water. Add yeast mixture to large bowl and mix into a dough. Add more flour until you have a dough that is soft but not sticky. Knead dough for 10 minutes by hand, 5 minutes in heavy-duty mixer fitted with dough hook or 1 minute in food processor.

4. Place dough in oiled bowl and turn to coat with oil all over. Cover with oiled plastic wrap and allow to rise in warm spot for about 1 hour. Dough should double in volume.

5. Punch dough down and knead in olives. Divide dough into two equal portions and form into balls. Roll each ball into 9-inch/23 cm circle.

6. Place circles on oiled baking sheet. Make lots of indentations in surface of dough with your fingers. Brush with olive oil and sprinkle with rosemary and coarse salt. Allow to rise for 5 to 10 minutes.

7. Bake on bottom shelf of preheated 425°F/220°C oven for 15 to 20 minutes, or until crust is crisp and brown.

PER SERVING

Calories	156
g carbohydrate	30
g fibre	3
g total fat	2
g saturated fat	trace
g protein	5

Good: folacin

mg cholesterol	0
mg sodium	433
mg potassium	107

GRAIN AND SEED BREAD

This bread freezes well and makes fabulous toast and sandwiches. The dough can be used to make rolls.

Makes 1 9x5 inch/2 L loaf (16 slices)

1 tsp	granulated sugar	5 mL
¼ cup	warm water	50 mL
1	package dry yeast	1
½ cup	cornmeal	125 mL
½ cup	rye or buckwheat flour	125 mL
1 cup	whole wheat flour	250 mL
2 cups	all-purpose flour (approx.)	500 mL
¼ cup	wheat bran	50 mL
1 tsp	salt	5 mL
1 cup	water	250 mL
2 tbsp	vegetable oil	25 mL
3 tbsp	honey	45 mL
1 tbsp	caraway seeds	15 mL
2 tbsp	sunflower seeds	25 mL

1. In small bowl, dissolve sugar in ¼ cup/50 mL warm water. Sprinkle yeast over top. Allow mixture to bubble up and double in volume, about 10 minutes.

2. In large bowl, mix together cornmeal, rye flour, whole wheat flour, 1 cup/250 mL all-purpose flour, bran and salt.

3. Stir down yeast mixture and combine with 1 cup/250 mL water, oil and honey. Stir liquid ingredients into flour mixture. Stir in caraway and sunflower seeds. Add additional all-purpose flour until you have a soft dough that is not sticky.

4. Knead dough for 10 minutes by hand, 5 minutes in heavy-duty mixer fitted with dough hook or 1 minute in food processor.

5. Place dough in lightly oiled bowl and turn until oiled all over. Cover with oiled plastic wrap and allow to rise in warm spot until doubled in bulk, about 1½ to 2 hours.

6. Punch dough down. Shape into loaf and place in non-stick, lightly oiled or parchment paper-lined loaf pan. Allow to rise until doubled again, about 1 hour.

7. Bake in preheated 400°F/200°C oven for 35 to 45 minutes. Remove from pan and cool on wire rack.

PER SLICE

Calories	150
g carbohydrate	28
g fibre	3
g total fat	3
g saturated fat	trace
g protein	4
mg cholesterol	0
mg sodium	145
mg potassium	121

DESSERTS

Apple Strudel

Baked Wild Rice Pudding Brûlée

Caramelized Fruit Crisp

Peach Cobbler

Fruit Salad with Marsala

Baked Apple Slices

Rosy Applesauce

Baked Alaska

Dried Fruit Compote

Pavlova with Berries and Flowers

Cinnamon Pear Cake with Caramel Coffee Sauce

Orange Polenta Cake with Mango and Orange Salad

Oatmeal Banana Cake

Gingerbread Angel Cake

Crispy Chocolate Cookies

Hermit Bar Cookies

Espresso Biscotti

APPLE STRUDEL

My husband loves apple desserts more than any other. I cannot make them often enough and can never make them as good as his memories of his mom's. But this one he adores.

If you like other fruits, try using 3 cups/750 mL each diced rhubarb and quartered strawberries (increase the sugar in the filling to ¾ cup/175 mL), instead of the apples.

This dessert freezes well baked or unbaked.

Makes 12 servings

6	apples (3 lb/1.5 kg)	6
½ cup	brown sugar	125 mL
½ tsp	cinnamon	2 mL
pinch	nutmeg	pinch
¼ cup	all-purpose flour	50 mL

Pastry:

¼ cup	dry breadcrumbs	50 mL
¼ cup	granulated sugar	50 mL
¼ cup	unsalted butter, melted, or vegetable oil	50 mL
¼ cup	water	50 mL
12	sheets phyllo pastry	12
1 tbsp	sifted icing sugar	15 mL

1. Peel, core and slice apples.

2. In large bowl, toss apples with brown sugar, cinnamon, nutmeg and flour. Reserve.

3. To assemble strudel, organize your work area and allow yourself as much counter space as possible. In shallow bowl, combine breadcrumbs and granulated sugar. In second bowl, combine butter and water. Have pastry brush at hand. Keep phyllo sheets covered with damp tea towel.

4. Place one sheet of phyllo on large baking sheet (this will be easier than having to transfer the strudel to the baking sheet once it has been rolled). Keep the rest of phyllo covered with tea towel. Brush single sheet of phyllo with butter/water mixture and sprinkle lightly with breadcrumb mixture. Top with 5 more sheets of phyllo, brushing and sprinkling each layer. Arrange half of apple mixture along one long end of pastry. Fold in about 1 inch/2.5 cm on both ends and gently roll up.

PER SERVING

Calories	212
g carbohydrate	41
g fibre	2
g total fat	5
g saturated fat	3
g protein	3
mg cholesterol	10
mg sodium	168
mg potassium	134

5. Repeat with remaining phyllo and filling on second baking sheet. Brush rolls with any remaining butter. Make 6 diagonal slashes through top layer of phyllo (so rolls will be easier to cut after they are baked).

6. Bake rolls in preheated 400°F/200°C oven for 15 minutes. Reduce heat to 350°F/180°C and bake for 40 minutes longer, or until apples are very tender.

7. Cool for at least 15 minutes before removing from baking sheets. With large spatula, gently transfer to serving board. Dust with icing sugar and cut into slices with sharp knife.

WORKING WITH PHYLLO PASTRY

- If your phyllo pastry is frozen, defrost it overnight in the refrigerator and allow the package to stand at room temperature for about 1 hour before using.

- Be organized. Have your fillings ready and all your equipment close at hand. Give yourself as much counter space as possible.

- Once you open the package, cover the phyllo that you are not using with a damp tea towel or a large piece of plastic wrap.

- Sprinkle breadcrumbs, sugar, ground nuts, etc., between the layers of phyllo for added texture and flavour.

- Use a large pastry brush to brush on the butter or oil.

- Extra pastry will keep in the refrigerator for a few weeks, or you can refreeze it if you wrap it well.

- Phyllo freezes beautifully, either baked or unbaked. Freeze small pastries in a single layer on a baking sheet lined with plastic wrap and then pack in bags when frozen.

- Mix some water with the butter so that it will go farther. You can also brush the pastry with egg white instead of butter or oil for an even lower-fat version.

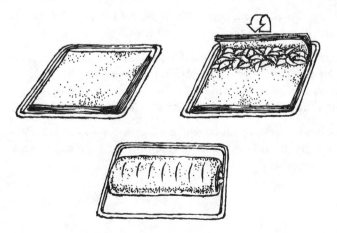

BAKED WILD RICE PUDDING BRÛLÉE

This is a combination of rice pudding and crème brûlée. Crème brûlée is a very popular dessert, but it is pretty rich. In this version, a creamy custard is made using rice as a thickener instead of egg yolks and cream. The result isn't the same, but spectacular nonetheless. This is also delicious without the "brûlée" — more like a traditional baked rice pudding.

Makes 8 servings

¾ cup	wild rice	175 mL
½ cup	short-grain rice	125 mL
½ cup	raisins, chopped dried apricots or dried cherries	125 mL
3	eggs	3
⅔ cup	granulated sugar	150 mL
2 tsp	vanilla	10 mL
pinch	cinnamon	pinch
pinch	nutmeg	pinch
2 cups	milk	500 mL
½ cup	brown sugar	125 mL

1. Bring large pot of water to boil. Add wild rice. Cook, uncovered, until very tender, about 1 hour. (The rice should be well cooked and out of its shell.) Drain.

2. Meanwhile, bring another pot of water to boil. Add short-grain rice and cook until tender, about 15 minutes. Add raisins and cook for 5 minutes longer. Drain.

3. In large bowl, whisk eggs with sugar. Add vanilla, cinnamon, nutmeg and milk. Stir in rices and fruit.

4. Pour mixture into lightly oiled 9-inch/2.5 L square baking dish. Bake in water bath (see sidebar) in preheated 350°F/180°C oven for 1 hour, or until custard is just set. Cool if desired (pudding can be served warm or very cold).

5. Just before serving, sift brown sugar over top of custard. Pat down gently and evenly. Broil carefully just until sugar melts and turns slightly golden.

BAIN MARIE

A water bath, or bain marie, acts like a double boiler but is used in the oven. It keeps the cooking temperature even for softer, creamier custards. I put a roasting pan filled with about 2 inches/5 cm water in the oven while it is preheating, then lower the pan of custard into it to bake. The water should be very hot by then and should come about halfway up the sides of the custard pan.

PER SERVING

Calories	301
g carbohydrate	63
g fibre	1
g total fat	3
g saturated fat	1
g protein	8

Good: riboflavin

mg cholesterol	83
mg sodium	61
mg potassium	305

CARAMELIZED FRUIT CRISP

The caramel adds another layer of flavour to this favourite dessert. Serve it with sorbet or yogurt cheese (page 229).

Makes 12 servings

½ cup	granulated sugar	125 mL
3 tbsp	cold water	45 mL
4	pears, peeled, cored and cut in large pieces	4
4	apples, peeled, cored and cut in large pieces	4
½ cup	dried apricots, cut in half	125 mL
⅓ cup	dried cherries	75 mL
¼ cup	thinly sliced candied ginger	50 mL

Topping:

1 cup	all-purpose flour	250 mL
⅔ cup	brown sugar or maple sugar	150 mL
1 tsp	cinnamon	5 mL
⅓ cup	soft margarine, cold, cut in bits	75 mL
½ cup	rolled oats	125 mL

1. Place sugar in large, deep non-stick skillet. Stir in cold water. Heat on medium-high until sugar dissolves. Stop stirring and cook until sugar turns a golden caramel colour, about 5 to 10 minutes. Do not allow mixture to burn.

2. Add pears, apples, apricots, cherries and ginger to skillet all at once. Stir just until coated with caramel. Heat gently for 1 minute.

3. Place fruit in 13 x 9-inch/3.5 L lightly oiled casserole or baking dish.

4. For topping, in large bowl, combine flour, brown sugar and cinnamon. Cut in margarine until it is in tiny bits. Stir in rolled oats.

5. Sprinkle topping over fruit. Bake in preheated 375°F/190°C oven for 45 to 60 minutes, or until fruit is very tender.

BROWN SUGAR AND MAPLE SUGAR

Although many people think that brown sugar is healthier than white sugar, brown sugar is simply white sugar with molasses added. Keep it in an airtight container. If it becomes hard, place a piece of apple or bread in the closed container overnight, and the sugar will soften.

Maple sugar can also be used in place of brown sugar; it will add a delicious flavour to your baked goods, although it can be hard to find (farmers' markets are a good source) and it is often quite expensive.

PER SERVING

Calories	268
g carbohydrate	55
g fibre	3
g total fat	6
g saturated fat	1
g protein	2

Good: iron

mg cholesterol	0
mg sodium	75
mg potassium	390

PEACH COBBLER

If it isn't peach season, use apples or pears. This dessert is also good made with fresh berries and plums. Serve it with sweetened yogurt cheese (page 229) if you wish.

Makes 8 servings

8	peaches, sliced	8
½ cup	granulated sugar	125 mL
3 tbsp	all-purpose flour	45 mL
½ tsp	cinnamon	2 mL

Topping:

1½ cups	all-purpose flour	375 mL
¾ cup	whole wheat flour	175 mL
⅓ cup	granulated sugar	75 mL
2 tsp	baking powder	10 mL
¾ tsp	baking soda	4 mL
pinch	salt	pinch
pinch	nutmeg	pinch
⅓ cup	soft margarine, cold, cut in bits	75 mL
1 cup	buttermilk *plus* 2 tbsp/25 mL	250 mL
2 tbsp	coarse sugar	25 mL

1. In large bowl, combine peaches with granulated sugar. Allow to sit for 15 minutes. Toss with flour and cinnamon. Spread over bottom of 12 x 8-inch/3 L baking dish.

2. To make topping, in large bowl, combine all-purpose flour, whole wheat flour, sugar, baking powder, baking soda, salt and nutmeg. Cut margarine into flour mixture until it is in very small pieces and mixture looks like fresh breadcrumbs. Drizzle 1 cup/250 mL buttermilk over top and gather dough together into ball. (If mixture doesn't come together, add a little more buttermilk.)

3. Gently pat out dough to thickness of ½ inch/1 cm and cut out 2-inch/5 cm circles. Arrange circles, overlapping, over peaches. Press scraps of dough together to create more circles (do not knead or work dough too much).

4. Brush topping with remaining 2 tbsp/25 mL buttermilk and sprinkle with coarse sugar. Bake at 375°F/190°C for 45 to 50 minutes until peaches are juicy and cooked and top has browned nicely.

PER SERVING

Calories	346
g carbohydrate	64
g fibre	3
g total fat	8
g saturated fat	1
g protein	6

Good: niacin

mg cholesterol	1
mg sodium	313
mg potassium	287

FRUIT SALAD WITH MARSALA

This simple salad is very refreshing and easy to prepare.

Makes 8 servings

¼ cup	apricot jam	50 mL
¼ cup	Marsala or orange juice	50 mL
2	pears, cored and cut in wedges	2
2	apples, cored and cut in wedges	2
2	oranges, peeled and segmented (see diagram)	2
2	grapefruit, peeled and segmented	2
1	small melon, seeded and cut in small wedges or balls	1
1 cup	seedless grapes	250 mL

1. In large bowl, whisk jam with Marsala until smooth.

2. Add pears, apples, oranges, grapefruit, melon and grapes, along with any juices collected from cutting fruit. Combine gently but well. Serve chilled.

MARSALA

Marsala is quite sweet, but when you are cooking with it, use the driest one you can find. It is a fortified wine that keeps well for a month or two after opening. You can use other sweet wines in its place, such as Vin Santo, ice wine (if you can afford it!), Madeira, port or a liqueur.

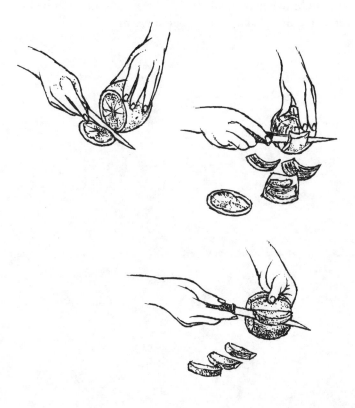

PER SERVING

Calories	150
g carbohydrate	36
g fibre	4
g total fat	1
g saturated fat	0
g protein	2

Excellent: vitamin C
Good: vitamin A

mg cholesterol	0
mg sodium	7
mg potassium	442

BAKED APPLE SLICES

I once ate something called "apple fries." They were deep-fried and very good. I decided to try making them the same way I cook oven-roasted potato fries (page 217), and they turned out even better than the fried version!

These are great as a snack or dessert. Serve them with yogurt cheese (page 229) or fruit sorbet. You can also serve them as a side dish with savoury foods such as pork or roast chicken.

Makes about 48 pieces

4	apples	4
⅓ cup	all-purpose flour	75 mL
⅓ cup	granulated sugar	75 mL
1½ tsp	cinnamon	7 mL

1. Peel, halve and core apples. Cut each half into 6 wedges.

2. In large bowl, combine flour, sugar and cinammon. Mix together well. Add apples and toss.

3. Spread apples in single layer on non-stick or parchment paper-lined baking sheet.

4. Bake in preheated 450°F/230°C oven for 15 to 20 minutes, or until browned and tender. Cool for a few minutes before removing from baking sheet. Serve warm.

APPLES

Everyone has a favourite variety of eating apple. But when you cook, you want an apple with a strong apple taste (rather than simply tart) that keeps its shape when baked. McIntosh, which are great for eating, turn into mush when they are cooked, whereas Golden Delicious, which are not my favourite for eating (because they lack crispness), are great for cooking. I also like to cook with Spy, Empire, Ida Red, Cortland and Royal Gala apples.

PER PIECE

Calories	15
g carbohydrate	4
g fibre	trace
g total fat	0
g saturated fat	0
g protein	trace
mg cholesterol	0
mg sodium	0
mg potassium	12

ROSY APPLESAUCE

The secret to making rosy-coloured applesauce is to leave the skins on the apples while they are cooking. To remove the skins, puree the sauce in a food mill (see diagram), or just puree the sauce in a food processor and don't worry about the little bits of peel. Or you can simply peel the apples first for a more traditionally coloured applesauce. You can also add about 1 tbsp/15 mL hot cinnamon candy hearts to the sauce while it cooks, for a really rosy colour. For apple butter, continue cooking until sauce is thick enough to spread.

Makes 8 servings

8	red apples	8
1 tsp	cinnamon	5 mL
½ cup	granulated sugar or maple sugar (page 267)	125 mL
½ cup	apple juice	125 mL

1. Cut apples in half and remove cores. Cut into chunks but do not peel.

2. Place apples in large saucepan and add cinnamon, sugar and juice. Bring to boil and reduce heat. Stirring occasionally, cook gently for about 30 minutes, uncovered, until apples are very tender and mixture is thick.

3. Puree sauce in food mill to remove skins. Serve warm or cold.

FOOD MILL

The old-fashioned food mill is one of my favourite pieces of kitchen equipment — it's the original food processor. I use it when I want to strain and puree at the same time (tomato sauce, applesauce or pureeing raspberries), or for mashing potatoes without overprocessing.

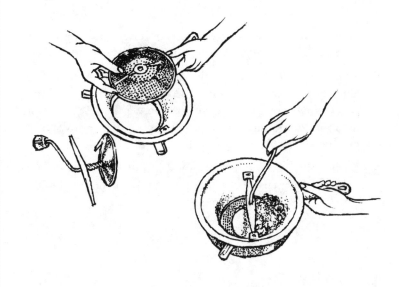

BAKED ALASKA

This old-fashioned dessert is making a big comeback (it always seemed like a miracle to me that you could put ice cream in the oven and the meringue would seal it so it wouldn't melt). It is still a real show-stopper, and this version is very low in fat.

There are all sorts of ways to make Baked Alaska. You can use different cake bases, different flavours of ice cream or sorbets and different meringue designs and shapes.

Makes 12 servings

Cake:

2	eggs	2
2	egg whites	2
½ cup	granulated sugar	125 mL
1 tsp	vanilla	5 mL
½ cup	all-purpose flour	125 mL
1 tsp	grated orange peel	5 mL

Filling:

2 cups	raspberry or mango sorbet	500 mL

Meringue:

6	egg whites	6
½ tsp	cream of tartar	2 mL
1½ cups	granulated sugar	375 mL
1 tsp	vanilla	5 mL

1. To make cake, with electric mixer, beat eggs and egg whites with sugar until very light — about 5 minutes. Add vanilla.

2. Sift flour over eggs and gently fold in, along with orange peel. Spread over bottom of 9-inch/23 cm non-stick or parchment paper-lined cake pan. Bake in preheated 350°F/180°C oven for 15 to 20 minutes, or until brown and spongy. Invert cake on rack and cool.

3. Meanwhile, soften sorbet just until spreadable. Spread over bottom of 8-inch/20 cm cake pan that has been lined with plastic wrap or foil. Freeze until firm.

PER SERVING	
Calories	210
g carbohydrate	47
g fibre	1
g total fat	1
g saturated fat	trace
g protein	4
mg cholesterol	36
mg sodium	48
mg potassium	108

4. Place cooled cake on piece of cardboard cut just to fit and place on baking sheet. Unmould sorbet onto cake and freeze until ready to coat with meringue.

5. To make meringue, just before assembling, beat egg whites with cream of tartar until opaque and light. Gradually beat in sugar and continue to beat until stiff. Beat in vanilla.

6. Pipe or spoon meringue over entire cake right down to cardboard to completely enclose sorbet. Freeze until ready to serve.

7. Just before serving, bake frozen cake in preheated 500°F/260°C oven for 2 to 3 minutes, or until nicely browned. Place cake on serving platter and serve immediately.

WORKING WITH EGG WHITES

In many recipes, egg whites are essential for making a dish light and airy. Try these tips to achieve the best results:

• Make sure your bowl and utensils are completely clean and grease free (a little oil or egg yolk in the bowl will stop the whites from beating to their greatest volume).

• Use a copper bowl if you have one (be sure to clean it out with salt and vinegar before using), but if not, simply use a stainless-steel or glass bowl and, before beating, add ¼ tsp/1 mL cream of tartar for every 4 egg whites.

• Do not add sugar to the egg whites until they have been beaten enough to become opaque; add the sugar very gradually.

• Use a balloon whisk to beat in the most air.

• Do not overbeat egg whites. They should be light and fluffy (you should be able to turn the bowl upside down without the whites falling out).

• When you are folding beaten egg whites into a heavier mixture, always stir in about one-quarter of the egg whites into the base first, to lighten it. Then gently fold in the remaining whites. It doesn't matter whether you fold the whites into the base or the base into the whites; just use the larger bowl.

DRIED FRUIT COMPOTE

See photo opposite page 256.

This can be served on its own or with yogurt cheese (page 229). It can also be served on top of plain cakes, in meringue or phyllo cups (pages 275 and 52), rolled in crêpes or as a base for a crisp or cobbler. The flavours are spicy and rich, and all kinds of dried fruits can be used.

Makes about 2 cups/500 mL

1 cup	prunes	250 mL
1 cup	dried apricots	250 mL
¼ cup	dried cherries	50 mL
¼ cup	chopped candied ginger	50 mL
1 cup	Marsala or orange juice	250 mL
¼ cup	lemon juice	50 mL
½ cup	maple syrup, honey or brown sugar	125 mL
1 cup	water	250 mL

1. Place prunes, apricots, cherries, ginger, Marsala, lemon juice, maple syrup and water in saucepan.

2. Bring to boil. Reduce heat and simmer gently for 10 to 15 minutes, or until fruit is tender. Serve warm or cold.

PER ½ CUP (125 mL)

Calories	375
g carbohydrate	90
g fibre	9
g total fat	trace
g saturated fat	0
g protein	3

Excellent: iron
Good: vitamin A; vitamin B$_6$

mg cholesterol	0
mg sodium	28
mg potassium	1273

See photo opposite page 257.

PAVLOVA WITH BERRIES AND FLOWERS

This dessert is too beautiful to believe, and it is low in fat. The trick to making a great pavlova is beating the egg whites properly (page 273), adding vinegar to the meringue at the last moment and baking it just to the point where the meringue is crunchy on the outside and marshmallowy on the inside.

If berries are not in season, try using mangoes, oranges, kiwi, bananas or caramelized apples or pears (page 228).

You can make individual pavlovas or shape the meringue into baskets and bake them until they are cooked through and firm. You can also use softened frozen yogurt or sorbet as a topping instead of yogurt cheese, but be sure to serve the dessert right away!

EDIBLE FLOWERS

If you can find them, edible flowers make a wonderful garnish for salads, soups and desserts. You can grow your own or buy them at an organic market (make sure they are pesticide-free). There are many varieties of edible flowers, including roses, nasturtiums, daisies, marigolds, impatiens, chive flowers, squash blossoms and pansies.

Makes 8 servings

4	egg whites	4
1 cup	granulated sugar	250 mL
2 tsp	white vinegar	10 mL
1½ cups	yogurt cheese (page 229)	375 mL
2 tbsp	honey or icing sugar	25 mL
1 tsp	vanilla	5 mL
4 cups	fresh berries	1 L
	fresh edible flowers (see sidebar)	

1. In large bowl, beat egg whites until light.

2. Gradually add sugar to egg whites and beat until firm. Beat in vinegar.

3. Outline 12-inch/30 cm circle on piece of parchment paper and place on baking sheet. Spoon egg whites inside circle shape and spread in loose waves. Bake in preheated 275°F/140°C oven for 2 hours. Remove from oven and cool. Freeze if not using immediately.

4. Meanwhile, in small bowl, combine yogurt cheese, honey and vanilla.

5. Just before serving, spread yogurt mixture over meringue. Top with berries and scatter flowers over top. Serve immediately.

PER SERVING

Calories	189
g carbohydrate	39
g fibre	2
g total fat	2
g saturated fat	1
g protein	7

Excellent: vitamin C
Good: riboflavin; vitamin B$_{12}$

mg cholesterol	5
mg sodium	68
mg potassium	291

Cinnamon Pear Cake with Caramel Coffee Sauce

This is a delicious coffee cake-style dessert that can be served with or without the sauce.

Makes 12 servings

1 cup	all-purpose flour	250 mL
½ cup	whole wheat flour	125 mL
1 tsp	baking soda	5 mL
2 tsp	cinnamon	10 mL
¼ tsp	nutmeg	1 mL
¼ tsp	cardamom	1 mL
⅓ cup	soft margarine	75 mL
1 cup	granulated sugar	250 mL
2	eggs	2
1 tsp	vanilla	5 mL
3	pears (preferably Bartlett), peeled, seeded and diced	3

Caramel Coffee Sauce:

1 cup	granulated sugar	250 mL
¼ cup	cold water	50 mL
¾ cup	coffee	175 mL

1. In bowl, combine flours, baking soda, cinnamon, nutmeg and cardamom.

2. In separate large bowl, cream margarine until light. Beat in sugar gradually. Add eggs, beating batter well after each addition. Add vanilla.

3. Stir dry ingredients into large bowl of batter, mixing just until combined. Quickly stir in pears.

4. Transfer batter to oiled 9-inch/2.5 L square baking dish. Bake in preheated 350°F/180°C oven for 40 to 45 minutes, or until cake comes away from sides of pan and centre springs back when lightly pressed. Cool for at least 15 minutes before serving.

PEARS

Pears really don't have much flavour unless they are ripe, but they are one of the few fruits that ripen after picking. I like to cook with Bartlett or Bosc pears the best.

PER SERVING

Calories	263
g carbohydrate	51
g fibre	2
g total fat	6
g saturated fat	1
g protein	3
mg cholesterol	36
mg sodium	177
mg potassium	96

5. Meanwhile, to make sauce, combine sugar and cold water in saucepan. Bring to boil, stirring, until sugar dissolves. Brush down any sugar crystals clinging to sides of pan with pastry brush dipped in cold water. Stop stirring but watch carefully. Allow sugar to boil and bubble until it turns golden, about 5 minutes.

6. Remove pan from heat. Stand back and carefully add coffee. Stir to combine. If mixture seems lumpy, return to heat until it melts down — a minute or two.

7. Serve cake with sauce drizzled over top.

COOKING WITH WINES AND LIQUEURS

I usually keep wine, brandy, dark rum and an orange liqueur on hand to use in cooking. The orange liqueur can be used when any fruit liqueur is called for.

Brandy, rum and liqueurs do not have to be refrigerated after opening, but wines will oxidize and go off quickly once they have been opened. Keep opened bottles in the refrigerator and use them up within a day or two or, if you plan to use the wine only for flavouring savoury dishes, pour a spoonful of olive oil into the bottle. The oil floats on the surface and blocks off the air, and the wine should keep, refrigerated, for a month or two.

You can also use non-alcoholic substitutes for wines and liqueurs, although the result will not be exactly the same as the original recipe.

- white wine: substitute chicken stock or vegetable juice in savoury dishes and light-coloured fruit juices (apple, orange or pineapple) in desserts

- red wine: substitute beef stock or tomato juice in savoury dishes and red fruit juices in desserts

- Marsala, Madeira or Port: substitute stock or vegetable juice in savoury recipes and fruit juice concentrates in dessert recipes

- fruit liqueurs: substitute fruit juice concentrate, citrus peel or vanilla

- brandy or rum: substitute fruit juice concentrates or concentrated stocks in savoury recipes and fruit purees or concentrated juices in desserts

Orange Polenta Cake with Mango and Orange Salad

This is a light, lovely cake that is moistened with the oranges, mango and juices (allow the juices to soak in like a trifle). The oranges and mangoes are also great served on their own, or they can be used as a topping for mango ice cream in meringue cups (page 275) or phyllo cups (page 52).

This cake can also be served with Dried Fruit Compote (page 274).

Makes 8 to 10 servings

1	egg	1
⅓ cup	soft margarine, melted	75 mL
½ cup	low-fat yogurt	125 mL
2 tbsp	orange juice concentrate	25 mL
1 tbsp	grated orange peel	15 mL
1 cup	cornmeal	250 mL
½ cup	all-purpose flour	125 mL
1½ tsp	baking powder	7 mL
1 cup	granulated sugar, divided	250 mL
4	egg whites	4

Mango and Orange Salad:

2	mangoes	2
4	oranges	4
½ cup	granulated sugar	125 mL
2 tbsp	cold water	25 mL
¼ cup	orange juice	50 mL

1. Lightly brush 9-inch/23 cm springform pan with oil and line bottom with round of parchment paper.

2. In large bowl, beat egg with melted margarine, yogurt, orange juice concentrate and orange peel.

3. In separate bowl, combine cornmeal, flour, baking powder and ½ cup/125 mL sugar.

4. In third bowl, beat egg whites until opaque and starting to froth. Beating constantly, slowly add remaining sugar. Beat until firm.

RASPBERRY SAUCE
Serve this with cakes, meringues, sorbet or ice cream.

Thaw two 10-oz/300 g packages frozen raspberries and drain, reserving juices. Puree with 2 tbsp/25 mL granulated sugar. Strain out seeds if you wish. Stir in 2 tbsp/25 mL orange or raspberry liqueur (or 1 tbsp/15 mL frozen orange juice concentrate) and enough reserved juice to make a sauce. (If you use sweetened frozen berries, omit the sugar and/or add a little lemon juice.)

Makes about 2 cups/500 mL

5. Add cornmeal mixture to yogurt mixture and combine. Fold in egg whites.

6. Spoon batter into prepared pan. Bake in preheated 350°F/180°C oven for 40 minutes, or until centre springs back when pressed gently. Cool on rack and then remove from pan.

7. Meanwhile, to prepare salad, cut mangoes and place in large bowl. Peel oranges and cut out segments (page 269).

8. Place sugar and cold water in medium saucepan. Bring to boil, stirring, until sugar dissolves. Stop stirring and brush down any sugar crystals on sides of pan with pastry brush dipped in cold water. Continue to cook, without stirring, until sugar is golden.

9. Remove sugar from heat and, standing back, add orange juice. Return to heat, stirring until smooth — about 1 minute. Cool.

10. Combine caramel mixture with oranges and mangoes. Serve cake with fruit and syrup on top.

PREPARING MANGOES

If you can, buy the yellow Alfonso mangoes, as they are sweeter and less fibrous than other varieties. To cut the mango, hold it upright on a cutting board. Cut right beside the pit to remove the largest oval-sized piece without cutting the pit. Do the same on the other side. Hold the oval in your hand and cut in a grid pattern without going through the skin (or your hand!). Pull the skin away from the fruit and cut it off. Remove as much fruit as possible from the pit (there isn't that much, but it is worth removing).

OATMEAL BANANA CAKE

This cake is delicious on its own, or you can make a glaze by combining icing sugar with just enough lemon juice to form a mixture that can be drizzled over each serving. You could also serve this with Dried Fruit Compote (page 274) or fruit salad.

Makes 12 servings

1 cup	rolled oats	250 mL
1¼ cups	boiling water	300 mL
¼ cup	soft margarine	50 mL
¾ cup	brown sugar	175 mL
⅓ cup	granulated sugar	75 mL
1 tsp	vanilla	5 mL
2	eggs	2
1	ripe banana, mashed	1
¾ cup	whole wheat flour	175 mL
¾ cup	all-purpose flour	175 mL
1 tsp	baking soda	5 mL
¾ tsp	cinnamon	4 mL
¼ tsp	nutmeg	1 mL

1. In bowl, combine rolled oats with boiling water. Allow to soften for 20 minutes. Reserve.

2. In large bowl, cream margarine with brown and white sugars until light. Add vanilla and eggs and beat well. Stir in mashed banana.

3. In separate bowl, combine whole wheat and all-purpose flours, baking soda, cinnamon and nutmeg.

4. Stir rolled oats into margarine mixture. Stir in flour mixture just until combined.

5. Transfer batter to oiled 12 x 8-inch/2.5 L baking pan and bake in preheated 350°F/180°C oven for 45 minutes, or until centre springs back when lightly touched.

PER SERVING

Calories	209
g carbohydrate	37
g fibre	2
g total fat	5
g saturated fat	1
g protein	4
mg cholesterol	36
mg sodium	165
mg potassium	160

GINGERBREAD ANGEL CAKE

Gingerbread spices taste especially wonderful in this angel food cake. It is light and delicate. If you prefer, omit the cinnamon, ginger and allspice for a plain cake.

You can serve the cake on its own, with a berry sauce or mixed berries, with fruit purees, fruit sorbets or with a light chocolate sauce. Or slice it into three layers, slather with sweetened yogurt cheese (page 229) and sprinkle with berries or edible flowers. This is also delicious served with fresh orange slices. Peel eight oranges, slice and toss with 2 tbsp/25 mL orange liqueur and 2 tbsp/25 mL orange marmalade.

Makes 12 servings

1½ cups	granulated sugar, divided	375 mL
1 cup	cake and pastry flour	250 mL
1 tsp	cinnamon	5 mL
1 tsp	ground ginger	5 mL
¼ tsp	allspice	1 mL
2 cups	egg whites (about 16)	500 mL
1 tsp	vanilla	5 mL
1 tsp	grated orange peel	5 mL

1. In bowl, sift ¾ cup/175 mL sugar with flour, cinammon, ginger and allspice.

2. With electric mixer, beat egg whites on medium speed until frothy. Turn speed to medium-high and continue to beat until opaque and light. Slowly add remaining ¾ cup/175 mL sugar, beating constantly. Add vanilla and orange peel.

3. Gently fold flour mixture into egg whites in three additions. Do not overfold, as you do not want to deflate the whites.

4. Very gently spoon batter into ungreased 10-inch/3 L tube pan. Bake in preheated 375°F/190°C oven for 35 to 45 minutes, or until cake tester comes out clean and dry and top of cake springs back when lightly touched.

5. Turn pan upside down onto rack so air can circulate and allow cake to cool. To remove cake from pan, use a long, thin knife to loosen sides. Use spatula or knife to loosen bottom (if pan has removable bottom, remove sides and then loosen bottom with knife).

GINGERBREAD ANGEL CAKE ROULADE

Spread batter over bottom of 17 x 11-inch/45 x 29 cm jelly roll pan lined with parchment paper. Bake in preheated 350°F/180°C oven for about 25 minutes. When cool, run knife around edges of cake. Sprinkle cake with icing sugar and invert onto clean tea towel. Remove pan and paper and trim edges of cake. Spread with sweetened yogurt cheese (page 229) and fresh berries and gently roll up cake lengthwise, using tea towel as guide.

PER SERVING

Calories	151
g carbohydrate	33
g fibre	trace
g total fat	trace
g saturated fat	0
g protein	5
mg cholesterol	0
mg sodium	67
mg potassium	72

CRISPY CHOCOLATE COOKIES

See photo opposite page 256.

My cousin Barbara Glickman has good taste in everything, including these cookies that she shared with me.

Makes 30 cookies

1 cup	rolled oats	250 mL
⅔ cup	all-purpose flour	150 mL
⅔ cup	granulated sugar	150 mL
⅓ cup	cocoa, sifted	75 mL
1 tsp	baking powder	5 mL
pinch	salt	pinch
2	egg whites	2
⅓ cup	corn syrup	75 mL
1 tsp	vanilla	5 mL
1 cup	crispy rice cereal	250 mL

1. In large bowl, combine oats, flour, sugar, cocoa, baking powder and salt. Stir together well.

2. In small bowl, whisk together egg whites, corn syrup and vanilla.

3. Add egg white mixture to large bowl and combine. Dough should be very stiff. Knead in cereal.

4. Drop batter by spoonfuls onto non-stick or parchment paper-lined baking sheet. Bake in preheated 350°F/180°C oven for 9 to 11 minutes.

COCOA

Cocoa has a deep, rich chocolate flavour but contains very little fat. It can be used in place of chocolate in some circumstances.

PER COOKIE

Calories	56
g carbohydrate	12
g fibre	1
g total fat	trace
g saturated fat	trace
g protein	1
mg cholesterol	0
mg sodium	32
mg potassium	24

HERMIT BAR COOKIES

Hermits are old-fashioned cookies that are chewy and gingery in flavour.

Makes about 36 squares

1 cup	all-purpose flour	250 mL
1 cup	whole wheat flour	250 mL
¾ tsp	baking powder	4 mL
¾ tsp	baking soda	4 mL
¾ tsp	cinnamon	4 mL
½ tsp	ground ginger	2 mL
½ tsp	nutmeg	2 mL
pinch	ground cloves	pinch
1	egg	1
1	egg white	1
¾ cup	brown sugar	175 mL
3 tbsp	molasses	45 mL
⅓ cup	vegetable oil	75 mL
½ cup	raisins	125 mL
¼ cup	chopped candied ginger	50 mL

1. In bowl, mix together flours, baking powder, baking soda, cinnamon, ground ginger, nutmeg and cloves.

2. In large bowl, beat egg and egg white with sugar, molasses and vegetable oil.

3. Add dry ingredients to egg mixture and combine thoroughly. Add raisins and candied ginger.

4. Pat batter into lightly oiled or parchment paper-lined 15 x 10-inch/40 x 25 cm baking sheet. Bake in preheated 375°F/190°C oven for 15 minutes, or until cooked through but not hard. Cut into squares while warm and cool on racks.

BAKING COOKIES
If your cookies tend to burn, try using two baking sheets at once. Place one on top of another the same size, for added insulation. Or, you can buy insulated cookie sheets.

PER SQUARE

Calories	78
g carbohydrate	14
g fibre	1
g total fat	2
g saturated fat	trace
g protein	1
mg cholesterol	6
mg sodium	36
mg potassium	108

ESPRESSO BISCOTTI

Biscotti — twice-baked cookies — are rather hard, dry Italian treats that are meant to be dipped into coffee, tea or Vin Santo so that they soften slightly. This recipe is a variation of one given to me by Nick Malgieri, one of New York's leading baking and dessert instructors, who teaches at my school each year.

Makes about 60 cookies

2 cups	all-purpose flour	500 mL
⅔ cup	granulated sugar	150 mL
1 tbsp	instant espresso powder	15 mL
½ cup	finely ground almonds	125 mL
½ tsp	baking powder	2 mL
½ tsp	baking soda	2 mL
½ tsp	cinnamon	2 mL
½ cup	whole unblanched almonds	125 mL
⅓ cup	honey	75 mL
⅓ cup	strong coffee, hot	75 mL

Dipping Sugar:

¼ cup	granulated sugar	50 mL
½ tsp	cinnamon	2 mL

1. In large bowl, combine flour, sugar, espresso powder, ground almonds, baking powder, baking soda and cinnamon. Stir together well.

2. Stir in whole almonds.

3. In small bowl, combine honey and coffee. Stir into flour mixture until stiff dough forms.

4. Divide dough in half. Shape each half into log about 15 inches/40 cm long.

5. Place logs at least 2 inches/5 cm apart on non-stick or parchment paper-lined baking sheet. Bake in preheated 350°F/180°C oven for 30 minutes, or until well risen, firm and golden. Be sure to bake them fully.

6. Cool logs for about 15 minutes and place on cutting board. Cut on diagonal into ½-inch/1 cm slices.

7. On plate, combine sugar and cinnamon. Dip each cookie into cinnamon sugar. Return cookies to pan, cut side down, and bake for 15 minutes longer, until dry and lightly coloured.

ORANGE HAZELNUT BISCOTTI
Omit espresso powder and chocolate. Add 1 tbsp/15 mL grated orange peel. Use orange juice instead of coffee. Use toasted whole and ground hazelnuts instead of the almonds.

PER COOKIE

Calories	45
g carbohydrate	8
g fibre	trace
g total fat	1
g saturated fat	trace
g protein	1
mg cholesterol	0
mg sodium	12
mg potassium	25

APPENDICES

FAT AND CHOLESTEROL

The average Canadian is getting about 38% of his or her calories from fat. Canada's Guidelines for Healthy Eating recommends that we reduce our fat intake to 30% or less of the day's calories. That means the average women should cut about 20 grams of fat from her diet every day and the average man should cut about 30 grams.

A recommended fat intake for the day should be:

    Man: 90 grams of fat or less
                (based on 30% of 3000 calories)

    Woman: 65 grams of fat or less
                (based on 30% of 2150 calories)

In a healthy diet, high-fat foods should be used sparingly and the recipes in *More HeartSmart Cooking with Bonnie Stern* reflect the thinking that to reduce fat you do not have to sacrifice taste.

In terms of what you are eating each day, research indicates that it is the excess fat (especially saturated fat) and not dietary cholesterol that has the greatest impact on your blood cholesterol levels. As blood cholesterol levels go up, the chances of having a heart attack or stroke also go up. Therefore, it is important to reduce your total fat intake, especially saturated fat.

HOW TO CALCULATE THE % OF CALORIES FROM FAT

- 1 gram of fat has 9 calories
- multiply the # of grams of fat by 9 and divide by the total number of calories in the food and then multiply by 100

      example: Baked Alaska (page 272) has 1 g of fat
                and 210 calories

                1 g fat x 9 cal/gm = 9

                divide by 210
                (total number of calories in one serving)

                = .04 x 100 = 4% of calories from fat

It is important to remember that the recommendation for 30% of calories from fat refers to your total diet and not on individual foods. Some foods will naturally be higher in fat and others lower.

FAT AND CHOLESTEROL VALUES

Below is a listing of ingredients that are commonly used in recipes — in your own and in this book. Lower-fat alternatives are given to assist you in selecting specific ingredients to lower the fat content in your favorite recipes.

Here are some common ingredients that may be of interest to you in terms of total fat, saturated fat and cholesterol contents:

Food	Total Fat (g)	Saturated Fat (g)	Cholesterol (g)
1 whole egg	5.0	1.5	214
2 egg whites	0	0	0
chicken breast, skinless (3½ oz/100 g raw)	1.2	0.3	58
lean, ground chicken (17% fat/3½ oz/100 g)	17	4.9	75
turkey breast, skinless (3½ oz/100 g raw)	1.6	.5	60
lean, ground turkey (17% fat/3½ oz/100 g)	17.1	4.6	71
1% milk (1 cup/250 mL)	2.6	1.6	10
2% milk (1 cup/250 mL)	4.7	2.9	18
buttermilk (1 cup/ 250 mL)	2.1	1.3	9
plain yogurt, 1.55% M.F. (1 cup/250 mL)	3.8	2.4	15
drained, plain yogurt (1.55% M.F. (1 cup/250 mL)	6.5	4.3	25
dry, unsalted, skim milk cottage cheese (1 cup/250 mL)	0.9	0.6	15
light ricotta cheese (1 cup/250 mL)	12.3	7.6	76
cottage cheese, 2% M.F. (1 cup/250 mL)	4.4	2.8	19
cottage cheese, 1% M.F. (1 cup/250 mL)	2.6	1.6	11
cheddar cheese (1 oz/30 g)	9.5	6	30
light cheddar cheese (1 oz/30 g)	5.4	3.7	18
partly skimmed mozzarella cheese (1 oz/30 g)	4.9	3.1	15
goat cheese, 22% M.F. (1 oz/30 g)	6.3	2.3	19
feta cheese, crumbled (2 tbsp/25 mL)	3.3	2.3	14
parmesan cheese, grated (1 tbsp/15 mL)	1.9	1.2	5

FAT SUBSTITUTES

As the population strives to reduce its fat intake, food manufacturers will try to reduce the fat in their foods. Sometimes they may be using a fake fat that is low in fat and possibly calories. The number of these products will increase with technological advances and consumer demand. Currently there are still many questions concerning the longterm safety of these products and they should be used with caution.

BLOOD CHOLESTEROL

When blood cholesterol is too high it settles on the inside walls of blood vessels. As it builds up, blood vessels become clogged and the blood can't flow properly to the heart and brain. When this happens, the chances of having a heart attack or stroke are greatly increased.

GOOD AND BAD BLOOD CHOLESTEROL

Cholesterol travels through the blood with other fats and protein. These are called lipoproteins. There are two key kinds of lipoproteins:

- Low Density Lipoprotein cholesterol (LDL-cholesterol), often called bad cholesterol, is linked to heart disease and stroke.
- High Density Lipoprotein (HDL- cholesterol) is a good form of cholesterol. HDL cholesterol is good for heart health.

TESTING BLOOD CHOLESTEROL

Blood tests can measure LDL-cholesterol, HDL-cholesterol and total cholesterol. The levels listed below are linked to a greater risk of heart disease and stroke.

- Total cholesterol greater than 6.2 mmol/L
- LDL-cholesterol greater than 4.14 mmol/L
- HDL-cholesterol less than 0.9 mmol/L

SODIUM

Salt and sodium are often used interchangeably, but actually they are not the same thing. Sodium is 40% of salt by weight ($\frac{1}{4}$ tsp/ 1 mL salt contains 575 mg sodium)

Although most Canadians can benefit from a reduced sodium intake, it is of particular importance to anyone who has high blood pressure and/or heart disease and stroke. Throughout *More HeartSmart Cooking* attempts were made to offer alternative ingredients to limit the intake of sodium. However, in some cases, as with the homemade chicken broth versus the canned, condensed chicken broth, there is a significant increase in the sodium values of the per serving content if the canned version is used. Although it is much more convenient to use canned broth, whenever possible, try to use **homemade chicken broth** in the recipes that call for it. If you use the alternative canned, condensed chicken broth in any of the recipes calling for it, don't add **"salt to taste"** as stated in the recipe since it will already be salty enough.

Here are some tips to help you reduce the salt and sodium that you are eating:
• limit the "salt to taste" in cooking or avoid it altogether
• avoid convenience foods such as dried and canned soups and mixes, TV dinners, casserole mixes and meat and poultry coating mixes
• limit highly salted snack foods such as potato chips, cheesies and salted nuts
• watch out for salt-preserved foods such as smoked, salted, cured or corned products like bacon, ham, smoked meats and fish, corned meats, and pepperoni-like luncheon meats
• use fresh or fresh frozen products whenever possible
• experiment with other spices and flavoring instead of the ones that contain "salt" like onion salt, garlic salt, celery salt, etc.

Be creative and experiment — you'll be amazed what great tastes you can get without using salt!

POTASSIUM
Sodium and potassium are two minerals that go hand-in-hand due to their functions within the body

Potassium is of particular importance to individuals who are taking diuretic medication for high blood pressure (hypertension). Some diuretics, if they are used over an extended period of time, cause a loss of potassium and others may, in contrast, cause an increase in potassium levels. Both of these side effects should be monitored by your physician if you are taking diuretics. As well, many people who are monitoring their sodium intakes use salt substitutes to flavour their meals — salt substitutes often contain potassium. Consult your physician before using a salt substitute.

* portion sizes are based on
Canada's Food Guide to
Healthy Eating, current
market units and
consumption practices.

Here are some food sources of potassium*:

Fruits:

apricots	orange juice
bananas	grapefruit juice
cantaloupe	raisins
nectarines	rhubarb
honeydew melons	kiwi
oranges	papaya
mangoes	

Vegetables:

artichoke	pumpkin
bamboo shoots	potato
beet greens	sweet potato
brussel sprouts	spinach
chard	winter squash
dried peas and beans	tomato
mushrooms	tomato juice
parsnips	

Other:

nuts	molasses
milk	wheat germ

GARLIC

By now, you may have heard that garlic has a vast and varied list of possible (potential) health benefits that have been attributed to consuming high amounts of this member of the onion family. Promoters of garlic (supplements) make countless health claims of how garlic can benefit you, but the main areas of interest in terms of heart disease and stroke are the claims suggesting that garlic can lower cholesterol and blood pressure. Unfortunately, after review of the studies that determined these findings, they have been found to be seriously flawed and thus, the results are inconclusive.

Currently there is no conclusive evidence to substantiate the health claims for the use of garlic; however, there is also no evidence that garlic can hurt you. So, go ahead and enjoy the robust and delicious flavour that garlic adds to many foods and recipes — Bonnie Stern offers a multitude of recipes within this book that do just that!

IRON

Iron is a mineral that your body needs to keep it working at its best. Iron is an important part of your blood because it carries the oxygen throughout the body which is needed for energy and it is also needed to make red blood cells.

Lately, there have been conflicting reports in the media regarding a possible link between high levels of stored iron and coronary artery disease (CAD) which is a form of heart disease. While there are some people who are predisposed to having high iron levels, for the majority of the population this should not be a concern (unless you are taking high doses of iron supplements). It is quite difficult to eat as many iron-containing foods as it would take to have high iron levels. Also, since most of the evidence does not support this link between iron and CAD, it is recommended that people continue to eat the foods that supply your daily requirements of iron.

A more common concern, especially among pre-menopausal women, is iron deficiency (iron levels in the blood are too low) or anemia where people are not getting enough iron from the foods that they are eating. For some people with heart disease, this can lead to serious difficulties if the need for surgery arises since it cannot be performed until the iron levels are back to normal. So, in this case, it is important to eat enough iron-containing foods to meet your iron needs.

The iron needs of adults are shown here:

Women	(19 – 49 years or pre-menopause)	13 mg/day
	(50+ years or post-menopause)	8 mg/day
Men	(19 – 75+ years)	9 mg/day

Here are some tips to help you get more iron:

- Meat, poultry, fish, eggs, enriched pastas and bread, whole grains, fortified cereals, and leafy green vegetables are all good sources of iron.
- Animal sources of iron are better absorbed by your body than plant sources of iron.
- Eating meat with vegetables helps the body absorb more of the iron from the vegetable sources.
- Cooking in iron pots (i.e., cast iron pans) adds iron to the foods you cook in them
- Eating foods high in vitamin C with meals helps the body absorb the iron within the meal better.
- Cut down on coffee and tea — compounds in them can interfere with the uptake of iron from the foods you eat.

CANADIAN DIABETES ASSOCIATION FOOD CHOICE SYSTEM

The following CDA Food Choice Values have been assigned to the recipes in this book in accordance with the Good Health Eating Guide (1994) which is used for meal planning by people with diabetes. The Food Choice Value for a certain serving size has been calculated for each recipe to make it easy to fit into a personalized meal plan. Servings must be measured carefully, since changing the serving size will increase or decrease the Food Choice Value assigned. Some recipes may include an inappropriate portion of a certain food group for a person with diabetes. For these recipes, it is recommended that the portions that are in excess be reduced to include them in a meal plan.

The Good Health Eating Guide (1994) reflects the Canadian Diabetes Association's position on the intake of sugar by people with diabetes. Simple sugars can be incorporated into a meal plan according to the information in the new Good Health Eating Guide (1994) and with the help of a dietitian-nutritionist.

The Food Choice System used in the Good Health Eating Guide (1994) is based on Canada's Food Guide To Healthy Eating. For more information on diabetes and the complete Good Health Eating Guide (1994), contact the Canadian Diabetes Association National Office:

15 Toronto Street, Suite 800, Toronto, Ontario, M5C 2E3
E-mail: info@cda-nat.org *Internet:* http://www.diabetes.ca

FOOD CHOICE VALUE PER SERVING

PG	RECIPE (PORTION SIZE)	STARCH	FRUITS & VEGETABLES	MILK	SUGARS	PROTEIN	FATS & OILS	EXTRA
34	Red Pepper, Feta and Garlic Hummos (1 tbsp: 1/32 of recipe)		½					
35	Creamy Salsa (1 tbsp: 1/32 of recipe)							1
36	Beet and Potato Skordalia (1 tbsp: 1/32 of recipe)							1
37	White Bean and Roasted Garlic Spread (1 tbsp: 1/24 of recipe)							1
38	Roasted Squash Spread (1 tbsp: 1/32 of recipe)		½					
39	Roasted Eggplant Spread (1 tbsp: 1/40 of recipe)							1
40	Grilled Vegetables with Chèvre Dip (1/8 of recipe)		1½			1	½	
41	Veggie Cheese Spread (1 tbsp: 1/32 of recipe)							1
42	Smoked Trout Spread (1 tbsp: 1/32 of recipe)							1
43	Cooked Salad (1 tbsp: 1/80 of recipe)							1
44	Wild Mushroom Bruschetta with Chèvre (1 piece: 1/20 of recipe)	½					½	
45	Roasted Garlic Pesto on Bruschetta (1 piece: 1/32 of recipe)	½					½	
46	Smoked Salmon Sushi (1 piece: 1/32 of recipe)	½						
48	Tortilla Rolls with Hummos and Grilled Eggplant (1 piece: 1/32 of recipe)	½						
50	Salad Rolls (1 roll: 1/16 of recipe)	½				½		
51	Smoked Cheese and Sweet Onion Quesadillas (1 wedge: 1/24 of recipe)	½	½			½		
52	Asparagus Tarts with Chèvre (1/8 of recipe)	1½				½	1½	
54	Chicken Satays with Peanut Sauce (1 skewer: 1/16 of recipe)				½	1		

PG	RECIPE (PORTION SIZE)	STARCH	FRUITS & VEGETABLES	MILK	SUGARS	PROTEIN	FATS & OILS	EXTRA
56	Winter Root Vegetable Soup (⅙ of recipe)		2			1		
58	Fresh Herb Soup with Ricotta Croutons (⅙ of recipe)	1½				1		1
60	Fresh Tomato Soup with Pesto Cream (⅙ of recipe)		1½			½	½	
61	Calconnan Soup (⅙ of recipe)	1	½			½	½	1
62	Butternut Squash Soup with Wild Mushroom Sauté (⅛ of recipe)	½	1½			½	½	
64	Corn Chowder with Herb Cheese (¼ of recipe)	3	½			1	½	
65	Curried Squash Soup (⅙ of recipe)		2			½	½	
66	White Bean and Spinach Soup (⅙ of recipe)	1				1½		1
67	Lemony Lentil Soup (⅙ of recipe)	1½				2		1
68	Tortilla Soup (⅙ of recipe)	½	½			2		1
69	Chicken Soup with Rice (⅙ of recipe)	1	½			1½		
70	Thai Chicken Noodle Soup (⅙ of recipe)	1	½			2		
72	Malka's Bouillabaisse (⅛ of recipe)	1½	½			5½		
74	Seafood Chowder (¼ of recipe)	2	½			4½		
75	Spicy Gazpacho (⅙ of recipe)	½	1				½	1
76	Cold Cucumber Tzatziki Soup (⅙ of recipe)	½		1½ 2%				1
78	Grilled Corn Salad (⅙ of recipe)	2½	½				1½	
79	Caesar Salad with Creamy Roasted Garlic Dressing (⅙ of recipe)	½				½	1	
80	Carrot Salad with Moroccan Dressing (⅙ of recipe)		1½					
81	Baked Beets with Mustard Horseradish Dressing (⅙ of recipe)		½					
82	Wheat Berry Salad (⅙ of recipe)	1½					½	
83	Tabbouleh Salad with Fresh Herbs (⅙ of recipe)	1					1	
84	Rice Salsa Salad (¼ of recipe)	2½					1	1
85	Spaghetti Salad with Roasted Garlic and Tomato Salsa (⅛ of recipe)	3					1½	
86	White Bean and Chopped Shrimp Salad (⅙ of recipe)	½	1½			3	½	
88	Chopped Tuna Salad (¼ of recipe)	2½	½			3		
89	Quinoa and Crab Salad with Cilantro Lime Dressing (⅙ of recipe)	2½			½	3		1
90	Wild Salad with Cranberry Vinaigrette (⅙ of recipe)	2	1			1½	1	
91	Chinese Chicken Salad (⅙ of recipe)	2			1	2½		
92	Asian Grilled Steak Salad (⅙ of recipe)		½		1	2½		1
94	Vietnamese Chicken Noodle Salad (⅙ of recipe)	2	½		½	2½		1
96	Spaghetti with Roasted Tomato Sauce (⅙ of recipe)	3	1			1		
97	Linguine with Hot Garlic Tomato Sauce (¼ of recipe)	4	½			½	1½	
98	Angelhair Pasta with Fresh and Cooked Tomato Sauce (¼ of recipe)	4	1			1	1	
99	Pasta with Tomato and Red Pepper Sauce (⅙ of recipe)	3½	1			½	½	
100	Penne with Tomatoes and Arugula (¼ of recipe)	4	1			½	1	
101	Trenne with Wild Mushrooms (⅙ of recipe)	4	½			½	1	

PG	RECIPE (PORTION SIZE)	STARCH	FRUITS & VEGETABLES	MILK	SUGARS	PROTEIN	FATS & OILS	EXTRA
102	Pasta with Roasted Cauliflower (¼ of recipe)	3				½	1½	
103	Bow Ties with Spring Vegetables (⅛ of recipe)	2	1			½		
104	Penne with Eggplant, Peppers and Ricotta (⅙ of recipe)	3	1			1½	1	
105	Spaghetti Rustica (⅙ of recipe)	4				1	½	
106	Spaghetti and Seafood Casserole (⅛ of recipe)	2½	1			4		
107	Broken Spaghetti with Fresh Salsa and Scallops (⅙ of recipe)	2½	1			2		
108	Pasta with Swordfish and Olives (⅙ of recipe)	3½	1			3½		
109	Fettuccine with Chicken and Mixed Peppers (⅙ of recipe)	2½	1			2½		
110	Sweet and Spicy Chicken Lo Mein (⅙ of recipe)	3½	1		1	3		
112	Soupy Chinese Noodles (⅙ of recipe)	2	½			3		
114	Portobello Mushroom Burgers with Roasted Garlic Mayonnaise (¼ of recipe)	2½	1½			1	2	1
116	Lentil and Mushroom Burgers (¼ of recipe)	3½				1	1	
117	Stuffed Baked Potatoes with Stir-fried Vegetables (¼ of recipe)	1½					½	
118	Risotto with Tomatoes and Beans (⅙ of recipe)	4½	½			1	½	
119	Rice Baked with Spinach, Feta and Dill (⅙ of recipe)	3				½	1	1
120	Polenta with Roasted Ratatouille (⅙ of recipe)	1	1½				½	
122	Fresh Herb and Vegetable Lasagna (⅙ of recipe)	2	1½			1½	½	
124	Baked Beans in Brewmaster's Barbecue Sauce (⅛ of recipe)	2	½		1	1½		
126	Couscous Soup with Vegetables and Charmoula (⅛ of recipe)	2	1			½	1	
128	Pizza with Black Bean Salsa (⅙ of recipe)	3				1½	1½	
129	Lentil and Wild Rice Salad with Feta (⅛ of recipe)	2	½			1	1	
130	Pizza Salad with Roasted Garlic Hummos (⅛ of recipe)	2	½			1	1½	
132	Spicy Singapore Noodles (¼ of recipe)	3	1		½	½	1½	
134	Chickpea and Couscous Salad (⅙ of recipe)	3				½	1	
135	Tofu and Onions Braised in Asian Barbecue Sauce with Noodles (¼ of recipe)	3	1		½	3		
136	Spicy Tofu with Eggplant and Mushrooms (¼ of recipe)	4	1			½	1	
138	Fried Rice with Grilled Tofu (¼ of recipe)	4	½			1	1	
140	Salmon Baked in Parchment wth Parsley Pesto (⅙ of recipe)					3		1
141	Salmon Fillets in Rice Paper Wrappers (⅙ of recipe)	½				3		
142	Salmon Patties with Fresh Dill (¼ of recipe)	½				1½		1
143	Glazed Swordfish (⅙ of recipe)				1	3		
144	Teriyaki Swordfish Burgers with Sweet Pickled Ginger Salsa (⅙ of recipe)	2½	1		½	2½		
146	Halibut with Rice Wine (⅙ of recipe)		½			2		
147	Oven-Roasted Sea Bass (⅙ of recipe)				½	3		
148	Sea Bass with Couscous Crust and Tomato Olive Vinaigrette (⅙ of recipe)	1½				3		
150	Cod Baked in Tomato Sauce with Onions (⅙ of recipe)		1			3		
151	Baked Red Snapper with Hot Chiles (⅙ of recipe)					5½		1

PG	RECIPE (PORTION SIZE)	STARCH	FRUITS & VEGETABLES	MILK	SUGARS	PROTEIN	FATS & OILS	EXTRA
152	Baked Fish with Mushroom Crust (¼ of recipe)		½			3½		1
154	Lightly Breaded Shrimp with Hot Garlic Sauce (⅙ of recipe)	½				2½		
156	Stir-fried Scallops (¼ of recipe)		1½		½	3		1
158	Steamed Fish with Spinach and Black Bean Sauce (¼ of recipe)		½			2½		
160	Barbecued Chicken Steaks (¼ of recipe)				½	3½		
161	Flattened Cumin-grilled Chicken Breasts with Garlic Couscous (⅙ of recipe)	2½	½			4½		
162	Twist and Shout Chicken Drumsticks (⅙ of recipe)	1				3½		
163	Chicken Burgers with Herbed Yogurt Sauce (⅙ of recipe)	2½		½ 2%		3		
164	Sweet and Sour Chicken Balls (⅙ of recipe)		1		1	3		
165	Chicken "Meatloaf" (⅛ of recipe)		1			4		
166	Baked Chicken with Vegetables and Balsamic Vinegar (⅙ of recipe)	1½	1			4		
167	Asian Chicken Thighs (⅙ of recipe)				½	2		
168	Hunter-style Chicken with Wild Mushrooms (⅙ of recipe)		1			3½		
170	Chicken Jambalaya (⅙ of recipe)	2½	½			2½		
172	Breaded Chicken Cutlets with Roasted Tomato Sauce (¼ of recipe)	1	1			3½		
174	Chicken Adobo (¼ of recipe)		½			4½		
175	Thai Chicken and Noodle Stir-fry (¼ of recipe)	4	½			4½		
176	Turkey Burgers with Old-fashioned Coleslaw (⅙ of recipe)	2½	1			3		
177	Turkey Paillards (¼ of recipe)					4		1
178	Roast Turkey Breast with Spinach Stuffing (⅙ of recipe)	½				4½		
180	Barbecued Butterflied Turkey Breast (⅙ of recipe)					5		
182	Beef and Broccoli with Baked Noodle Cake (¼ of recipe)	3	1			3½	½	
184	Grilled Steak Sandwiches wth Barbecued Onion Sauce (⅛ of recipe)	3	1		1	2½		
186	Shepherd's Pie with Garlic Mashed Potatoes (⅛ of recipe)	1½	2			2		
188	Polenta with Wild Mushroom and Meat Ragout (¼ of recipe)	1½	1½			2	½	
190	Giant Hamburger with Homemade Chili Sauce (1/10 of recipe)	3	1			2		
192	Shishkebab-flavoured Butterflied Leg of Lamb (⅛ of recipe)				½	4		
193	Lamb Chops with Cashew Nut Couscous (¼ of recipe)	3½	½			1½	½	
194	Osso Bucco (Braised Veal Shanks) (⅛ of recipe)	2½	2			3½		
196	Sweet and Sour Cabbage Casserole (⅙ of recipe)	1½	1		1½	2½	½	
198	Braised Lamb Shanks with White Bean Puree (⅛ of recipe)	1	1			3		
200	Barbecued Lamb Chili (⅛ of recipe)	5	1		½	4		1
202	Baked Pork Chops with Barbecue Sauce (⅙ of recipe)	1½	½		1½	4		
203	Pork Tenderloin with Hoisin (¼ of recipe)				½	4½		
204	Cajun Glazed Ham (1/16 of recipe)				1	3		
206	Green Beans with Garlic (⅙ of recipe)		½					
207	Asparagus with Thai Dipping Sauce (¼ of recipe)				½	½		1

PG	RECIPE (PORTION SIZE)	STARCH	FRUITS & VEGETABLES	MILK	SUGARS	PROTEIN	FATS & OILS	EXTRA
208	Glazed Beets with Balsamic Vinegar (⅙ of recipe)		½		½		½	
209	Sauteed Greens (⅙ of recipe)		½				½	
210	Stir-fried Broccoli with Ginger (¼ of recipe)		½				½	
211	Roasted Fennel with Tomatoes (¼ of recipe)		1				1	
212	Caramelized Onions (¼ of recipe)		1				½	
213	Wild Mushrooms with Herbs (¼ of recipe)		½				½	
214	Sweet Potato Mash (⅙ of recipe)	2½					½	
215	Buttermilk Mashed Potatoes (¼ of recipe)	2	½					
216	Mashed Baked Squash (⅙ of recipe)		2			½		
217	Roasted "French-fried" Potatoes (¼ of recipe)	3						
218	Mashed Root Vegetables (¼ of recipe)	2	1½					
219	Glazed Winter Vegetables with Maple and Ginger (⅙ of recipe)		1		½		½	
220	Spicy Rice Pilaf (⅙ of recipe)	2½					½	
221	Basmati Rice Pilaf with Garam Masala (⅛ of recipe)	2½					½	
222	Israeli Couscous with Squash and Peppers (⅙ of recipe)	1	1			½	½	
223	Barley and Wild Mushroom Risotto (⅙ of recipe)	2				½	½	
224	Risotto with Rapini (⅛ of recipe)	2½	½			½	½	
226	Breakfast Brûlée (⅙ of recipe)		½	2 2%	2	½		
227	Wild Rice Blueberry Pancakes (1 pancake: ⅙ of recipe)	1½		½ 1%	½	½	½	
228	Buckwheat Crêpes with Caramelized Apples (⅛ of recipe)	1	1½		2		1	
229	Yogurt Cheese (1 tbsp: 1/24 of recipe)							1
230	Summer Crêpes with Berry Berry Salad (2 crepes: ⅙ of recipe)	1½	2		1½	1	½	
232	Breakfast Honey Bread (1 slice: 1/12 of recipe)	2			½		1	
234	Lemon Polenta Waffles (1 waffle: ⅛ of recipe)	1½				½	½	
235	Baked Potatoes with Tuna Salad and Lemon Mayonnaise (¼ of recipe)	1½	½			1½		
236	Pasta Frittata (⅛ of recipe)	1				½	1	
237	Feta and Spinach Frittata Sandwiches (⅙ of recipe)	4				2		
238	Chicken Burritos with Cooked Tomato Salsa (1 burrito: ⅛ of recipe)	1	½			1½		
240	Grilled Chicken Sandwiches with Charmoula (⅙ of recipe)	2½	1			3		
242	Chilly Cappuccino (1 drink: ½ of recipe)			1 1%	3		½	
243	Fara's European Fruit Salad "Drink" (1 drink: ⅛ of recipe)		1½		½			
244	Tropical Smoothie (1 drink: ½ of recipe)		2½		1			
244	Yogurt Fruit Shake (1 drink: ½ of recipe)		2½	½ 2%				
246	Blueberry Bran Muffins (1 muffin: 1/18 of recipe)	1			1½		1	1
247	Rhubarb Cinnamon Muffins (1 muffin: 1/12 of recipe)	1½			1½		1	
248	Apple Spice Muffins (1 muffin: 1/12 of recipe)	1	1		1		1	
249	Lemon Poppy Seed Muffins (1 muffin: 1/12 of recipe)	1½			1½		1½	
250	Cappuccino Muffins (1 muffin: 1/12 of recipe)	1½			1		1	
251	Mini Berry Cornmeal Muffins (1 muffin: 1/24 of recipe)	1					½	

PG	RECIPE (PORTION SIZE)	STARCH	FRUITS & VEGETABLES	MILK	SUGARS	PROTEIN	FATS & OILS	EXTRA
252	Cheddar Sage Biscuits (1 biscuit: $\frac{1}{12}$ of recipe)	1					1	
253	Buttermilk Drop Biscuits (1 biscuit: $\frac{1}{10}$ of recipe)	1	½		½		½	
254	Prince Edward Island Dinner Rolls (1 bun: $\frac{1}{12}$ of recipe)	1½					½	
256	Banana Bread (1 slice: $\frac{1}{12}$ of recipe)	1	½		1		1	
257	Beer Bread with Rosemary (1 slice: $\frac{1}{12}$ of recipe)	1½			½			
258	Potato Sweet Rolls (1 roll: $\frac{1}{18}$ of recipe)	1½			½		½	
259	Baked Boston Brown Bread (1 slice: $\frac{1}{10}$ of recipe)	1	½		1			
260	Smoky Cornbread with Corn and Peppers ($\frac{1}{12}$ of recipe)	2				½	1	
261	Whole Wheat Focaccia (1 piece: $\frac{1}{8}$ of recipe)	2					½	
262	Grain and Seed Bread (1 slice: $\frac{1}{16}$ of recipe)	1½			½		½	
264	Apple Strudel ($\frac{1}{12}$ of recipe)	1	1		1½		1	
266	Baked Wild Rice Pudding Brûlée ($\frac{1}{8}$ of recipe)	1½	1	½ 1%	2½		½	
267	Caramelized Fruit Crisp ($\frac{1}{12}$ of recipe)	½	2		2½		1	
268	Peach Cobbler ($\frac{1}{8}$ of recipe)	2	1		2		1½	
269	Fruit Salad with Marsala ($\frac{1}{8}$ of recipe)		2½		½			
270	Baked Apple Slices ($\frac{1}{48}$ of recipe)		½					
271	Rosy Applesauce ($\frac{1}{8}$ of recipe)		2		1			
272	Baked Alaska ($\frac{1}{12}$ of recipe)	½			4	½		
274	Dried Fruit Compote ($\frac{1}{4}$ of recipe)		4½		3½			
275	Pavlova with Berries and Flowers ($\frac{1}{8}$ of recipe)		½	½ 2%	3	½		
276	Cinnamon Pear Cake with Caramel Coffee Sauce ($\frac{1}{12}$ of recipe)	1	½		3		1	
278	Orange Polenta Cake with Mango and Orange Salad ($\frac{1}{8}$ of recipe)	1½	1		3½		2	
280	Oatmeal Banana Cake ($\frac{1}{12}$ of recipe)	1			2		1	
281	Gingerbread Angel Cake ($\frac{1}{12}$ of recipe)	1			2½		1	
282	Crispy Chocolate Cookies (1 cookie: $\frac{1}{30}$ of recipe)				1			
283	Hermit Bar Cookies (1 square: $\frac{1}{36}$ of recipe)	½			½		½	
284	Espresso Biscotti (1 cookie: $\frac{1}{60}$ of recipe)	½						

INDEX

A

Alcohol
  cooking with, 277
  intake, 12
  substitutes, 277
Angel Cake, Gingerbread, 281
Angelhair Pasta with Fresh and Cooked
  Tomato Sauce, 98
Appetizers. *See also* 33–54.
  Asparagus with Thai Dipping Sauce, 207
  Barley and Wild Mushroom Risotto, 223
  Lightly Breaded Shrimp with Hot
    Garlic Sauce, 154
  Ricotta Croutons, 58
  Roasted "French-fried" Potatoes, 217
  Whole Wheat Focaccia, 261
  Wild Mushroom Sauté, 62
Apples, 270
  Apple Spice Muffins, 248
  Apple Strudel, 264
  Baked Apple Slices, 270
  Buckwheat Crêpes with Caramelized
    Apples, 228
  Rosy Applesauce, 271
Arugula
  Penne with Tomatoes and Arugula, 100
Asian
  Asian Chicken Thighs, 167
  Asian Coleslaw, 177
  Asian Grilled Steak Salad, 92
  Black Bean Sauce, 156
  Glazed Swordfish, 143
  Halibut with Rice Wine, 146
  ingredients for Asian cooking, 92
  Salmon Fillets in Rice Paper
    Wrappers, 141
  Spicy Singapore Noodles, 132
  Spicy Tofu with Eggplant and
    Mushrooms, 136
  Steamed Fish with Spinach and Black
    Bean Sauce, 158
  Stir-fried Scallops, 156
  Tofu and Onions Braised in Asian
    Barbecue Sauce with Noodles, 135
Chinese:
  Beef and Broccoli with Baked Noodle
    Cake, 182
  Chinese Chicken Salad, 91
  Hoisin Marinade, 154
  Soupy Chinese Noodles, 112
  Stir-fried Broccoli with Ginger, 210
  Sweet and Spicy Chicken Lo Mein,
    110
Filipino:
  Chicken Adobo, 174

Japanese:
  Smoked Salmon Sushi, 46
  Teriyaki Swordfish Burgers with
    Sweet Pickled Ginger Salsa, 144
Thai:
  Asparagus with Thai Dipping Sauce,
    207
  Chicken Satays with Peanut Sauce, 54
  Salad Rolls, 50
  Sweet and hot Thai chili sauce, 94
  Thai Chicken and Noodle Stir-fry, 175
  Thai Chicken Noodle Soup, 70
Vietnamese:
  Vietnamese Chicken Noodle Salad, 94
Asparagus, 207
  Asparagus Tarts with Chèvre, 52
  Asparagus with Thai Dipping Sauce, 207
  Bow Ties with Spring Vegetables, 103
  Roasted Asparagus, 210

B

Bain marie, 266
Baked Alaska, 272
Baked Apple Slices, 270
Baked Beans in Brewmaster's Barbecue
  Sauce, 124
Baked Beets with Mustard Horseradish
  Dressing, 81
Baked Boston Brown Bread, 259
Baked Chicken with Vegetables and
  Balsamic Vinegar, 166
Baked Fish with Mushroom Crust, 152
Baked Pork Chops with Barbecue
  Sauce, 202
Baked Potatoes with Tuna Salad and
  Lemon Mayonnaise, 235
Baked Red Snapper with Hot Chiles, 151
Baked Wild Rice Pudding Brûlée, 266
Bananas
  Banana Bread, 256
  Oatmeal Banana Cake, 280
  Smoothies, 243
Barbecue. *See also* Grilled.
  Barbecue Sauce, 202
  Barbecued Butterflied Turkey Breast,
    180
  Barbecued Chicken Steaks, 160
  Barbecued Lamb Chili, 200
  Barbecued Onion Sauce, 184
  Brewmaster's Barbecue Sauce, 124
Barley and Wild Mushroom Risotto, 223
Basil, 120, 175
  Fresh Tomato Soup with Pesto
    Cream, 60
  Pesto Sauce, 60

Roasted Garlic Pesto on Bruschetta, 45
Basmati Rice Pilaf with Garam Masala,
  221
Beans, 125. *See also* Chickpeas; Lentils.
  Baked Beans in Brewmaster's
    Barbecue Sauce, 124
  Black turtle beans, 128
  Braised Lamb Shanks with White
    Bean Puree, 198
  Pizza with Black Bean Salsa, 128
  Risotto with Tomatoes and Beans, 118
  Spaghetti Rustica, 105
  White Bean and Chopped Shrimp
    Salad, 86
  White Bean and Roasted Garlic
    Spread, 37
  White Bean and Spinach Soup, 66
  White Bean Puree, 199
Beef, 185. *See also* Beef, Ground.
  Asian Grilled Steak Salad, 92
  Beef and Broccoli with Baked Noodle
    Cake, 182
  Grilled Steak Sandwiches with
    Barbecued Onion Sauce, 184
Beef, Ground. *See also* Beef.
  Giant Hamburger with Homemade
    Chili Sauce, 190
  Polenta with Wild Mushroom and
    Meat Ragout, 188
  Shepherd's Pie with Garlic Mashed
    Potatoes, 186
  Sweet and Sour Cabbage Casserole, 196
Beer Bread with Rosemary, 257
Beets
  Baked Beets with Mustard Horseradish
    Dressing, 81
  Beet and Potato Skordalia, 36
  Glazed Beets with Balsamic Vinegar, 208
  Winter Root Vegetable Soup, 56
Berries. *See also* individual berries.
  Berry Berry Salad, 230
  Breakfast Brûlée, 226
  Mini Berry Cornmeal Muffins, 251
  Pavlova with Berries and Flowers, 275
Berry Berry Salad, 230
Biscotti
  Espresso Biscotti, 284
  Orange Hazelnut Biscotti, 284
Biscuits
  Buttermilk Drop Biscuits, 253
  Cheddar Sage Biscuits, 252
Black Bean Salsa, Pizza with, 128
Black bean sauce, 156
Black Bean Sauce, Steamed Fish with
  Spinach and, 158

297

C

Blood pressure, 288, 289
Blueberries
  Blueberry Bran Muffins, 246
  Wild Rice Blueberry Pancakes, 227
Boiled Rice, 171
Boston Brown Bread, Baked, 259
Bouillabaisse, Malka's, 72
Bow Ties with Spring Vegetables, 103
Braised Lamb Shanks with White Bean
  Puree, 198
Bran, 246
  Blueberry Bran Muffins, 246
Breaded Chicken Cutlets with Roasted
  Tomato Sauce, 172
Breads. See also 245-262; Tortillas.
  Breadcrumbs, 153
  Breakfast Honey Bread, 232
  Roasted Garlic Pesto on Bruschetta,
  45
  Wild Mushroom Bruschetta with
  Chèvre, 44
Breakfast. See also 225-244.
  Breakfast Brûlée, 226
  Breakfast Honey Bread, 232
Brewmaster's Barbecue Sauce, 124
Broccoli
  Beef and Broccoli with Baked Noodle
  Cake, 182
  Stir-fried Broccoli with Ginger, 210
Broken Spaghetti with Fresh Salsa and
  Scallops, 107
Brunch. See Breakfast.
Bruschetta
  Roasted Garlic Pesto on Bruschetta, 45
  Wild Mushroom Bruschetta with
  Chèvre, 44
Brussels sprouts
  Glazed Winter Vegetables with Maple
  and Ginger, 219
Buckwheat Crêpes with Caramelized
  Apples, 228
Bulgur
  Tabbouleh Salad with Fresh Herbs, 83
Burgers
  Chicken Burgers with Herbed Yogurt
  Sauce, 163
  Giant Hamburger with Homemade
  Chili Sauce, 190
  Lentil and Mushroom Burgers, 116
  Portobello Mushroom Burgers with
  Roasted Garlic Mayonnaise, 114
  Teriyaki Swordfish Burgers with Sweet
  Pickled Ginger Salsa, 144
  Turkey Burgers with Old-fashioned
  Coleslaw, 176
Butter, Pear, 258
Buttermilk, 253
  Buttermilk Drop Biscuits, 253
  Buttermilk Mashed Potatoes, 215
Butternut Squash Soup with Wild
  Mushroom Sauté, 62

C

Cabbage
  Asian Coleslaw, 177
  Calconnan Soup, 61
  Old-fashioned Coleslaw, 176
  Sweet and Sour Cabbage Casserole, 196
Caesar Salad with Creamy Roasted
  Garlic Dressing, 79
Caffeine intake, 12
Cajun Glazed Ham, 204
Cakes
  Cinnamon Pear Cake with Caramel
  Coffee Sauce, 276
  Gingerbread Angel Cake, 281
  Gingerbread Angel Cake Roulade, 281
  Oatmeal Banana Cake, 280
  Orange Polenta Cake with Mango and
  Orange Salad, 278
Calconnan Soup, 61
Calories from fat, 285
Canada's Food Guide to Healthy
  Eating, 10, 11, 13-14
Cancer, 17
Cappuccino Muffins, 250
Caramel Coffee Sauce, 276
Caramelized Fruit Crisp, 267
Caramelized Onions, 212
Carrots
  Asian Coleslaw, 177
  Carrot Salad with Moroccan Dressing,
  80
  Glazed Winter Vegetables with Maple
  and Ginger, 219
  Old-fashioned Coleslaw, 176
  Winter Root Vegetable Soup, 56
Cashew Nut Couscous, 193
Casseroles. See also Stews.
  Chicken Jambalaya, 170
  Osso Bucco (Braised Veal Shanks), 194
  Rice Baked with Spinach, Feta and
  Dill, 119
  Shepherd's Pie with Garlic Mashed
  Potatoes, 186
  Spaghetti and Seafood Casserole, 106
  Sweet and Sour Cabbage Casserole, 196
Cauliflower
  Pasta with Roasted Cauliflower, 102
Charmoula, 127, 240
Cheddar Sage Biscuits, 252
Cheese, 189. See also Chèvre; Feta;
  Yogurt Cheese.
  Cheddar Sage Biscuits, 252
  Fresh Herb Soup with Ricotta
  Croutons, 58
  Parmesan cheese, 118
  Parmesan Cheese Crisps, 118
  Penne with Eggplant, Peppers and
  Ricotta, 104
  Pizza with Black Bean Salsa, 128
  Smoked Cheese and Sweet Onion
  Quesadillas, 51

Chèvre, 40
  Asparagus Tarts with Chèvre, 52
  Grilled Vegetables with Chèvre Dip,
  40
  Wild Mushroom Bruschetta with
  Chèvre, 44
Chicken. See also 159-175.
  Chicken Adobo, 174
  Chicken Burgers with Herbed
  Yogurt Sauce, 163
  Chicken Burritos with Cooked
  Tomato Salsa, 238
  Chicken Jambalaya, 170
  Chicken "Meatloaf," 165
  Chicken Satays with Peanut Sauce, 54
  Chicken Soup with Rice, 69
  Chicken Stock, Homemade, 57
  Chinese Chicken Salad, 91
  Fettucine with Chicken and Mixed
  Peppers, 109
  Grilled Chicken Sandwiches with
  Charmoula, 240
  Salad Rolls, 50
  Soupy Chinese Noodles, 112
  Sweet and Spicy Chicken Lo Mein,
  110
  Thai Chicken Noodle Soup, 70
  Tortilla Soup, 68
  Vietnamese Chicken Noodle Salad,
  94
  Wild Salad with Cranberry Vinaigrette,
  90
Chickpeas
  Chickpea and Couscous Salad, 134
  Jalapeño and Cilantro Hummos, 34
  Red Pepper, Feta and Garlic Hummos,
  34
  Tortilla Rolls with Hummos and
  Grilled Eggplant, 48
Chiles, 239
Chili
  Barbecued Lamb Chili, 200
  Chili Sauce, 191
Chilly Cappuccino, 242
Chinese. See also Asian.
  Chinese Chicken Salad, 91
Chocolate Cookies, Crispy, 282
Cholesterol
  blood, 17, 287
  dietary, 285
  fat and, 11, 285
  nutrition claims, 24
  types of, 287
  values, 286
Chopped Tuna Salad, 88
Chowder, Seafood, 74
Cilantro, 190
  Cilantro Lime Dressing, 89
  Jalapeño and Cilantro Hummos, 34
Cinnamon Pear Cake with Caramel
  Coffee Sauce, 276

Clams
  Malka's Bouillabaisse, 72
Cobbler, Peach, 268
Cocoa, 282
Cod Baked in Tomato Sauce with
  Onions, 150
Coffee
  Cappuccino Muffins, 250
  Caramel Coffee Sauce, 276
  Chilly Cappuccino, 242
  Espresso Biscotti, 284
Cold Cucumber Tzatziki Soup, 76
Coleslaw
  Asian Coleslaw, 177
  Old-fashioned Coleslaw, 176
Compote, Dried Fruit, 274
Cooked Salad, 43
Cooked Tomato Salsa, 238
Cookies, 283
  Crispy Chocolate Cookies, 282
  Espresso Biscotti, 284
  Hermit Bar Cookies, 283
  Orange Hazelnut Biscotti, 284
Corn, 88
  Corn Chowder with Herb Cheese,
    64
  Grilled Corn Salad, 78
  Smoky Cornbread with Corn and
    Peppers, 260
Cornmeal
  Lemon Polenta Waffles, 234
  Mini Berry Cornmeal Muffins, 251
  Orange Polenta Cake with Mango
    and Orange Salad, 278
  Polenta with Roasted Ratatouille,
    120
  Polenta with Wild Mushroom and
    Meat Ragout, 188
  Smoky Cornbread with Corn and
    Peppers, 260
Couscous, 146, 161
  Chickpea and Couscous Salad, 134
  Couscous Soup with Vegetables and
    Charmoula, 126
  Flattened Cumin-grilled Chicken
    Breasts with Garlic Couscous, 161
  Israeli Couscous with Squash and
    Peppers, 222
  Lamb Chops with Cashew Nut
    Couscous, 193
  Sea Bass with Couscous Crust and
    Tomato Olive Vinaigrette, 148
Crab
  Quinoa and Crab Salad with Cilantro
    Lime Dressing, 89
Cranberries
  Cranberry Sauce, 179
  Cranberry Vinaigrette, 90
  Wild Salad with Cranberry
    Vinaigrette, 90
Creamy Roasted Garlic Dressing, 79

Creamy Salsa, 35
Crêpes, 231
  Buckwheat Crêpes with Caramelized
    Apples, 228
  Summer Crêpes with Berry Berry
    Salad, 230
Crisp, Caramelized Fruit, 267
Crispy Chocolate Cookies, 282
Croutons
  Homemade Croutons, 74
  Parmesan Cheese Crisps, 118
  Ricotta Croutons, 58
Cucumbers, 83
  Cold Cucumber Tzatziki Soup, 76
Cumin, 222
  Flattened Cumin-grilled Chicken
    Breasts with Garlic Couscous, 161
Curried Squash Soup, 65

D

Desserts. *See also* 263-284.
  Breakfast Brûlée, 226
  Dessert Phyllo Cups, 52
  Smoothies, 243
  Summer Crêpes with Berry Berry
    Salad, 230
  Tropical Smoothie, 244
  Yogurt Cheese Dessert Topping, 229
Diabetes, 26, 291-296
Dill
  Rice Baked with Spinach, Feta and
    Dill, 119
  Salmon Patties with Fresh Dill, 142
Dips. *See also* Sauces.
  Beet and Potato Skordalia, 36
  Chèvre Dip, 40
  Citrus Dipping Sauce, 92
  Cooked Salad, 43
  Creamy Roasted Garlic Dressing, 79
  Creamy Salsa, 35
  Hot Garlic Sauce, 154
  Hummos, 48
  Jalapeño and Cilantro Hummos, 34
  Peanut Dressing, 91
  Red Pepper, Feta and Garlic
    Hummos, 34
  Roasted Eggplant Spread, 39
  Thai Dipping Sauce, 207
  Veggie Cheese Spread, 41
  White Bean and Roasted Garlic
    Spread, 37
  White Bean Puree, 199
  Yogurt Cheese Dip, 229
Diuretic medication, 288
Dressings. *See* Salad dressings.
Dried Fruit Compote, 274
Drinks
  Chilly Cappuccino, 242
  Fara's European Fruit Salad "Drink,"
    243
  Smoothies, 243

Tropical Smoothie, 244
Yogurt Fruit Shake, 244

E

Eating out, 25-26
Edible flowers, 275
Eggplant, 39
  Penne with Eggplant, Peppers and
    Ricotta, 104
  Roasted Eggplant Spread, 39
  Spicy Tofu with Eggplant and
    Mushrooms, 136
  Tortilla Rolls with Hummos and
    Grilled Eggplant, 48
Eggs, 26, 237, 273
  Baked Alaska, 272
  Baked Wild Rice Pudding Brûlée, 266
  Buckwheat Crêpes with Caramelized
    Apples, 228
  Feta and Spinach Frittata Sandwiches,
    237
  Gingerbread Angel Cake, 281
  Pasta Frittata, 236
  Pavlova with Berries and Flowers, 275
  Summer Crêpes with Berry Berry
    Salad, 230
  Wild Rice Blueberry Pancakes, 227
Entertaining, 31
Espresso Biscotti, 284

F

Fara's European Fruit Salad "Drink," 243
Fat
  and cholesterol, 285, 286
  intake, 10
  monounsaturated, 11
  nutrition claims, 24
  omega-3, 11
  polyunsaturated, 11
  reducing, 10, 16, 22, 25-26, 110, 187,
    286
  saturated, 11
  sources, 11, 25
  substitutes, 287
  trans fatty acids, 11
Fennel
  Bow Ties with Spring Vegetables, 103
  Roasted Fennel with Tomatoes, 211
Feta
  Feta and Spinach Frittata Sandwiches,
    237
  Lentil and Wild Rice Salad with Feta,
    129
  Red Pepper, Feta and Garlic
    Hummos, 34
  Rice Baked with Spinach, Feta and
    Dill, 119
Fettuccine with Chicken and Mixed
  Peppers, 109
Fibre
  intake, 17

nutrition claims, 24
sources, 17, 22, 25
Filipino. *See* Asian.
Fish and Seafood. *See also* 139-158;
  individual fish.
  Fish Stock, Homemade, 57
  Malka's Bouillabaisse, 72
  Seafood Chowder, 74
  Spaghetti and Seafood Casserole, 106
Flattened Cumin-grilled Chicken
  Breasts with Garlic Couscous, 161
Flowers, edible, 275
Focaccia, Whole Wheat, 261
Food Choice System, Canadian
  Diabetes Association, 291-296
Food Guide to Healthy Eating,
  Canada's, 10, 11, 13-14
Food mill, 271
Food preparation tips, 10
Fresh Herb and Vegetable Lasagna, 122
Fresh Herb Soup with Ricotta
  Croutons, 58
Fresh Tomato Salsa, 107
Fresh Tomato Soup with Pesto Cream, 60
Fried Rice with Grilled Tofu, 138
Frittatas
  Feta and Spinach Frittata Sandwiches,
    237
  Pasta Frittata, 236
Fruit, 16, 17. *See also* individual fruits.
  Berry Berry Salad, 230
  Caramelized Fruit Crisp, 267
  Dried Fruit Compote, 274
  Fara's European Fruit Salad "Drink,"
    243
  Fruit Salad with Marsala, 269
  Smoothies, 243
  Tropical Smoothie, 244
  Yogurt Fruit Shake, 244

G
Garlic, 130, 289
  Caesar Salad with Creamy Roasted
    Garlic Dressing, 79
  Garlic Bread, 257
  Garlic Couscous, 161
  Green Beans with Garlic, 206
  Lightly Breaded Shrimp with Hot
    Garlic Sauce, 154
  Linguine with Hot Garlic Tomato
    Sauce, 97
  Pizza Salad with Roasted Garlic
    Hummos, 130
  Portobello Mushroom Burgers with
    Roasted Garlic Mayonnaise, 114
  Red Pepper, Feta and Garlic Hummos,
    34
  Roasted Garlic, 131
  Roasted Garlic and Balsamic Dressing,
    87
  Roasted Garlic Pesto on Bruschetta, 45

Shepherd's Pie with Garlic Mashed
  Potatoes, 186
Spaghetti Salad with Roasted Garlic
  and Tomato Salsa, 85
White Bean and Roasted Garlic
  Spread, 37
Garnishes. *See also* Croutons.
  Salad garnishes, 86
  Soup garnishes, 62
Gazpacho, Spicy, 75
Giant Hamburger with Homemade
  Chili Sauce, 190
Ginger, 71, 144
  Glazed Winter Vegetables with Maple
    and Ginger, 219
  Stir-fried Broccoli with Ginger, 210
  Teriyaki Swordfish Burgers with Sweet
    Pickled Ginger Salsa, 144
Gingerbread Angel Cake, 281
Gingerbread Angel Cake Roulade, 281
Glazed Beets with Balsamic Vinegar, 208
Glazed Swordfish, 143
Glazed Winter Vegetables with Maple
  and Ginger, 219
Goat cheese. *See* Chèvre.
Grains, 16, 17. *See also* Barley; Bulgur;
  Corn; Couscous; Oats; Polenta;
  Quinoa; Rice; Wehani.
  Grain and Seed Bread, 262
  Wheat Berry Salad, 82
Gravy, 178
Green Beans with Garlic, 206
Greens, Sauteed, 209
Grilled, 185
  Asian Chicken Thighs, 167
  Asian Grilled Steak Salad, 92
  Barbecued Butterflied Turkey Breast,
    180
  Barbecued Chicken Steaks, 160
  Barbecued Lamb Chili, 200
  Chicken Burgers with Herbed Yogurt
    Sauce, 163
  Chicken Satays with Peanut Sauce, 54
  Flattened Cumin-grilled Chicken
    Breasts with Garlic Couscous, 161
  Fried Rice with Grilled Tofu, 138
  Giant Hamburger with Homemade
    Chili Sauce, 190
  Grilled Chicken Sandwiches with
    Charmoula, 240
  Grilled Corn Salad, 78
  Grilled Steak Sandwiches with
    Barbecued Onion Sauce, 184
  Grilled Vegetables with Chèvre Dip, 40
  Shishkebab-flavoured Butterflied Leg
    of Lamb, 192
  Swordfish Kebabs, 143
  Teriyaki Swordfish Burgers with Sweet
    Pickled Ginger Salsa, 144
  Tortilla Rolls with Hummos and
    Grilled Eggplant, 48

Turkey Burgers with Old-fashioned
  Coleslaw, 176
Ground Beef. *See* Beef, Ground.

H
Halibut with Rice Wine, 146
Ham, Cajun Glazed, 204
Heart disease, 11, 287, 289, 290
Herbs. *See also* individual herbs.
  Chicken Burgers with Herbed Yogurt
    Sauce, 163
  Corn Chowder with Herb Cheese, 64
  Fresh Herb and Vegetable Lasagna,
    122
  Fresh Herb Soup with Ricotta
    Croutons, 58
  Herb Topping, 195
  Light Herb Cheese, 64
  Tabbouleh Salad with Fresh Herbs, 83
  Wild Mushrooms with Herbs, 213
Hermit Bar Cookies, 283
Hoisin
  Hoisin Marinade, 154
  Pork Tenderloin with Hoisin, 203
Homestyle Sushi, 46
Hot Garlic Sauce, 154
Hummos
  Jalapeño and Cilantro Hummos, 34
  Red Pepper, Feta and Garlic Hummos,
    34
  Roasted Garlic Hummos, 130
  Tortilla Rolls with Hummos and
    Grilled Eggplant, 48
Hunter-style Chicken with Wild
  Mushrooms, 168

I
Iron, 290
Israeli Couscous with Squash and
  Peppers, 222

J
Jalapeño and Cilantro Hummos, 34
Jambalaya, Chicken, 170
Japanese. *See* Asian.

K
Kebabs
  Shishkebab-flavoured Butterflied Leg
    of Lamb, 192
  Swordfish Kebabs, 143
Kids, cooking for, 27-28

L
Lactose-intolerant, cooking for the, 30
Lamb
  Barbecued Lamb Chili, 200
  Braised Lamb Shanks with White Bean
    Puree, 198
  Lamb Chops with Cashew Nut
    Couscous, 193

Shishkebab-flavoured Butterflied Leg of Lamb, 192
Lasagna, Fresh Herb and Vegetable, 122
Leeks, 132
  Bow Ties with Spring Vegetables, 103
  Calconnan Soup, 61
  Fresh Herb Soup with Ricotta Croutons, 58
Legumes, 17, 18. See also Beans, Lentils.
Lemon grass, 70
Lemon Mayonnaise, 235
Lemon Polenta Waffles, 234
Lemon Poppy Seed Muffins, 249
Lemony Lentil Soup, 67
Lentils, 116
  Lemony Lentil Soup, 67
  Lentil and Mushroom Burgers, 116
  Lentil and Wild Rice Salad with Feta, 129
Light Herb Cheese, 64
"Light" products, homemade, 188-189
Lightly Breaded Shrimp with Hot Garlic Sauce, 154
Linguine with Hot Garlic Tomato Sauce, 97
lower-fat salad dressings, 87

M

Malka's Bouillabaisse, 72
Mangoes, 279
  Mango and Orange Salad, 278
  Mango and Red Pepper Salsa, 163
Maple syrup
  Glazed Winter Vegetables with Maple and Ginger, 219
Margarine, 18
Marinade, Hoisin, 154
Marsala, 269
  Fruit Salad with Marsala, 269
Mashed Baked Squash, 216
Mashed potatoes
  Buttermilk Mashed Potatoes, 215
  Garlic Mashed Potatoes, 186
  Sweet Potato Mash, 214
Mashed Root Vegetables, 218
Mayonnaise
  Lemon Mayonnaise, 235
  lower-fat mayonnaise, 189
  Roasted Garlic Mayonnaise, 114
  substitutes, 25
Meal planning, 15-18
Meat and alternatives, 16, 18
Meatless main courses. See also 113-138; Pancakes.
  Barley and Wild Mushroom Risotto, 223
  Feta and Spinach Frittata Sandwiches, 237
  Pasta Frittata, 236
  Risotto with Rapini, 224
Menu planning, 19-21

Meringues
  Baked Alaska, 272
  Pavlova with Berries and Flowers, 275
Milk products, 16, 18
Mini Berry Cornmeal Muffins, 251
Moroccan Dressing, 80
Muffins, 251
  Apple Spice Muffins, 248
  Blueberry Bran Muffins, 246
  Cappuccino Muffins, 250
  Lemon Poppy Seed Muffins, 249
  Mini Berry Cornmeal Muffins, 251
  Rhubarb Cinnamon Muffins, 247
Mushrooms. See also Wild Mushrooms.
  Baked Fish with Mushroom Crust, 152
  Lentil and Mushroom Burgers, 116
Mussels
  Malka's Bouillabaisse, 72
  Spaghetti and Seafood Casserole, 106
Mustard Horseradish Dressing, 81

N

Nori, 46
Nutrients, 10
  nutrient analysis, 32
Nuts, 11, 193
  Lamb Chops with Cashew Nut Couscous, 193
  Pine nuts, 45

O

Oats
  Crispy Chocolate Cookies, 282
  Oatmeal Banana Cake, 280
Oils, 11, 25
  olive oil, 11, 188, 198
  sesame oil, 11, 136
Old-fashioned Coleslaw, 176
Olives
  olive oil, 188, 198
  Pasta with Swordfish and Olives, 108
One-pot meals. See Casseroles; Stews.
Onions, 44, 51
  Barbecued Onion Sauce, 184
  Caramelized Onions, 212
  Cod Baked in Tomato Sauce with Onions, 150
  Smoked Cheese and Sweet Onion Quesadillas, 51
  Tofu and Onions Braised in Asian Barbecue Sauce with Noodles, 135
Oranges
  Orange Hazelnut Biscotti, 284
  Orange Polenta Cake with Mango and Orange Salad, 278
Osso Bucco (Braised Veal Shanks), 194
Oven-roasted Sea Bass, 147

P

Pancakes. See also Waffles.
  Wild Rice Blueberry Pancakes, 227

Parmesan Cheese Crisps, 118
Parsnips
  Mashed Root Vegetables, 218
  Winter Root Vegetable Soup, 56
Pastas. See also 95-112.
  Beef and Broccoli with Baked Noodle Cake, 182
  Chinese Chicken Salad, 91
  Pasta Frittata, 236
  Pasta with Roasted Cauliflower, 102
  Pasta with Swordfish and Olives, 108
  Pasta with Tomato and Red Pepper Sauce, 99
  Spaghetti Salad with Roasted Garlic and Tomato Salsa, 85
  Spicy Singapore Noodles, 132
  Thai Chicken and Noodle Stir-fry, 175
  Thai Chicken Noodle Soup, 70
  Tofu and Onions Braised in Asian Barbecue Sauce with Noodles, 135
  Vietnamese Chicken Noodle Salad, 94
Pavlova with Berries and Flowers, 275
Peach Cobbler, 268
Peanut Dressing, 91
Peanut Sauce, 54
Pearl pasta. See Israeli couscous.
Pears, 276
  Cinnamon Pear Cake with Caramel Coffee Sauce, 276
  Pear Butter, 258
Penne with Eggplant, Peppers and Ricotta, 104
Penne with Tomatoes and Arugula, 100
Peppers, 239, 241
  Baked Red Snapper with Hot Chiles, 151
  Cooked Salad, 43
  Fettucine with Chicken and Mixed Peppers, 109
  Israeli Couscous with Squash and Peppers, 222
  Jalapeño and Cilantro Hummos, 34
  Mango and Red Pepper Salsa, 163
  Pasta with Tomato and Red Pepper Sauce, 99
  Penne with Eggplant, Peppers and Ricotta, 104
  Red Pepper, Feta and Garlic Hummos, 34
  Smoky Cornbread with Corn and Peppers, 260
Pesto
  Fresh Tomato Soup with Pesto Cream, 60
  Pesto Sauce, 60
  Roasted Garlic Pesto on Bruschetta, 45
  Salmon Baked in Parchment with Parsley Pesto, 140
Phyllo pastry, 265
  Apple Strudel, 264
  Asparagus Tarts with Chèvre, 52

Dessert Phyllo Cups, 52
Physical activity, 11-12
Pine nuts, 45
Pies
  Shepherd's Pie with Garlic Mashed
    Potatoes, 186
Pita Chips, 35
Pizza
  Pizza Salad with Roasted Garlic
    Hummos, 130
  Pizza with Black Bean Salsa, 128
Polenta
  Lemon Polenta Waffles, 234
  Orange Polenta Cake with Mango and
    Orange Salad, 278
  Polenta with Roasted Ratatouille, 120
  Polenta with Wild Mushroom and
    Meat Ragout, 188
Pork
  Baked Pork Chops with Barbecue
    Sauce, 202
  Pork Tenderloin with Hoisin, 203
Portobello Mushroom Burgers with
  Roasted Garlic Mayonnaise, 114
Potassium, 288-289
Potatoes
  Baked Potatoes with Tuna Salad and
    Lemon Mayonnaise, 235
  Beet and Potato Skordalia, 36
  Buttermilk Mashed Potatoes, 215
  Calconnan Soup, 61
  Fresh Herb Soup with Ricotta
    Croutons, 58
  Mashed Root Vegetables, 218
  Potato Salad, 84
  Potato Sweet Rolls, 258
  Roasted "French-fried" Potatoes, 217
  Shepherd's Pie with Garlic Mashed
    Potatoes, 186
  Stuffed Baked Potatoes with Stir-fried
    Vegetables, 117
  Sweet Potato Mash, 214
Prince Edward Island Dinner Rolls, 254
Pulses. See Beans; Lentils.

Q
Quesadillas
  Pizza with Black Bean Salsa, 128
  Smoked Cheese and Sweet Onion
    Quesadillas, 51
Quick and easy dinners, 30-31
Quinoa, 89
  Quinoa and Crab Salad with Cilantro
    Lime Dressing, 89

R
Rapini, 224
  Risotto with Rapini, 224
  Spaghetti Rustica, 105
Raspberries
  Breakfast Brûlée, 226

Raspberry Sauce, 278
Ratatouille, Roasted, 120
Red Pepper, Feta and Garlic Hummos, 34
Red Snapper. See Snapper, Red.
Rhubarb Cinnamon Muffins, 247
Rice, 171
  Baked Wild Rice Pudding Brûlée, 266
  Basmati Rice Pilaf with Garam Masala,
    221
  Boiled Rice, 171
  Chicken Jambalaya, 170
  Chicken Soup with Rice, 69
  Fried Rice with Grilled Tofu, 138
  Lentil and Wild Rice Salad with Feta,
    129
  Rice Baked with Spinach, Feta and
    Dill, 119
  Rice Salsa Salad, 84
  Risotto with Rapini, 224
  Risotto with Tomatoes and Beans, 118
  Spicy Rice Pilaf, 220
  Steamed Rice, 171
  Sticky Rice, 171
  Sweet and Sour Cabbage Casserole,
    196
  Wehani, 90
  Wild rice, 129
  Wild Rice Blueberry Pancakes, 227
  Wild Salad with Cranberry Vinaigrette,
    90
Rice paper wrappers, 141
  Salad Rolls, 50
  Salmon Fillets in Rice Paper Wrappers,
    141
Rice vermicelli, 112
  Salad Rolls, 50
  Soupy Chinese Noodles, 112
  Spicy Singapore Noodles, 132
  Thai Chicken Noodle Soup, 70
  Vietnamese Chicken Noodle Salad, 94
Rice vinegar, 184
Ricotta Croutons, 58
Risotto
  Barley and Wild Mushroom Risotto,
    223
  Risotto with Rapini, 224
  Risotto with Tomatoes and Beans, 118
Roast Turkey Breast with Spinach
  Stuffing, 178
Roasted Asparagus, 210
Roasted Eggplant Spread, 39
Roasted Fennel with Tomatoes, 211
Roasted "French-fried" Potatoes, 217
Roasted Garlic, 131
Roasted Garlic and Balsamic Dressing, 87
Roasted Garlic and Tomato Salsa, 85
Roasted Garlic Mayonnaise, 114
Roasted Garlic Pesto on Bruschetta, 45
Roasted Ratatouille, 120
Roasted Squash Spread, 38
Roasted Tomato Sauce, 96

Rolled Oats. See Oats.
Rolls
  Potato Sweet Rolls, 258
  Prince Edward Island Dinner Rolls,
    254
Rosy Applesauce, 271
Rutabagas
  Mashed Root Vegetables, 218
  Winter Root Vegetable Soup, 56

S
Saffron, 72
Salad dressings
  Cilantro Lime Dressing, 89
  Citrus Dipping Sauce, 92
  Cranberry Vinaigrette, 90
  Creamy Roasted Garlic Dressing, 79
  Lemon Sesame Dressing, 94
  lower-fat salad dressings, 87
  Moroccan Dressing, 80
  Mustard Horseradish Dressing, 81
  Peanut Dressing, 91
  Roasted Garlic and Balsamic Dressing, 87
  Roasted Garlic and Tomato Salsa, 85
  Salsa Vinaigrette, 82
  Tomato Balsamic Dressing, 87
  Tomato Olive Vinaigrette, 148
Salad Rolls, 50
Salads. See also 77-94.
  Asparagus with Thai Dipping Sauce, 207
  Chickpea and Couscous Salad, 134
  Lentil and Wild Rice Salad with Feta,
    129
  Pizza Salad with Roasted Garlic
    Hummos, 130
Salmon
  Salmon Baked in Parchment with
    Parsley Pesto, 140
  Salmon Fillets in Rice Paper Wrappers,
    141
  Salmon Patties with Fresh Dill, 142
  Smoked Salmon Sushi, 46
  Spaghetti and Seafood Casserole, 106
Salsa Vinaigrette, 82
Salsas
  Black Bean Salsa, 128
  Cooked Tomato Salsa, 238
  Creamy Salsa, 35
  Fresh Tomato Salsa, 107
  Mango and Red Pepper Salsa, 163
  Roasted Garlic and Tomato Salsa, 85
  Sweet Pickled Ginger Salsa, 144
  Tomato Salsa, 84
Salt. See also Sodium.
  limiting, 12, 189, 288
  substitutes, 288
Sandwiches
  Breaded Chicken Cutlets with Roasted
    Tomato Sauce, 172
  Feta and Spinach Frittata Sandwiches,
    237

Grilled Chicken Sandwiches with Charmoula, 240
Grilled Steak Sandwiches with Barbecued Onion Sauce, 184
lower-fat sandwich spreads, 240
Tortilla Rolls with Hummos and Grilled Eggplant, 48
Sauces, Dessert
Caramel Coffee Sauce, 276
Raspberry Sauce, 278
Sauces, Savoury
Barbecue Sauce, 202
Barbecued Onion Sauce, 184
Brewmaster's Barbecue Sauce, 124
Charmoula, 127
Chili Sauce, 191
Cranberry Sauce, 179
Herbed Yogurt Sauce, 163
Hoisin Marinade, 154
Hot Garlic Sauce, 154
Peanut Sauce, 54
Pesto Sauce, 60
Roasted Tomato Sauce, 96
Sweet and Sour Sauce, 164
Teriyaki Sauce, 144
Tomato and Red Pepper Sauce, 99
Wild Mushroom and Meat Ragout, 188
Sauteed Greens, 209
Scallops
Broken Spaghetti with Fresh Salsa and Scallops, 107
Seafood Chowder, 74
Stir-fried Scallops, 156
Sea bass
Oven-roasted Sea Bass, 147
Sea Bass with Couscous Crust and Tomato Olive Vinaigrette, 148
Spaghetti and Seafood Casserole, 106
Seafood Chowder, 74
Seasonings
Black bean sauce, 156
Cumin, 222
Five-spice powder, 135
Garam masala, 221
Saffron, 72
Spices, 126
Sesame
Lemon Sesame Dressing, 94
sesame oil, 136
sesame seeds, 80
Shallots, 44
Shepherd's Pie with Garlic Mashed Potatoes, 186
Shishkebab-flavoured Leg of Lamb, 192
Shopping, 23
healthy shopping checklist, 22
reading labels, 23–24
Shrimp
Lightly Breaded Shrimp with Hot Garlic Sauce, 154

Malka's Bouillabaisse, 72
Seafood Chowder, 74
Spaghetti and Seafood Casserole, 106
White Bean and Chopped Shrimp Salad, 86
Skewers, 54
Smoked Cheese and Sweet Onion Quesadillas, 51
Smoked Salmon Sushi, 46
Smoked Trout Spread, 42
Smoky Cornbread with Corn and Peppers, 260
Smoothies, 243
Tropical Smoothie, 244
Snapper, Red
Baked Red Snapper with Hot Chiles, 151
Sodium. See also Salt.
content in canned, condensed chicken broth, 287–288
reducing, 287, 288
Soups, 66, 70. See also 55–76.
Couscous Soup with Vegetables and Charmoula, 126
Soupy Chinese Noodles, 112
Spaghetti, 107
Broken Spaghetti with Fresh Salsa and Scallops, 107
Spaghetti and Seafood Casserole, 106
Spaghetti Rustica, 105
Spaghetti Salad with Roasted Garlic and Tomato Salsa, 85
Spaghetti with Roasted Tomato Sauce, 96
Spice grinders, 216
Spices. See Seasonings.
Spicy Gazpacho, 75
Spicy Rice Pilaf, 220
Spicy Singapore Noodles, 132
Spicy Tofu with Eggplant and Mushrooms, 136
Spinach
Feta and Spinach Frittata Sandwiches, 237
Rice Baked with Spinach, Feta and Dill, 119
Roast Turkey Breast with Spinach Stuffing, 178
Steamed Fish with Spinach and Black Bean Sauce, 158
White Bean and Spinach Soup, 66
Spreads
Charmoula, 240
Jalapeño and Cilantro Hummos, 34
lower-fat sandwich spreads, 240
Pear Butter, 258
Red Pepper, Feta and Garlic Hummos, 34
Roasted Eggplant Spread, 39
Roasted Garlic Hummos, 130
Roasted Squash Spread, 38

Smoked Trout Spread, 42
Veggie Cheese Spread, 41
White Bean and Roasted Garlic Spread, 37
White Bean Puree, 199
Squash, 63
Butternut Squash Soup with Wild Mushroom Sautè, 62
Curried Squash Soup, 65
Israeli Couscous with Squash and Peppers, 222
Mashed Baked Squash, 216
Roasted Squash Spread, 38
Steamed Fish with Spinach and Black Bean Sauce, 158
Steamed Rice, 171
Stews. See also Casseroles.
Chicken Adobo, 174
Hunter-style Chicken with Wild Mushrooms, 168
Sticky Rice, 171
Stir-fried
Stir-fried Broccoli with Ginger, 210
Stir-fried Scallops, 156
Thai Chicken and Noodle Stir-fry, 175
Stock, 56–57
Chicken Stock, Homemade, 57
Fish Stock, Homemade, 57
Roasted Vegetable Stock, Homemade, 57
Vegetable Stock, Homemade, 57
Stroke, 287
Stuffed Baked Potatoes with Stir-fried Vegetables, 117
Sugar, 267
Summer Crêpes with Berry Berry Salad, 230
Sushi
Homestyle Sushi, 46
Smoked Salmon Sushi, 46
Sweet and hot Thai chili sauce, 94
Sweet and Sour Cabbage Casserole, 196
Sweet and Sour Chicken Balls, 164
Sweet and Spicy Chicken Lo Mein, 110
Sweet potatoes
Mashed Root Vegetables, 218
Sweet Potato Mash, 214
Swordfish
Glazed Swordfish, 143
Pasta with Swordfish and Olives, 108
Swordfish Kebabs, 143
Teriyaki Swordfish Burgers with Sweet Pickled Ginger Salsa, 144

T

Tabbouleh Salad with Fresh Herbs, 83
Tarts
Asparagus Tarts with Chèvre, 52
Teenagers, cooking for, 29
Teriyaki Swordfish Burgers with Sweet Pickled Ginger Salsa, 144

Thai. *See also* Asian.
  Thai basil, 175
  Thai Chicken and Noodle Stir-fry,
    175
  Thai Chicken Noodle Soup, 70
Tofu, 137
  Fried Rice with Grilled Tofu, 138
  Spicy Singapore Noodles, 132
  Spicy Tofu with Eggplant and
    Mushrooms, 136
  Tofu and Onions Braised-in Asian
    Barbecue Sauce with Noodles, 135
Tomatoes, 170
  Angelhair Pasta with Fresh and
    Cooked Tomato Sauce, 98
  Breaded Chicken Cutlets with Roasted
    Tomato Sauce, 172
  Broken Spaghetti with Fresh Salsa and
    Scallops, 107
  Cod Baked in Tomato Sauce with
    Onions, 150
  Cooked Salad, 43
  Cooked Tomato Salsa, 238
  Creamy Salsa, 35
  Fresh Tomato Soup with Pesto Cream,
    60
  Linguine with Hot Garlic Tomato
    Sauce, 97
  Pasta with Tomato and Red Pepper
    Sauce, 99
  Penne with Tomatoes and Arugula, 100
  Rice Salsa Salad, 84
  Risotto with Tomatoes and Beans,
    118
  Roasted Fennel with Tomatoes, 211
  Spaghetti Salad with Roasted Garlic
    and Tomato Salsa, 85
  Spaghetti with Roasted Tomato Sauce,
    96
  Spicy Gazpacho, 75
  Tomato Balsamic Dressing, 87
  Tomato Olive Vinaigrette, 148
Tortilla Chips, 35
Tortillas, 200, 238
  Chicken Burritos with Cooked
    Tomato Salsa, 238
  Pizza with Black Bean Salsa, 128
  Smoked Cheese and Sweet Onion
    Quesadillas, 51
  Tortilla Rolls with Hummos and
    Grilled Eggplant, 48
  Tortilla Soup, 68
"Total diet" approach to food and
    activity, 9
  cornerstones of healthy living, 9-12
  meal planning, 15-18
  menu planning chart, 19-20
  menu planning checklist, 21
Trace elements, 10
Trenne with Wild Mushrooms, 101
Tropical Smoothie, 244

Trout
  Smoked Trout Spread, 42
Tuna
  Baked Potatoes with Tuna Salad and
    Lemon Mayonnaise, 235
  Chopped Tuna Salad, 88
Turkey
  Barbecued Butterflied Turkey Breast,
    180
  Gravy, 178
  Roast Turkey Breast with Spinach
    Stuffing, 178
  Turkey Burgers with Old-fashioned
    Coleslaw, 176
  Turkey Paillards, 177
Turnips
  Mashed Root Vegetables, 218
  Winter Root Vegetable Soup, 56
Twist and Shout Chicken Drumsticks,
  162

U
Utensils for a low-fat kitchen, 187

V
Veal
  Osso Bucco (Braised Veal Shanks), 194
Vegetables, 16, 17. *See also* 205-224;
  individual vegetables.
  Baked Chicken with Vegetables and
    Balsamic Vinegar, 166
  Bow Ties with Spring Vegetables, 103
  Couscous Soup with Vegetables and
    Charmoula, 126
  Fresh Herb and Vegetable Lasagna, 122
  Grilled Vegetables with Chèvre Dip, 40
  Polenta with Roasted Ratatouille, 120
  Roasted Vegetable Stock, Homemade, 57
  Stuffed Baked Potatoes with Stir-fried
    Vegetables, 117
  Vegetable Stock, Homemade, 57
  Veggie Cheese Spread, 41
  Winter Root Vegetable Soup, 56
Vegetarian, 28-29
  Vegetarian main courses. *See* Meatless
    main courses.
Veggie Cheese Spread, 41
Vietnamese. *See also* Asian.
  Vietnamese Chicken Noodle Salad, 94
Vinaigrettes
  Cranberry Vinaigrette, 90
  Salsa Vinaigrette, 82
  Tomato Olive Vinaigrette, 148
Vinegar
  Baked Chicken with Vegetables and
    Balsamic Vinegar, 166
  Glazed Beets with Balsamic Vinegar,
    208
  Rice vinegar, 184
  Roasted Garlic and Balsamic Dressing,
    87

Tomato Balsamic Dressing, 87
Vitamins, 10

W
Waffles
  Lemon Polenta Waffles, 234
Wasabi, 47
Wehani, 90
  Wild Salad with Cranberry Vinaigrette,
    90
Wheat Berry Salad, 82
White Bean and Chopped Shrimp
  Salad, 86
White Bean and Roasted Garlic Spread,
  37
White Bean and Spinach Soup, 66
Whole Wheat Focaccia, 261
Wild mushrooms, 115
  Barley and Wild Mushroom Risotto,
    223
  Butternut Squash Soup with Wild
    Mushroom Sauté, 62
  Hunter-style Chicken with Wild
    Mushrooms, 168
  Portobello Mushroom Burgers with
    Roasted Garlic Mayonnaise, 114
  Spaghetti Rustica, 105
  Spicy Tofu with Eggplant and
    Mushrooms, 136
  Trenne with Wild Mushrooms, 101
  Wild Mushroom and Meat Ragout, 188
  Wild Mushroom Bruschetta with
    Chèvre, 44
  Wild Mushrooms with Herbs, 213
  Wild Rice Blueberry Pancakes, 227
  Wild Salad with Cranberry Vinaigrette,
    90
Winter Root Vegetable Soup, 56
Worcestershire sauce, 117
Wraps, 200

Y
Yeast, 255
Yogurt
  Cold Cucumber Tzatziki Soup, 76
  Yogurt Fruit Shake, 244
Yogurt cheese
  Breakfast Brûlée, 226
  Chèvre Dip, 40
  Chicken Burgers with Herbed Yogurt
    Sauce, 163
  Creamy Salsa, 35
  Grilled Chicken Sandwiches with
    Charmoula, 240
  Light Herb Cheese, 64
  Smoked Trout Spread, 42
  Veggie Cheese Spread, 41
  Yogurt Cheese, 229
  Yogurt Cheese Dessert Topping, 229
  Yogurt Cheese Dip, 229